Customizing Microsoft Teams

Build custom apps and extensions for your business using
Power Platform and Dataverse in Microsoft Teams

Gopi Kondameda

BIRMINGHAM—MUMBAI

Customizing Microsoft Teams

Group Product Manager: Alok Dhuri
Publishing Product Manager: Akshay Dani
Senior Editor: Kinnari Chohan
Technical Editor: Pradeep Sahu
Copy Editor: Safis Editing
Project Coordinator: Deeksha Thakkar
Proofreader: Safis Editing
Indexer: Tejal Soni
Production Designer: Jyoti Chauhan
Marketing Coordinators: Rayyan Khan and Deepak Kumar

First published: April 2023

Production reference: 1170323

Published by Packt Publishing Ltd.
Livery Place
35 Livery Street
Birmingham
B3 2PB, UK.

ISBN 978-1-80107-538-1

www.packtpub.com

First, I dedicate this book to my loving wife, Komala, and my sons, Rohit and Rahul. You are the foundation of my life and the source of my strength. Your unwavering support has made this book possible, and I feel blessed to have you in my life.

I would also like to dedicate this book to the memory of my grandfather and father, for their sacrifices and for exemplifying my power of determination. I am who I am today because of them.

To my mother, for her unconditional love and support, and to my father-in-law, for his love, blessings, and support back home, allowing me to focus on my career here. I am grateful to have him in my life and for the role he has played over the last 15 years.

Lastly, I would like to extend my gratitude to my dear friends: Subbu, who keeps me grounded; Suresh, my "anna" (elder brother); Chandra, whom I fondly call "C Anna"; and my extended family of Dunkin boys. You all keep me motivated and make me laugh. A big shoutout to all of you, especially Umesh – the most dependable coffee companion and trusted advisor; Chandu – always just a phone call away; and Prasad – who has been a witness to many important events in my life.

To my family back home, Padma, Sridhar, and Seshu (Chinni), thank you.

Thank you all!

Contributors

About the author

Gopi Kondameda is a seasoned IT professional with over 20 years of experience as a senior cloud solution architect, SharePoint Saturday Speaker, developer, and trainer. He specializes in various Microsoft technologies, including Microsoft Teams apps, Power Platform, and Microsoft 365 SharePoint. He has extensive experience in building custom business applications using code, low-code, and no-code solutions. Gopi is skilled in managing the Microsoft 365 cloud platform and modernizing solutions. He has excellent communication and collaboration abilities, enabling him to work effectively with business leaders, IT professionals, and end users to identify requirements and design effective solutions. As a senior cloud solution architect, he guides and supports clients in their cloud journey, helping them leverage the cloud to improve scalability, security, and performance.

I want to thank all the people who have been close to me and helped shape my career.

To the project coordinator, Deeksha Thakkar, and the senior editor, Kinnari Chohan – a big thank you to both of you!. You are the reason this book was completed.

About the reviewer

Sharon Sumner is a highly accomplished technology executive with over 20 years of experience in the IT industry. She is the CEO of Business Cloud Integration, a leading provider of Microsoft-based solutions, using their Casper365 tools to empower organizations.

As a Microsoft MVP for Business Applications and M365 Apps & Services, Sharon is a recognized expert in the field and a sought-after keynote speaker and consultant. In addition, Sharon is an esteemed technical community leader and board member of the Microsoft Global Community Initiative. Her commercial accomplishments have earned her a reputation as a visionary leader in the industry, and she is passionate about driving innovation and empowering businesses to succeed.

Table of Contents

Part 2: Microsoft Teams Customization with Tools and Techniques

3

Microsoft Graph API   83

4

Microsoft Teams PowerShell   105

5

Microsoft Teams Customization Using the SharePoint Framework (SPFx)   115

6

Microsoft Teams Authentication   135

Part 3: Microsoft Teams Customization with Low-Code and No-Code

7

Microsoft Dataverse for Teams   151

8

Microsoft Teams App Templates   191

9

Microsoft Viva   217

10

Microsoft Teams Third-Party Apps   237

Index   259

Other Books You May Enjoy   268

Preface

Microsoft Teams is a versatile collaboration platform that offers many features and tools to facilitate virtual work within teams, including chat, meetings, file sharing, and real-time collaboration. However, the wide range of built-in apps, third-party apps, and custom app integrations available to users sets Teams apart from other collaboration tools. Teams has become a one-stop-shop for all collaboration needs, eliminating the need for multiple tools and platforms. This leads to improved productivity, better communication, and enhanced teamwork from one location.

With the rise of hybrid work, virtual teamwork has made Microsoft Teams an essential tool for businesses and organizations to maintain connectivity and productivity among team members. In addition, Teams offers several customization options to users, allowing them to tailor their experience based on their preferences and needs. Overall, Microsoft Teams is a robust platform that can enhance the efficiency and productivity of remote teams, which ultimately leads to better collaboration and results.

In addition to exploring the different types of apps available on Microsoft Teams, this book will provide you with a good understanding of the Microsoft Teams app architecture. We will cover the prerequired configurations necessary to have apps available in your tenant, including how to manage app policies and permissions.

Furthermore, this book will delve into building custom apps for Microsoft Teams, utilizing various options and supporting technologies/APIs for building these apps. We will explore how to use different development tools (such as Visual Studio) and programming languages (such as JavaScript and TypeScript) to build and customize apps that meet your specific needs.

This book will provide you with the knowledge and skills to create a powerful and efficient workspace using Microsoft Teams and its various apps. From understanding the architecture to building custom apps, you will be equipped with the tools and techniques to optimize your use of Microsoft Teams and achieve your goals more effectively.

Who this book is for

This book is perfect for cloud architects, Teams admins, Teams developers, and citizen developers looking to optimize their use of Microsoft Teams and its various apps. It provides a comprehensive understanding of the Microsoft Teams app architecture, configuration, and development using the different development tools and APIs that are available for Teams. So, whether you want to design or develop apps, or just want to understand how Microsoft Teams can host customization, this book is for you. Its practical approach equips you with the knowledge and skills required to enhance your collaboration, productivity, and efficiency within your organization using Microsoft Teams and its apps.

Cloud architects can benefit from this book by gaining a comprehensive understanding of the Microsoft Teams app architecture and its integration with Microsoft 365 apps/services and learning how to design and manage apps in Teams.

Teams admins can benefit from this book by learning how to manage and configure apps within Teams to meet their organization's and team members' specific needs.

Teams developers can learn how to build and customize apps using the different development tools, programming languages, and APIs that are available for Teams.

Citizen developers can also benefit from this book by gaining the knowledge and skills required to develop custom apps for Teams, even without extensive coding experience.

What this book covers

Chapter 1, Introducing Microsoft Teams Apps, introduces you to the Microsoft Teams platform's extensibility, providing an overview of custom app architecture and configuration prerequisites. It is a critical starting point for building custom apps and integrations for Teams.

Chapter 2, Microsoft Teams Apps and Bots, provides a detailed overview of the various components of Teams apps, including tabs, apps, connectors, messaging extensions, cards, task modules, and notifications. You will learn how these components can expose and integrate various solutions within Teams, enhancing collaboration and productivity.

Chapter 3, Microsoft Graph API, helps you to thoroughly understand the Graph API and its functionality. You will then learn how to leverage the Microsoft Graph API to work with Teams, providing practical insights into its potential applications.

Chapter 4, Microsoft Teams PowerShell, gives an overview of the PowerShell module for provisioning and managing Teams and its associated groups. You will gain a comprehensive understanding of the Microsoft Teams PowerShell topics and their practical applications.

Chapter 5, Microsoft Teams Customization Using the SharePoint Framework (SPFx), introduces the **SharePoint Framework** (**SPFx**), a modern development model for SharePoint, and how it can be used to bring customizations to Microsoft Teams. It covers the history of SharePoint development and the open source tools needed to develop SPFx components.

Chapter 6, Microsoft Teams Authentication, focuses on authentication and authorization options for creating custom Microsoft Teams tabs, including **single sign-on** (**SSO**) and related topics.

Chapter 7, Microsoft Dataverse for Teams, covers Microsoft Dataverse for Teams, a low-code data platform built into Microsoft Teams. You will learn how to build solutions using Power Apps, Power Automate, and Power Virtual Agents within Teams.

Chapter 8, Microsoft Teams App Templates, covers Microsoft's community-driven app templates initiative for building ready-to-deploy app templates for common scenarios, which organizations can easily install and use through GitHub. These open source templates provide instructions for deployment and usage, making it easier for businesses to utilize Teams' app capabilities.

Chapter 9, Microsoft Viva, covers Microsoft Viva as an integrated employee experience platform, with modules such as Viva Topics, Viva Connections, Viva Insights, and Viva Learning in Microsoft Teams and Microsoft 365. It supports individuals' and teams' connection, insight, purpose, and growth.

Chapter 10, Microsoft Teams Third-Party Apps, discusses third-party app integration and Microsoft Dynamics 365 app integration with Microsoft Teams. The focus is on ISV-built Teams apps, with the previous chapters covering built-in and custom apps.

To get the most out of this book

A basic understanding of Microsoft 365 and its technologies is essential for effectively utilizing this book on Microsoft Teams apps. Knowledge of Power Platform, APIs, and PowerShell will also be beneficial when creating apps.

Software/hardware covered in the book	Operating system requirements
Node.js v16 LTS, npm, Gulp, Yeoman	Windows
Visual Studio Code	
Microsoft Teams PowerShell	
CLI for Microsoft 365	

Download the color images

We also provide a PDF file that has color images of the screenshots and diagrams used in this book. You can download it here: `https://packt.link/ZNpMg`.

Conventions used

There are a number of text conventions used throughout this book.

`Code in text`: Indicates code words in text, database table names, folder names, filenames, file extensions, pathnames, dummy URLs, user input, and Twitter handles. Here is an example: "Later, you can also run this command with `@latest` as `npm install -g @pnp/cli-microsoft365@ latest` to update the CLI for Microsoft 365 to the latest version."

Bold: Indicates a new term, an important word, or words that you see onscreen. For instance, words in menus or dialog boxes appear in **bold**. Here is an example: "When you click on **Permissions**, you have the following options, shown in the screenshot."

> **Tips or important notes**
> Appear like this.

Get in touch

Feedback from our readers is always welcome.

General feedback: If you have questions about any aspect of this book, email us at customercare@ packtpub.com and mention the book title in the subject of your message.

Errata: Although we have taken every care to ensure the accuracy of our content, mistakes do happen. If you have found a mistake in this book, we would be grateful if you would report this to us. Please visit www.packtpub.com/support/errata and fill in the form.

Any errata related to this book can be found at https://github.com/PacktPublishing/ Customizing-Microsoft-Teams.

Piracy: If you come across any illegal copies of our works in any form on the internet, we would be grateful if you would provide us with the location address or website name. Please contact us at copyright@packt.com with a link to the material.

If you are interested in becoming an author: If there is a topic that you have expertise in and you are interested in either writing or contributing to a book, please visit authors.packtpub.com.

Share Your Thoughts

Once you've read *Customizing Microsoft Teams*, we'd love to hear your thoughts! Scan the QR code below to go straight to the Amazon review page for this book and share your feedback.

https://packt.link/r/1801075387

Your review is important to us and the tech community and will help us make sure we're delivering excellent quality content.

Download a free PDF copy of this book

Thanks for purchasing this book!

Do you like to read on the go but are unable to carry your print books everywhere?

Is your eBook purchase not compatible with the device of your choice?

Don't worry, now with every Packt book you get a DRM-free PDF version of that book at no cost.

Read anywhere, any place, on any device. Search, copy, and paste code from your favorite technical books directly into your application.

The perks don't stop there, you can get exclusive access to discounts, newsletters, and great free content in your inbox daily

Follow these simple steps to get the benefits:

1. Scan the QR code or visit the link below

https://packt.link/free-ebook/9781801075381

2. Submit your proof of purchase

3. That's it! We'll send your free PDF and other benefits to your email directly

Part 1: Microsoft Teams Customization Exploring the Architecture and Components

In this part, you are introduced to the extensibility of Microsoft Teams and its custom app architecture. It explains the various components of Teams apps, including tabs, apps, connectors, messaging extensions, cards, task modules, and notifications, and how they enhance collaboration and productivity within Teams. This part is a crucial starting point for building custom apps and integrations.

This section includes the following chapters:

- *Chapter 1, Introducing Microsoft Teams Apps*
- *Chapter 2, Microsoft Teams Apps and Bots*

1
Introducing Microsoft Teams Apps

In this first chapter of the book, we'll start with how Microsoft Teams has grown fast as a platform in a very short time. Our focus will mostly be on the context of apps and reviewing various types of apps, such as built-in, third-party, and custom, that are hosted on Microsoft Teams, a few examples that'll help you understand the apps better.

This book is all about building or hosting customizations on Microsoft Teams; the Teams customizations come in various shapes, such as tabs, apps, web services, and message extensions, just to name a few. To build these apps, you need to have some prior knowledge of supporting technologies such as Azure, Microsoft 365, and Power Platform. In this chapter, we will also review these prerequisites and will go into detail in later chapters on an as-needed basis. However, I highly recommend you spend time reading relevant books for a deeper and broader understanding of these supporting concepts, which is beyond the scope of this book.

Finally, we'll conclude this chapter by getting ourselves acquainted with the prerequisites of admin and configuration. These are required for making your tenant ready for custom apps and understanding the core permission and set-up policies available through Microsoft Teams administration. A typical developer may not have access to the Teams administration but understanding various policies will help them think through and generate intelligent conversations with a Teams administrator for the required configuration and setup at the tenant level.

These are the main topics we'll be covering in this chapter:

- Overview of Microsoft Teams as a platform
- Exploring the Microsoft Teams app architecture
- Exploring the core services used for the development of Teams
- Microsoft Teams admin, configuration, and prerequisites such as Azure, Microsoft 365, and Power Platform

So, let's get started!

Overview of Microsoft Teams as a platform

According to Microsoft's data, Teams is the fastest-growing app in Microsoft's suite. It started as a group chat-based utility and developed into an updated version of Skype with features such as chat, calls, and meetings. However, Microsoft Teams has grown as a platform for collaboration and is now home to various apps that are used by almost every organization every day.

Microsoft has even made Microsoft Teams an integral part of Windows 11 by pinning it to the taskbar. With the spread of the Covid pandemic, the need to work remotely and the concept of hybrid work have had an unprecedented surge and become the new norm. Understandably, there is a high demand for teleconference solutions such as Microsoft Teams, Zoom, Slack, Webex, and so on. In my opinion, the winner here is Microsoft Teams, as it goes beyond communication features such as chat, voice, and meetings. It has evolved as a platform for hosting apps so that businesses can do their day-to-day work without leaving Microsoft Teams.

Every organization prioritizes business productivity; most of the leadership wants to make Microsoft Teams sticky, bringing all the required tools for the job to one location and providing access to enterprise applications, custom applications, and even the intranet to Teams – so Teams has become a one-stop-shop for all things needed by members of IT.

In recent publications (*Microsoft FY22 Q2 Commercial Highlights*), they announced that Microsoft Teams' active users have hiked up to 270 million per month.

In this book, we are going to focus on various customization options that will help IT workers to make their day-to-day business scenarios easier. Here are a few examples:

- Opening a ticket or escalating in ServiceNow (`www.servicenow.com`) without leaving Microsoft Teams
- Using DevOps tools such as Jira Cloud and GitHub to build, test, and release software directly in Teams
- Consuming Azure-hosted FAQs or QnA Maker bots in Microsoft Teams
- Using no-code Power Apps, Power Automate, and chatbots easily
- Using Teams app templates such as **Appointment Manager**, an app template for conducting virtual appointments through Teams
- Using Building Access, a Power Platform-based full-blown app to support building occupancy by helping employees with on-site facility access adhere to social distancing rules
- Using Viva Connections, which acts as a gateway to monitor employee experience in Microsoft Teams

These are a few sample scenarios that highlight Microsoft Teams' role as a platform to host various customizations. Our focus is to learn how to build these customizations for end users with no code or very little code and complex solutions for developers with code. General best practices in Power Apps development are using a fusion development approach with blended groups of teams with low code or no code (also called citizen developers) and professional developers.

Exploring the Microsoft Teams app architecture

The customization of Microsoft Teams refers to bringing all the applications that a business needs to use daily to one location and integrating chats, meetings, calls, and files into it to be more productive. This will help business users stick to one tool and access all apps and services, which thereby avoids switching between multiple applications or services.

Classification of apps

You can bring most of the apps and services used in your organization and incorporate them into Teams as an app. These apps are grouped into the following three categories, mostly based on who created them.

Microsoft apps

Microsoft Teams comes with a set of built-in apps; these are built by Microsoft. One of the examples of Microsoft apps is shown here:

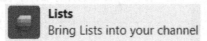

Figure 1.1 – Lists app

With this Lists app, you can create a new SharePoint list or use an existing SharePoint list and add it as a tab to any Teams channel. More precisely, you can create a custom list, import it from Excel, or generate one from an existing or predefined list template. The following screenshot shows various templates of list options:

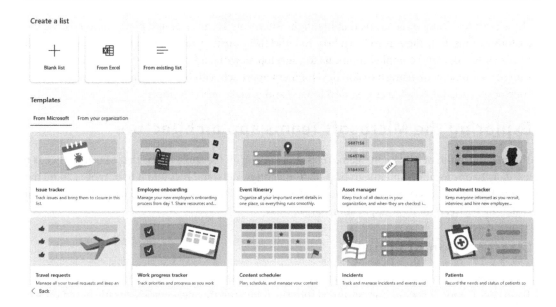

Figure 1.2 – Various list options through the Microsoft Lists app

Here's another example of a Microsoft-provided app:

Tasks by Planner and To Do

Microsoft, Productivity, Project management

Figure 1.3 – The Tasks by Planner and To Do app

Tasks by Planner and To Do is an app to simplify tasks. It combines the tasks from To Do and Planner. So, in essence, this combines To Do and Planner's utilities in one location.

Figure 1.4 shows the page that displays any tasks that were created by you or have been assigned to you in Planner or To Do.

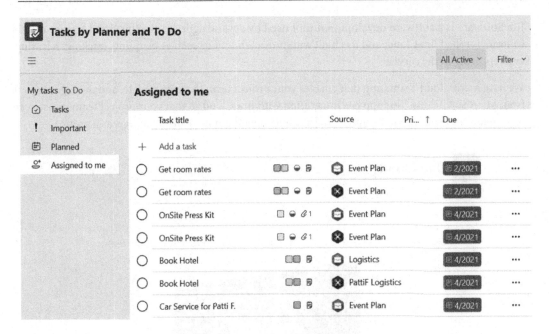

Figure 1.4 – The Tasks by Planner and To Do app

These tasks are automatically categorized into four lists as listed here:

- **Tasks** – all the tasks you've created
- **Important** – any task marked as **Important**
- **Planned** – tasks marked with a due date
- **Assigned to me** – tasks that are assigned to you

Third-party apps

Microsoft works with various developers and partners to build apps that work in Microsoft Teams. These are Microsoft-certified third-party apps; with certified apps, Microsoft provides assurance that you can trust them and that they comply with strong security principles that protect data and privacy.

Some of these third-party apps may require subscription services or licenses to purchase for consumption. An example of this kind of app is shown in the following screenshot:

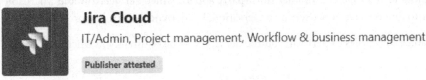

Figure 1.5 – Third-party Jira Cloud app

Jira Software is a software development tool used by several agile teams; the cloud service of this software is called Jira Cloud, and it is built with project functions such as planning, tracking, releasing, and reporting in the service.

We have a Jira Cloud Teams app that enables your project team to track, update, and manage projects from Microsoft Teams. This app has integration with Jira Cloud so that your project team or user can receive notifications, create or update tickets, and view them in Teams meetings as a group.

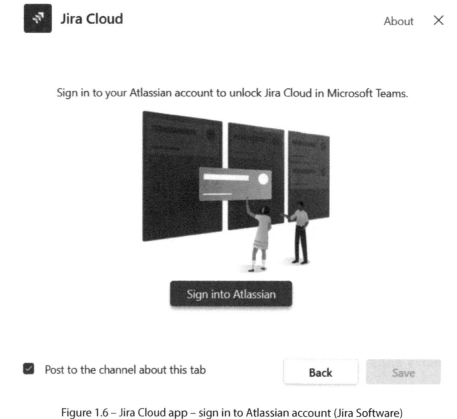

Figure 1.6 – Jira Cloud app – sign in to Atlassian account (Jira Software)

ServiceNow Virtual Agent

ServiceNow Virtual Agent is another third-party app for which ServiceNow and Microsoft partnered together to give ServiceNow users a conversational experience with a live or virtual agent.

This enables employees to perform routine ServiceNow tasks directly in Microsoft Teams.

Consider the following few scenarios:

- Employees can access ServiceNow's Employee Center embedded directly within Microsoft Teams

- IT service desk agents can reach out to employee requests directly in Microsoft Teams to resolve questions about open tickets

- Actionable notifications within Microsoft Teams enable employees to stay up to date on their tickets

Figure 1.7 – Now Virtual Agent

This app (Now Virtual Agent) is free with Microsoft Teams, and users of this app are required to have an appropriate ServiceNow license. For a better experience and range of features, it is recommended to have ITSM Pro/HR Pro, as the standard license doesn't cover many use cases. The following figure shows the experience of ServiceNow Virtual Agent in Teams:

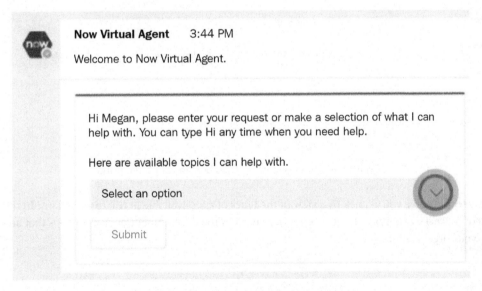

Figure 1.8 – Now Virtual Agent in Teams

Custom apps

In addition to Microsoft-provided and third-party-provided apps, as an organization, you can also build custom apps using various Teams integration strategies. These types of apps are called custom apps. We will spend a good amount of time in this book on building custom apps using various technologies such as Microsoft Power Platform, Azure, and the **SharePoint Framework (SPFx)**.

The Landings, as shown next, is an example of a custom app:

Figure 1.9 – The Landings custom app

Custom apps are typically created and approved by your organization's IT team and shared with you or a group you're in. These custom apps are usually designed based on your requirements.

Through the Teams App Store, you can see the custom apps built in your organization.

Figure 1.10 – View of custom apps built in your organization

This section gave you a quick overview of the types of apps available in Microsoft Teams. In the next section, we'll learn more about core services used in the development of custom apps that are built by your organization.

Exploring the core services used for the development of Teams

Before moving on to learning more about custom apps in Microsoft Teams, it is good to have some understanding of the following technologies:

- Azure
- Microsoft 365
- Power Platform

These concepts will be used in most of the apps that you are going to build and host in Teams. Let us have a look at each of them in brief.

Azure

Azure is the core platform that Microsoft Teams is built and hosted on; it takes advantage of core Azure features such as scaling, global footprint, redundancy, and disaster recovery. In this book, we are focusing on apps in Microsoft Teams and these apps can also use Azure services. We will briefly discuss a few of those Azure services, although it would be good for you to explore more about these services as a self-study.

Azure App Service

Azure App Service enables you to quickly build and host web apps, mobile backends, and RESTful APIs in the programming language of your choice without worrying about infrastructure. This **platform as a service** (**PaaS**) is offered by Azure so that you can focus on developing your application while the platform takes care of infrastructure needs and scaling based on your business requirements. Speaking of scaling, you can scale your app up or down by adding or removing resources based on demand, which helps control infrastructure costs. Scale-out is another option, increasing the machine instances that your app running on.

QnA Maker

QnA Maker is a cloud-based service that allows you to create a natural conversational layer over your data. QnA Maker lets you import a **knowledge base** (**KB**) of question and answer pairs from any FAQs, support websites, manuals, or documents. It also answers questions with the best answers from the QnA in your KB automatically.

Conversational applications are the most common scenario in which to use QnA Maker. A common scenario would be to create a FAQ bot with no code:

- Best practices: `https://aka.ms/QnAMakerBestPractices`
- Documentation: `https://aka.ms/QnAMakerDocumentation`
- QnA Maker portal: `https://aka.ms/QnAMakerPortal`

Azure Blob Storage

Azure Blob Storage is an optimized solution for storing massive amounts of unstructured data that doesn't adhere to a particular data model or definition, such as text or binary data. This helps you create data lakes for your analytics needs and provides storage to build powerful cloud-native and mobile apps.

Blob Storage is designed for the following:

- Bringing images or documents directly to a browser
- Storing files for distributed access
- Streaming video and audio
- Writing log files
- Storing data for backup and restoration, disaster recovery, and archiving
- Storing data for analysis by an on-premises or Azure-hosted service

These are the resources that Blob storage offers:

- **The storage account**: A storage account provides a unique namespace in Azure for your data.
- **A container in the storage account**: A container organizes a set of blobs, like a directory in a filesystem. A storage account can include an unlimited number of containers, and a container can store an unlimited number of blobs.
- **A blob in a container**

You can see the relationship between various resources in the following screenshot:

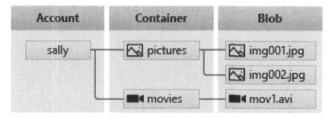

Figure 1.11 – Representation of the relationship between blob storage resources

Azure Storage supports three types of blobs:

- **Block blobs**: Defined by a list of blocks and predominantly used to store objects such as documents, images, video, and so on.

- **Append blobs**: An append blob is comprised of blocks and is optimized for append operations, used mostly for scenarios such as logging, big data analytics, output, and so on.

- **Page blobs**: These are collections of 512-byte pages with the ability to read/write arbitrary ranges of bytes. Also, page blobs are designed for random read/write operations, such as for IaaS disks, Azure Event Hubs, and block-level backup.

Azure Functions

Azure Functions is a serverless event-driven solution that extends Azure App Service on less infrastructure, thereby saving a lot of costs. As a developer, you focus on code and the rest will be handled by Azure Functions.

The following are a few common scenarios for using Azure Functions:

- Building a web API
- Time-based processing
- Images added
- Building a serverless workflow
- Responding to database changes
- Creating reliable message queue systems
- Processing data in real time
- Real-time bot messaging

You can write functions in C#, Java, JavaScript, PowerShell, or Python.

Azure Cognitive Services

Cognitive Services is a collection of intelligent APIs that you can embed into your app, as these REST APIs are very easy to implement. These services can span Vision, Speech, Language, Knowledge, and Web search. There are a variety of domains that give apps a human side, including Speech, Decision, Language, and Vision. Speech-to-text is one feature of the Speech service.

The following figure shows domain-specific pre-trained models:

Figure 1.12 – Screenshot of domain-specific pre-trained models

Microsoft 365

Microsoft 365 is he platform with the most compliant cloud-based subscription service and brings the best tools together with security and compliance.

SharePoint is the technology part of Microsoft 365 that underpins Teams. So, every Microsoft Team instance has a SharePoint site underneath, as well as an Office 365 group.

Office 365 is a service that connects a variety of collaboration tools across Office 365. You can create an Office 365 Group from a SharePoint page or a SharePoint administrator can create one from SharePoint Online Administration.

You can go to the SharePoint start page by clicking on the app launcher and selecting the SharePoint tile or by clicking on **SharePoint** in the global navigation bar from any site in SharePoint.

Figure 1.13 – SharePoint start page | + Create site

The preceding screen shows you the + **Create site** option on the SharePoint start page; the following screen shows the option to create a site in the **SharePoint admin center** window:

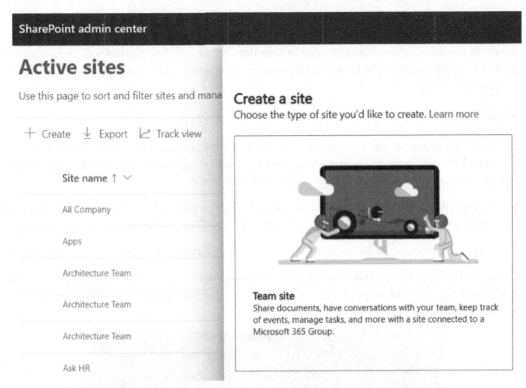

Figure 1.14 – SharePoint admin center | + Create | Team site

Power Platform

Power Platform is a low-code or no-code platform that lets you build end-to-end solutions with custom apps using Power Apps, automation processes using Power Automate, and intelligent bots using **Power Virtual Agents** (**PVA**), as well as analyze data with Power BI.

This diagram represents all the services from Power Platform in a row:

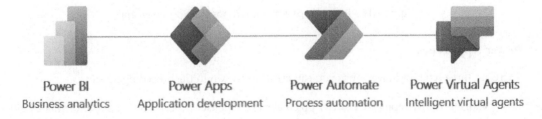

Figure 1.15 – Power Platform services

Power BI

Power BI provides insights into the value of your data; it can visualize most of your organization's data on the platform. With the **Power BI** tab, you can embed interactive reports into Microsoft Teams channels and chats.

Power Apps

Microsoft Power Apps is a SaaS for creating and using custom business apps across different mobile and web platforms. Through this, you can connect to various enterprise systems and data sources that may be used in your organization, such as SAP ERP and Oracle.

Power Apps enables you to build applications with no code or very little code. It will help businesses write their application with minimal help and support from IT organizations.

These apps can be shared with co-workers and even with guests across the web, tablets, and mobile devices.

To view the existing Power Apps or to create new ones, go to `https://web.powerapps.com`. From there, you can click **Apps** on the left-hand side to view existing apps and **+ New app** to create a new Power App.

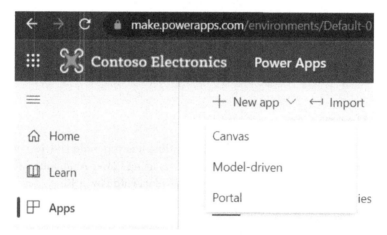

Figure 1.16 – Power Apps with options for creating a new app

Power Apps types

There are three types of Power Apps you can create as shown in the preceding figure:

- **Canvas**: Canvas apps are Power Apps that start with user experience or data, and will be built using concepts such as screens, controls, formulas, and connections.

- **Model-driven**: Model-driven apps are apps that start with data models in tables of Dataverse. They are built with components such as site maps, tables, forms, views, charts, dashboards, business processes, and Power Automate.

- **Portal**: Power Apps portals are external-facing websites that allow users outside your organization to create and modify data in Dataverse tables. These users can be signed via various identities or access content anonymously.

Power Automate

Power Automate helps businesses work smarter by automating workflows with personal productivity and various business apps and services across your organization. In addition, you can also integrate a Power App with Power Automate.

To view the existing Power Automate functionality or to add to it, go to `https://flow.microsoft.com`.

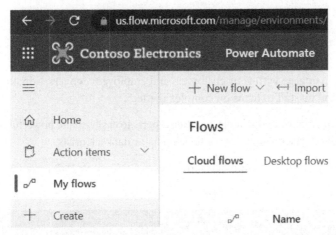

Figure 1.17 – Power Automate with the option to create new flows

Triggers

Always have one to start Power Automate. You can have the following type of triggers to start Power Automate

- Scheduled Power Automate
- The Power Apps button
- SharePoint items, files, emails, contacts created, HTTP triggers, or webhooks

Actions

You can have as many actions as you like after the trigger condition is successfully met.

The following figure is a sample Power Automate action with a trigger when a new item is created in SharePoint:

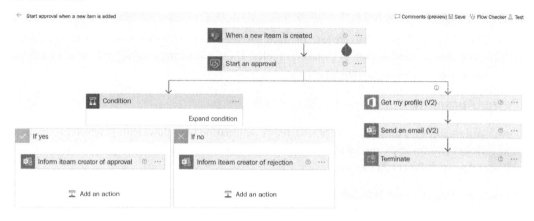

Figure 1.18 – Sample Power Automate

PVA

With PVA, you can engage with your customers and employees conversationally. It resolves routine issues easily, freeing up staff to focus on complex matters.

PVA enables you to empower your subject matter experts to easily create powerful bots using a guided, no-code graphical interface – no need for developers or data scientists.

We will discuss more of these technologies in *Chapter 7, Microsoft Dataverse for Teams*.

To work on PVA or add to it, go to `https://powerva.microsoft.com/`.

Figure 1.19 – PVA

Microsoft Teams admin, configuration, and prerequisites such as Azure, Microsoft 365, and Power Platform

If you want to start building various customization options such as apps, bots, and tabs (discussed in detail in the next chapter) for Microsoft Teams to use in your tenant, you should prepare your Microsoft 365 tenant for these customizations by configuring the required policies and settings in the Microsoft Teams admin center.

The Teams admin center is a single place to configure various settings and policies to control the behavior of all three types of apps (Microsoft, third-party, and custom): `https://admin.teams.microsoft.com`. You need to be a Teams Administrator or a Global/Tenant Admin to access and adjust the policies or settings in the Teams admin center.

> **Note**
>
> There are many types of Teams policies, such as those related to messaging, phone, voice, apps, and so on. Policies are a collection of configuration elements and can be assigned per user, group, or tenant (organization-wide). As this book is about Teams app customizations, our focus is mostly on policies that concern apps.
>
> In addition to policies, you can also control the configuration through settings – settings meaning a collection of configuration elements that can only be controlled at the tenant level.

You have the following options on the left-hand side to control Microsoft Teams apps for end users and their assignments at the user, group, or tenant level:

> **Note:**
>
> Assigning policies at the user level or tenant level is mostly clear based on the name; when it comes to groups, you can assign the policies to a group of users with a security group or distribution list.

Policies/Settings	Assignment
App Permissions	User
App Setup	Group
Org-Wide	Tenant

You can log in to the Teams admin center directly at `https://admin.teams.microsoft.com` or you can access the Teams admin center through the admin portal at `https://admin.microsoft.com`.

It will look as follows on your screen:

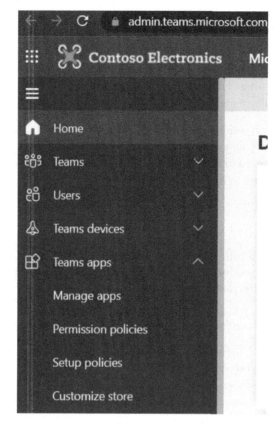

Figure 1.20 – Teams apps administration

Teams apps have the following options for the configuration of the app's permissions and settings:

- **Manage apps** – org-wide settings
- **Permission policies**
- **Setup policies**

Let us discuss these in detail in the following sub-sections.

Org-wide app settings

Org-wide app settings can control the apps available to your whole organization. Permissions and set-up policies can't be more permissive than org-wide app settings, so org-wide settings override any custom policies that you assign to users.

By navigating to the Teams admin center | **Teams apps** | **Manage apps** | **Org-wide app settings**, you can control the third-party apps and custom apps for your organization's tenant:

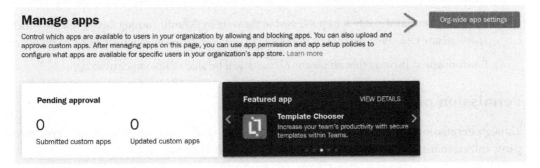

Figure 1.21 – Accessing Org-wide app settings through Manage apps

The following screenshot shows the various options available for org-wide settings:

Figure 1.22 – Org-wide app settings

From *Figure 1.22*, we can see how these org-wide settings can be controlled:

- **Allow third-party apps**: Turning this off will block all users from installing any third-party apps
- **Allow any new third-party apps published to the store by default**: Turning this on will allow users to install any new third-party apps published to the store based on their app permission policy
- **Custom apps**: Turning this off means no users will be able to upload custom apps

Permission policies

Through **Permission policies**, you can control the availability of apps (such as Microsoft apps, third-party, and custom apps that are built in-house) to Microsoft Teams users.

You can do this through the following actions:

- Creating custom app permission policies
- Controlling the apps available for various users and groups

Creating custom app permission policies

Through the Teams admin center | **Teams apps** | **Permission policies** | **App permission policies**, you can create a custom app permission policy by clicking on + **Add** and selecting the permissions that you want for various app types.

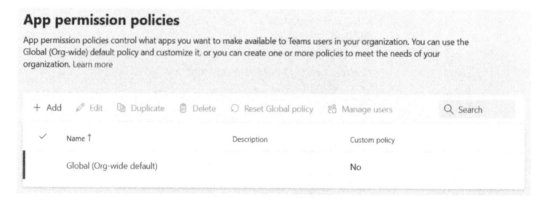

Figure 1.23 – App permission policies view

The following screenshot shows the various options that you can include for each type of app (**Microsoft apps**, **Third-party apps**, and **Custom apps**) in the custom policy:

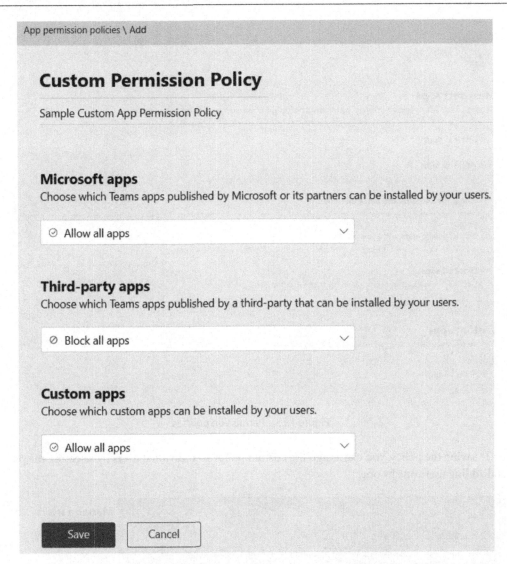

Figure 1.24 – Creating a custom app permission policy

You can select one of the following policy options from the dropdown as the permission policy for each type of app:

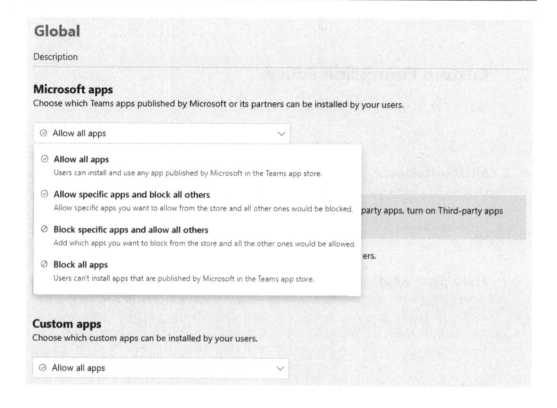

Figure 1.25 – Permission policies

After saving the policy, you can assign the custom policy to individual users by selecting the policy and adding users one by one.

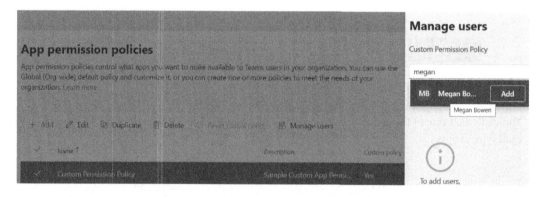

Figure 1.26 – Assigning a custom policy to individual users

When you block apps through an app permission policy, the users who are affected by this policy are unable to install the blocked apps from the Teams store.

In a nutshell, allowing all apps would be the least restrictive, and blocking all apps the most restrictive.

Setup policies

Setup policies will make the approved apps in your organization more accessible to Teams users. This will let you customize Teams by pinning the apps that are most important to the users—you can pin the apps to the left rail (on your desktop) or app bar (from your mobile) and set the order of the apps as they appear. This also includes all three types of apps – Microsoft-built, third-party, and custom. In addition to this, you can control who (such as the developers) can upload custom apps that they have built. The process of uploading custom apps is also called *side-loading*.

You have two built-in app setup policies that are included with the Microsoft Teams admin center:

- **Global (org-wide default)**: Applies to all users – you can pin apps that should be available to all users

- **Frontline worker**: You can assign this to frontline workers

> **Note**
> Frontline workers are employees that work directly with customers or the public, providing services and support and selling products, or employees directly involved in the manufacturing and distribution of products or services.

You can customize the built-in app setup policies by selecting the policy and clicking on **Edit**. Once you are in the policy, you can control the ability to upload a custom app or allow users to pin apps through the following features:

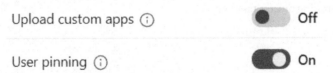

Figure 1.27 – App setup policies

Let's see what each function deals with:

- **Upload custom apps**: This determines whether a user can upload a custom app package to the Teams app. Turning it on lets you create or develop a custom app to be used personally or across your organization without having to submit it to the Teams app store.

- **User pinning**: With this policy, the user's existing app pins will be added to the list of pinned apps, and users can rearrange, add, and remove pins as they choose.

You can pin more apps through the + **Add apps** option on the following screen:

Pinned apps

Choose the order apps are pinned in the app bar in Teams. Learn more

+ Add apps   ↑ Move up   ↓ Move down   ✕ Remove | **7** items

✓	Name	App ID	Publisher
	Activity	14d6962d-6eeb-4f48-8890-de55454bb136	Microsoft Corporation
	Chat	86fcd49b-61a2-4701-b771-54728cd291fb	Microsoft Corporation
	Teams	2a84919f-59d8-4441-a975-2a8c2643b741	Microsoft Corporation
	Calendar	ef56c0de-36fc-4ef8-b417-3d82ba9d073c	Microsoft Corporation
	Calling	20c3440d-c67e-4420-9f80-0e50c39693df	Microsoft Corporation
	Files	5af6a76b-40fc-4ba1-af29-8f49b08e44fd	Microsoft Corporation
	The Landings	4009f8e6-2300-4fc8-8728-f6b9c1eaad16	Contoso Electronics

Figure 1.28 – Sample view of pinned apps

Pinning apps will give Teams users easy access by showcasing the important apps in your organization.

If the admin allows user pinning, the users can pin any existing app; however, if an admin pins apps, the latter configuration always take precedence.

You can also choose the apps that can be installed through this policy.

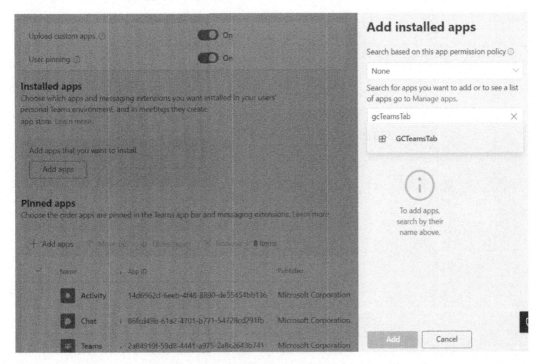

Figure 1.29 – Installing apps through the setup policies

Figure 1.29 shows you where to install the apps through the setup policy.

Summary

Congratulations on getting through the first chapter! In this chapter, you learned about the context behind custom apps for Microsoft Teams and the pre-configuration requirements for your Microsoft 365 tenant to support custom apps via its setup and permission policies. You also learned about supporting technologies that are very important in custom app development and hosting.

The next chapter will dive into various types of customizations that you can build into Microsoft Teams.

2
Microsoft Teams Apps and Bots

You can use Office 365 applications such as Microsoft Office products, Planner, SharePoint, Power Apps, and Power BI as first-party apps for a customized experience on Microsoft Teams, which enables your everyday business users to do all their work within Teams instead of switching between apps.

Beyond first-party apps (Microsoft apps), the next level of customization will come from **Independent Software Vendor** (**ISV**) apps such as ServiceNow, Salesforce, Adobe, and so on, which will enhance the business user's experience within Teams and prevent the need to switch between apps during work.

To achieve a higher level of customization in Microsoft Teams, custom-built apps can also be developed within your organization to enhance the user experience. This chapter will cover the different types of custom apps that can be created and the process of building them.

By customizing the Teams apps, you can make functionality from various solutions or applications available to end users through tabs, apps, connectors, messaging extensions, cards, task modules, and notifications, enhancing their overall experience.

This chapter covers the following main topics:

- Exploring App Studio
- Understanding how to use tabs
- Utilizing bots
- Getting to know more about webhooks and connectors
- Using messaging extensions
- Exploring the use of adaptive cards

Imagine a place where all the enterprise apps and services you require are available at one location, making your business users' daily lives much easier. Let us learn more about how to make that happen in this chapter!

Exploring App Studio/Developer Portal

Microsoft Teams App Studio was a low-code tool that enabled users to create custom Teams apps and bots without writing any code – this app was available from Microsoft Teams Store. In February 2022, Microsoft announced that the Microsoft Teams App Studio tool has been deprecated and will no longer be supported. Instead, they recommend developers use the new Teams Developer Portal, which provides more advanced tools and capabilities for building custom Teams apps and bots.

Microsoft Teams App Studio was used to create, package, and distribute custom Teams apps in a very simplified manner using a graphical interface. As Microsoft Teams App Studio was phased out, Developer Portal provides a dedicated app management console available via the web user interface or as a Teams app. All your existing apps created through Microsoft Teams App Studio will also be available in the Developer Portal app.

Developer Portal acts as a hub for Teams apps and is the new tool for configuring and registering managing Teams apps. Developer Portal will not produce any code for your app or host your app.

To access Developer Portal, go to `https://dev.teams.microsoft.com/` and click on **Apps**.

Figure 2.1 – The Developer Portal web UI

You can also install Developer Portal as a Teams app from the Teams Store, as shown here.

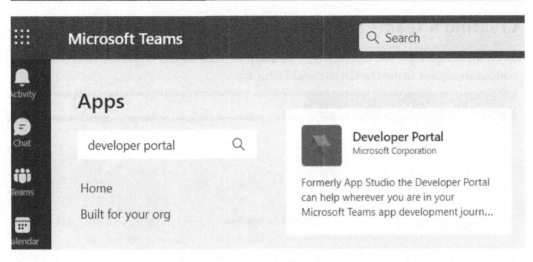

Figure 2.2 – Developer Portal Teams app

With the Developer Portal Teams app installed, you can create custom Microsoft Teams apps and bots; we will explore the different configuration elements involved in building a Teams app using Developer Portal.

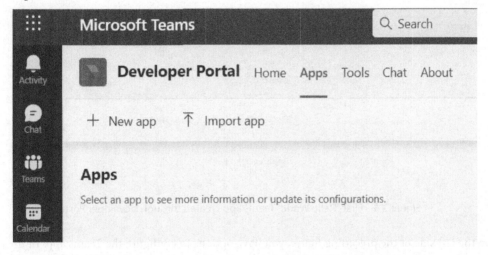

Figure 2.3 – Developer Portal Teams app

The preceding figure shows the Teams app view of Developer Portal, which serves as the central hub for creating and managing Teams apps. Here, you can access a range of resources such as templates, sample code, debugging tools, and detailed documentation to assist you in the app development process.

Creating a Teams app with Developer Portal

As shown in *Figure 2.3*, you can click on **+ New app** to create a Hello World app and review all the configuration pages in the Developer Portal Teams app.

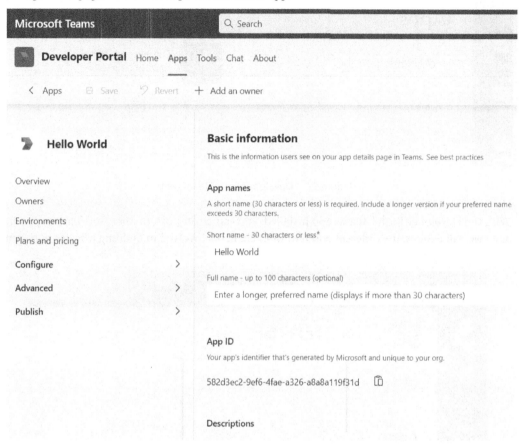

Figure 2.4 – First "Hello World" Teams app created through Developer Portal

On the left side of the preceding figure, you have options to configure the Teams app. In the next sections, we will review these configurations and options for configuring the "Hello World" Teams app.

Overview

On the **Overview** page, as shown in *Figure 2.5*, you have a few sections, such as **Teams store validation**, which validates your app against the Microsoft Teams test cases; the other section is **Active Users (Preview)**, where you can see your app's total number of users.

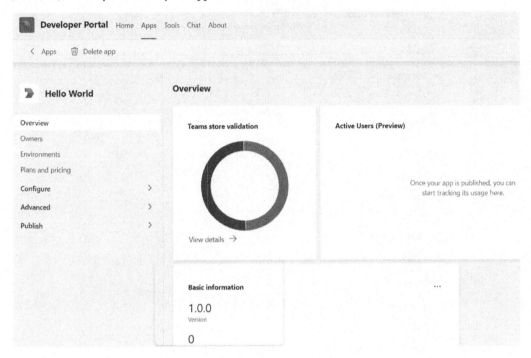

Figure 2.5 – Overview page of the app

Owners

Each app has an **Owners** area for sharing the app with other members; you can also share an app with an **Owner** or **Operative** role. The **Operative** role has the same permissions as the **Owner** role, except **Owner** can delete an app.

Figure 2.6 – The Owners page

The **Owners** page lists all the users that have access to the app and the role they have on the app. The following figure shows you to add an owner for your app.

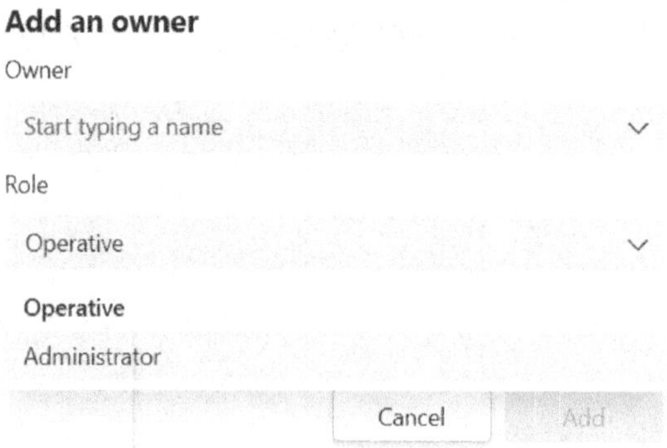

Add an owner

Owner

Start typing a name ⌄

Role

Operative ⌄

Operative

Administrator

Cancel | Add

Figure 2.7 – Sharing an app

As shown in the preceding figure, you type in the owner and pick the **Role** type to share the app with the user.

Environments

In Microsoft Teams, you can create and configure environments (such as development, staging, and production) and environment-specific variables to move your app and manage and evaluate the behavior of your app in each environment in a controlled way before deploying it to production.

You could use environment variables to store URLs for different backend services in development, staging, and production environments. You can then reference these URLs in your app's code to connect to the correct backend service for each environment.

By using environments and variables in this way, you can ensure that your app behaves as expected in each environment, and you can easily deploy your app to production with confidence.

These variables will help us to set up in-app configuration instead of hardcoded values.

Select + **Add an environment** to create an environment, and + **Add a variable** to create configuration variables, as shown in the following screenshot.

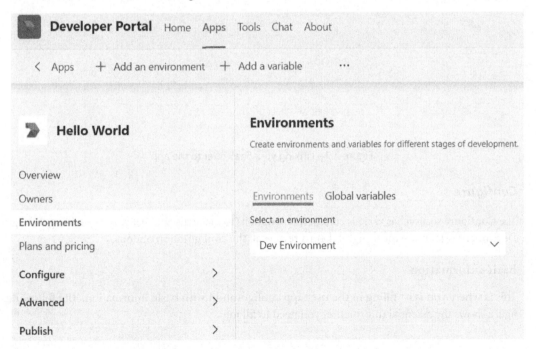

Figure 2.8 – Environments/Global variables for your app

Plans and pricing

If you are an ISV, you can create **Software-as-a-Service (SaaS)** offers so that customers can buy your SaaS-based technical apps. On the **Plans and pricing** screen here, you can set up your **Publisher ID** and **Offer ID** information.

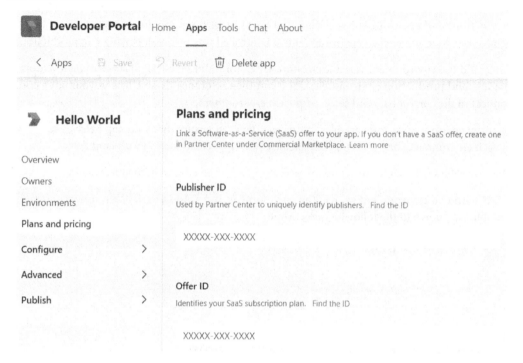

Figure 2.9 – Linking your SaaS offer to the app

Configure

The **Configure** section has various configuration options to make the app that you are building through Developer Portal more meaningful. Let us review all the configuration options.

Basic information

This is where you start filling in the user app configuration with basic information. The following figure shows the essential information you need to fill in.

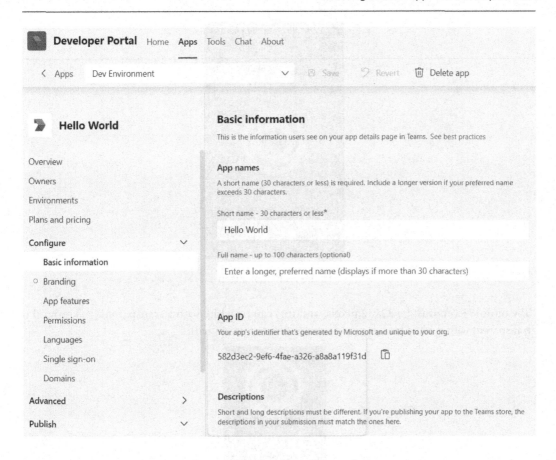

Figure 2.10 – User app configuration

Branding

You can create a custom icon for your app, with an option to update the color icon and outline icon in PNG format. The color version of your icon should be 192x192 pixels and your icon symbol should be 96x96 pixels. The latter can be of any color, but the icon must be on a solid or fully transparent square background. Here is an example:

Figure 2.11 – Color icon

The outline icon must be 32x32 pixels, and this can be white with a transparent background or transparent with a white background (as colors are not permitted):

Figure 2.12 – Outline icon

These icons need to meet the following size requirements for your app to pass the Teams Store review:

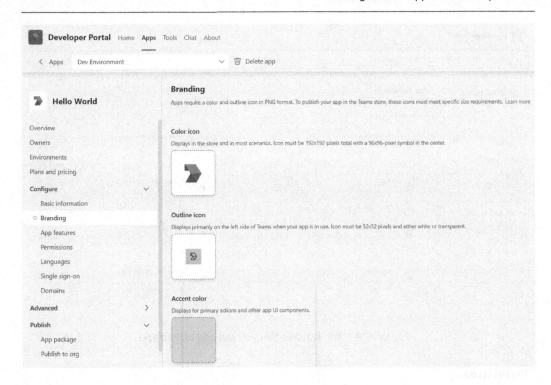

Figure 2.13 – Branding icons

App features

You can add various features based on what you plan for your app to do through the **App features** section; we will discuss these features in the next section. The following screenshot shows the distinct options available in **App features**.

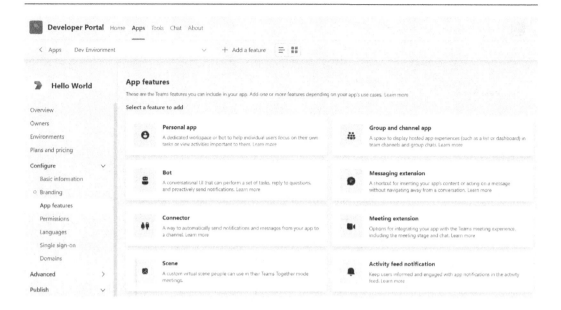

Figure 2.14 – App features that you can add to your app

Permissions

You can also set up permissions for the app you build through Developer Portal; you can add two types of permission to your app:

- **Device permissions**: With Microsoft Teams apps, you can easily integrate various device capabilities, such as the camera, QR codes, barcode scanner, photo gallery, microphone, and location with apps. With tools such as the Microsoft Teams JavaScript client SDK, you can set up requests for the required permissions to access a device's capabilities. Here are these permissions:

  - **Get the user's location**
  - Native features of the user's device, such as the camera, microphone, and speakers
  - User notifications
  - **Send and receive Musical Instrument Digital Interface (MIDI) information**
  - **Open links in external apps**

- **Team and chat permissions**: The **Resource-Specific Consent (RSC)** permissions model will let team owners and chat owners grant consent for an app to access and modify a team's and a chat's data, respectively.

The Teams app **Device permissions** section is where you specify whether your app requires access to specific devices such as the camera, microphone, speakers, and user's location. You can select the device features that your app needs to access.

The **team and chat permissions** section is where you can specify the permissions your app needs to access specific team and chat features, such as the ability to read and write messages, access teams and channels, and manage team settings.

The following screenshot shows the various permissions you can integrate into your app.

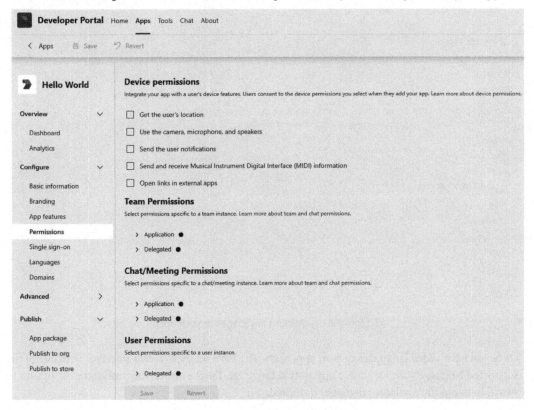

Figure 2.15 – Teams app permissions

Languages

Your app may have requirements to support multiple languages; you can configure additional languages for your app, and through this **Languages** page, you can provide pointers to additional language files. The following screenshot shows you the options to add other languages to your app on Microsoft Teams.

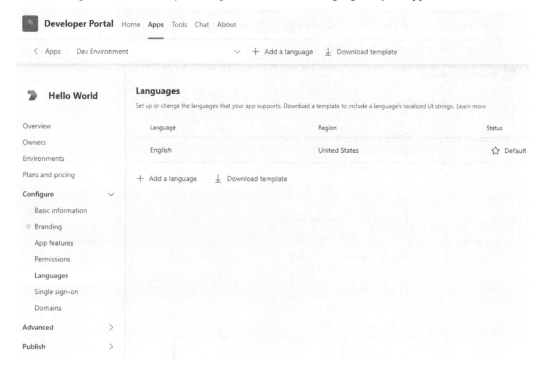

Figure 2.16 – Adding languages to your app

Once you have added languages to your app, users who have set their Teams interface with one of the supported languages can view your app in that language. Furthermore, they will have the option to switch between the available languages if desired.

Single sign-on

Single Sign-On (SSO) is critical for app authentication as most of the users in an organization may not want to have multiple auth prompts.

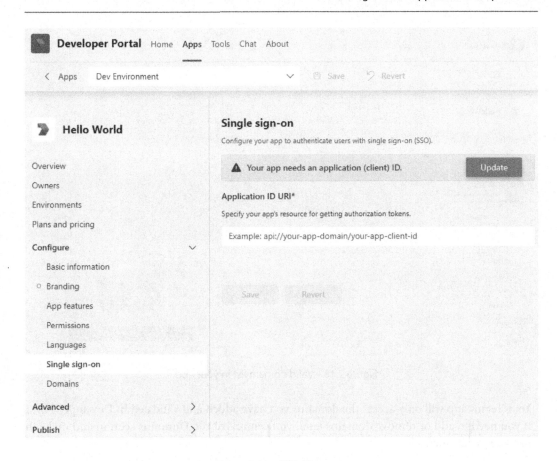

Figure 2.17 – SSO for an app

Setting up SSO for your app enables Microsoft Teams users to sign in to your app using their Teams account credentials without requiring a separate username and password. This provides a seamless user experience and eliminates the need for multiple authentication prompts.

Domains

You can add all valid domains for the websites your app will load within Teams through this page. The following screen lets you add the domains that your app needs.

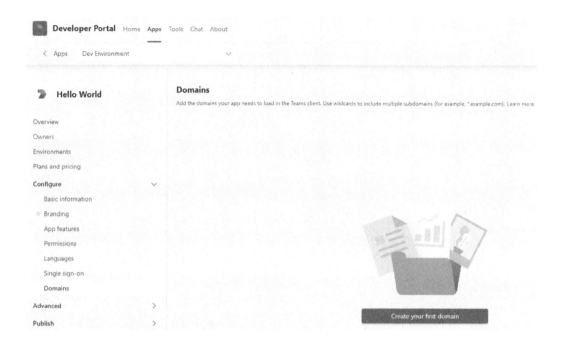

Figure 2.18 – Valid domain list in your app

Your Teams app will only access the domains you have added and validated in Developer Portal. If you need to add or remove domains later, you can revisit the **Domains** section and make the necessary adjustments.

Advanced

Within **Developer Portal**, you have advanced settings that enable you to configure complex settings for your app. You can enhance your app's behavior with these settings to better meet your users' needs.

App content

The following screen allows you to configure options related to displaying a loading indicator while content is loading, as well as enabling **Full-screen mode** to display apps without an app header.

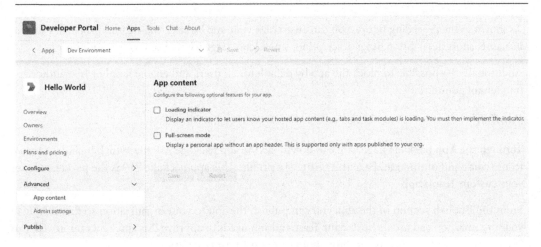

Figure 2.19 – App content under Advanced

Admin settings

App developers can allow users to customize certain aspects of their Teams app via the Teams admin center. However, this functionality is only available for apps published in the Teams Store.

The following screenshot highlights the specific options that can be modified using this menu:

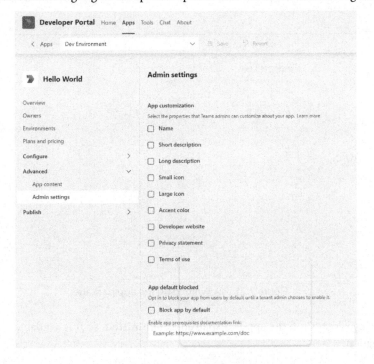

Figure 2.20 – Customizing your Teams app

As shown in the preceding figure, you can customize your app by selecting various properties such as its name, short description, long description, small icon, large icon, accent color, and more.

Additionally, it's possible to block the app by default for all users and enable it only when authorized by a tenant admin.

Publish

Through the **App package** page, you can download the app package ZIP file, which includes the two icons (color and outline) and a `manifest.json` file. This app package ZIP is the package file for your custom Teams app.

From the **Publish** section of the app, you can publish the app to your organization so that people in your organization can use it. Next, your Teams admin needs to approve this app. Once approved, this app will be available in the Teams Store under the **Build for your org** tab.

From the same **Publishi** section, you also have the option to publish the app to the Teams Store. An app validation tool checks your app package and validates it against the Microsoft test cases so it can be published to the Teams Store.

The following screenshot shows **App package** with all your app's configuration details, features, resources, and other required things.

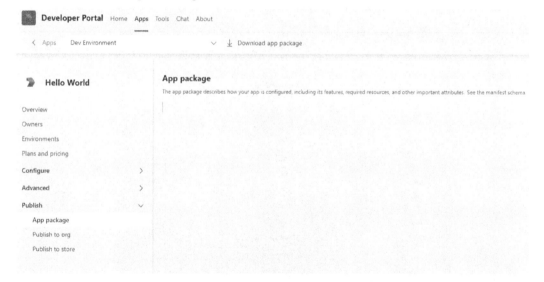

Figure 2.21 – Downloading the app package

In the following screenshot, the app is displayed as **Submitted**, so it is available to people within your organization.

Publish to your org (Contoso)

Make your app available to people in your org. Once approved by your IT admin, your app will be featured in the Teams store under **Built for your org**. Learn more

Version	Status
1.0.0	Submitted

Figure 2.22 – Publish to your org

As a Teams admin, you can log in and see the submitted app waiting for approval:

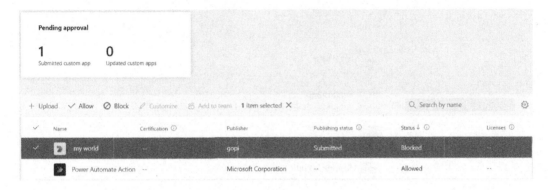

Figure 2.23 – Teams admin app submission

As a Teams admin, you can publish this app and change the status to **Allowed**:

Figure 2.24 – Approved app through the Teams admin center

Once the **my world** app gets approved by a Teams admin, it can be added to Teams:

Figure 2.25 – Approved app in Apps

You were able to create a new app through Developer Portal; all the aforementioned steps allow you to create a new app and publish it within your organization.

Teams Toolkit for Visual Studio Code

Teams Toolkit for Visual Studio Code is a plugin that enables developers to create, debug, and deploy Microsoft Teams apps directly from Visual Studio Code. Teams Toolkit is available as an extension for Visual Studio Code, so the first step is to install this extension.

The following screenshot depicts adding the Teams Toolkit extension in Visual Studio Code.

Figure 2.26 – Searching for Teams Toolkit and clicking Install to install it

After installing the Teams Toolkit extension, you will see the Teams logo in the left bar of Visual Studio Code. When you click on it, you will see an option to create a new Teams app.

Select the **Teams | Create a new Teams** app option from the list, and then follow the prompts to provide the required information, such as the app name, description, and icon.

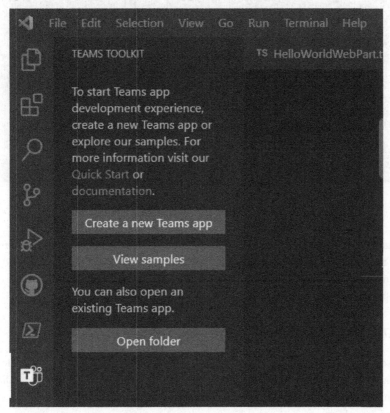

Figure 2.27 – Creating a new Teams app through the Teams Toolkit extension

When you click on **Create a new Teams app**, you can choose the type of app you want to create; there are pre-built templates, including a Teams **Tab** app, a **Bot** app, and **Messaging Extension**.

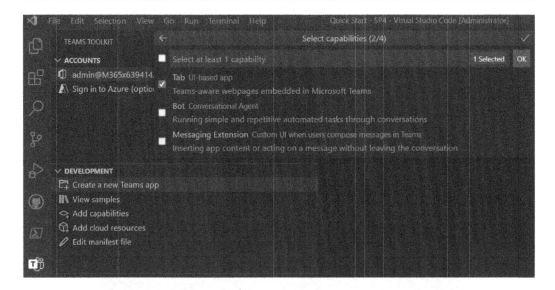

Figure 2.28 – Click on the Teams icon in the sidebar – Create a new Teams app

Once you have made all the necessary selections, Teams Toolkit will generate a new project for your Teams app. You can then code your app by opening the new project in Visual Studio Code and making the desired modifications. By leveraging Teams Toolkit for Visual Studio Code, you can rapidly create, test, and deploy top-notch Teams apps.

The Microsoft Teams JavaScript client SDK

The Microsoft Teams JavaScript client SDK is a set of libraries and is part of the Microsoft Teams developer platform. It makes it easy to integrate your services with Teams, whether you develop custom apps for your enterprise or SaaS applications for teams around the world.

@microsoft/teams-js - npm (npmjs.com) will give you all the details to start using the Microsoft Teams JavaScript client SDK.

The following steps are for installing the Teams JavaScript SDK with npm or yarn; after these steps, you will be able to create Teams apps with the JavaScript client SDK:

```
npm
npm install --save @microsoft/teams-js
yarn
yarn add @microsoft/teams-js
```

You can create various Teams apps with the Yeoman generator, as shown in the following screenshot.

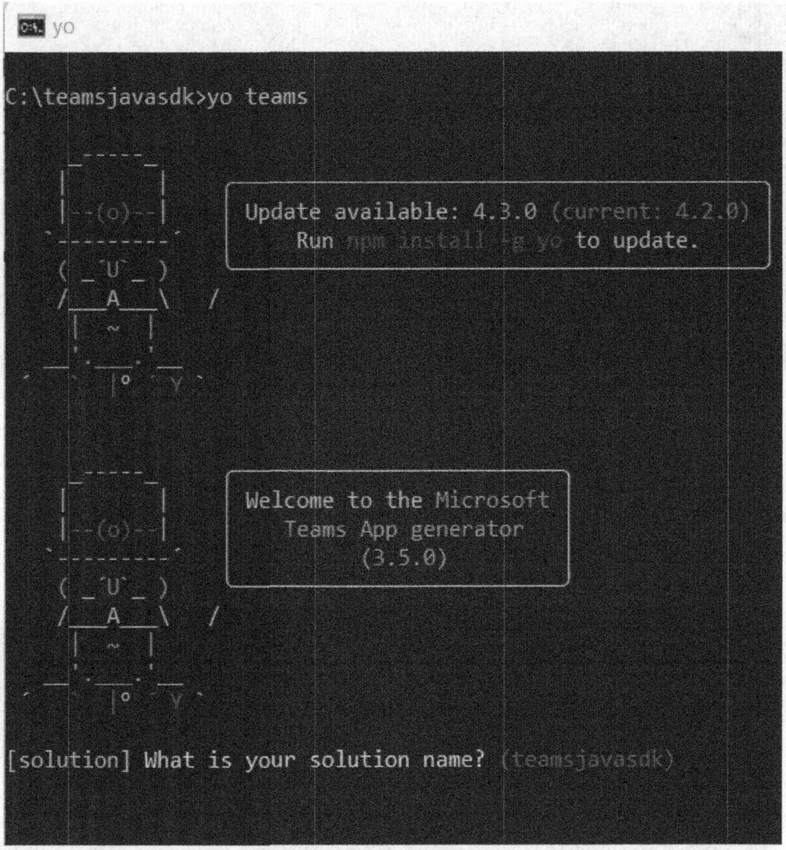

Figure 2.29 – Instantiating Teams with your teams

To create Teams apps using the Yeoman generator, you must go through a series of interactive prompts, which will assist you in determining the specific project type you require. The process has been designed to be user-friendly and intuitive, making it easy to specify the exact features and functionalities needed for your Teams project. Then, by following the prompts and answering the questions, you can rapidly generate a customized project that meets your unique requirements.

The following figure displays the questions and samples to respond to for you to create the Teams app:

```
[solution] What is your solution name? teamsjavasdk
[solution] Where do you want to place the files? Use the current folder
[solution] Title of your Microsoft Teams App project? teamsjavasdk
[solution] Your (company) name? (max 32 characters) GCTEST
[solution] Which manifest version would you like to use? v1.9
[solution] Quick scaffolding Yes
[solution] What features do you want to add to your project? (Press <space> to
selection)
>(*) A Tab
 ( ) A bot
 ( ) An Outgoing Webhook
 ( ) A Connector
 ( ) A Message Extension Command
 ( ) Localization support
```

Figure 2.30 – Scaffolding for the project

Based on your answers to all the questions, it creates a Teams app project. You can see the project created in Visual Studio Code in the following figure:

Figure 2.31 – Teams app project from the SDK

The Microsoft Teams JavaScript client SDK is a powerful tool for building custom Teams apps that can enhance the productivity and collaboration of Teams users. The libraries provided by the Microsoft Teams JavaScript client SDK offer a comprehensive set of APIs for building custom Teams apps.

Understanding how to use tabs

Tabs in Microsoft Teams provide a rich and interactive area for users to access important information and services directly within a Teams app. Tabs can be accessed through dedicated channels or chats and are a great way to provide access to **Line-of-Business (LOB)** data or services.

Two types of tabs are available in Teams: built-in tabs and custom tabs.

Built-in tabs come pre-configured within Teams and include popular services such as Planner, OneNote, and Stream. On the other hand, custom tabs can be created and configured by app developers to meet the specific needs of their users. By creating custom tabs, developers can integrate their app's data and services directly into Teams, providing users with a seamless and integrated experience.

The following screenshot highlights the flexibility given to team owners and members, as they can add tabs to Teams channels or chats. This allows users to customize their Teams experience and access the information they need in a more organized and efficient way.

Figure 2.32 – Clicking + Add a tab for a channel

Every new team has a default **General** channel, including the three tabs shown in *Figure 2.32*. You can also create additional channels in the team chat based on your own preferences or the team's purpose.

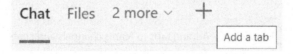

Figure 2.33 – Clicking + Add a tab for a chat

When we click the plus icon, we have various tab options that we can add.

Built-in tab

Several built-in tabs can be added to enhance the functionality and user experience of Teams channels. These tabs offer various features and functionalities that enable Teams users to access essential information and services directly within the Teams environment.

The following screenshot displays a few of the built-in tabs available that can be added to Teams channels:

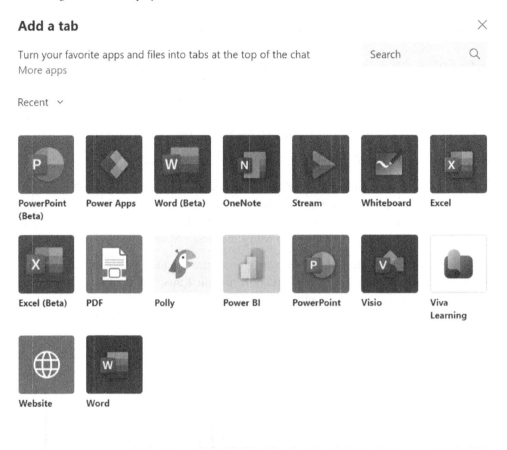

Figure 2.34 – Adding tabs to Teams channels and chats

Utilizing the tab feature allows you to seamlessly embed your content into any channel or chat within Teams, allowing for streamlined access and collaboration. In addition, this enables you to have conversations or meetings centered around the embedded content within the same channel or chat, fostering a more cohesive and efficient workflow.

Custom tabs

Developer Portal offers personal apps, which enable developers to create a set of tabs exclusively for individual use. These tabs can be used for various purposes, such as displaying a web page (i.e., a home tab) or providing a chatbot interface (i.e., a chat tab).

The following screenshot shows an example of the custom tabs you can add with custom links.

Figure 2.35 – Tabs in a personal app

These tabs allow you to bring rich content into Teams through built-in or custom tabs. Now, we will discuss bots.

Utilizing bots

A bot is a type of Teams app that facilitates user conversation with text, cards, or speech. It could be a simple Q&A or a more complex feature that is tailored to the specific services being offered.

Bots are also called chatbots or conversational bots. Conversational bots will have users interact with your web service through text, interactive cards, and task modules. In the end, a bot is just a REST endpoint.

We have an SDK that helps us build the conversational model for a bot and powerful AI tools such as **Language Understanding (LUIS)** to help power our bot. LUIS is cloud-based conversational AI that applies intelligence to predict the flow of conversation with a user and meet what they are asking for.

A significant advantage of these bots is that you can publish your bot to several different channels that help connect your bot to users.

Creating an FAQ bot with QnA Maker

We discussed QnA Maker in *Chapter 1, Introducing Microsoft Teams Apps*. You can go to `https://www.qnamaker.ai` to build a **Frequently Asked Questions (FAQ)** bot.

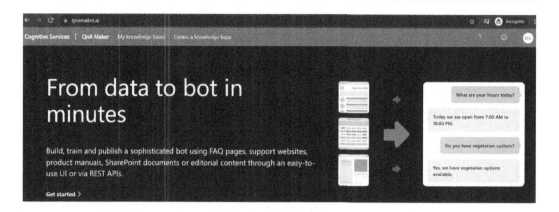

Figure 2.36 – Signing into QnA Maker (qnamaker.ai)

The QnA **Knowledge Base** (**KB**) will use a particular source for its Q&A pairs; you create a Q&A service with the KB you want to use for your given scenario. QnA Maker extracts all possible pairs of questions and answers from the user-provided content – FAQ URLs, documents, and editorial content.

Creating an FAQ bot

By using QnA Maker in Azure Cognitive Services, we can create an FAQ bot with no code. QnA Maker enables you to power a Q&A service for FAQ documents or URLs.

As a first step, you create a KB, as shown in the following figure. Then, you can go to `https://www.qnamaker.ai/Create` to set up QnA Maker.

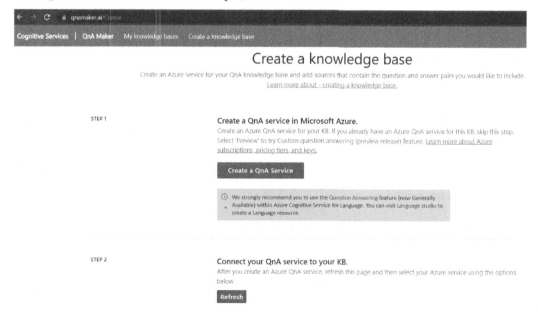

Figure 2.37 – Clicking on Create a knowledge base

Follow these steps to create the FAQ bot:

1. **Create a Q&A service**: You can create a Q&A service in the Azure portal with all the required information and then return it to QnA Maker.

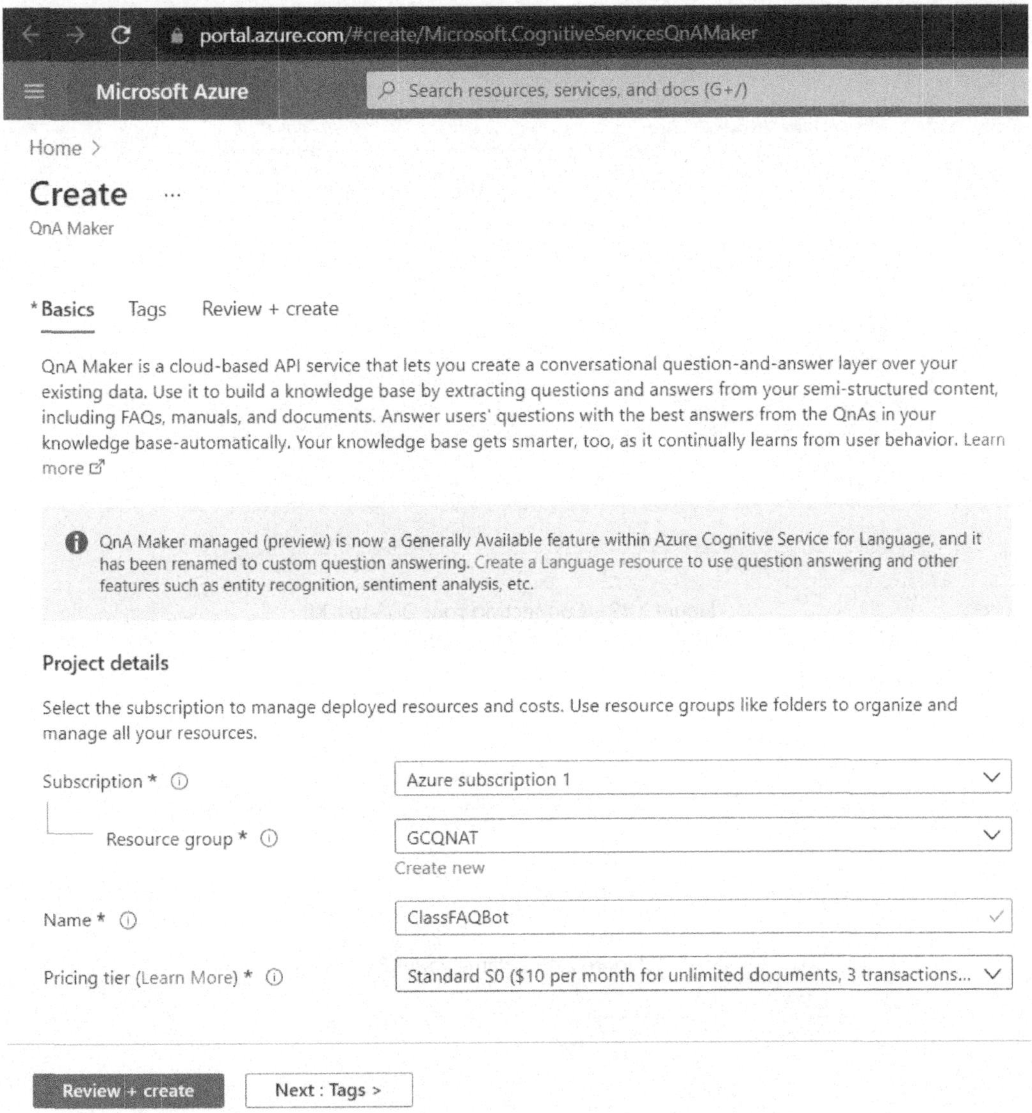

Figure 2.38 – Creating a Q&A service in Azure

2. Click **Refresh** and select your AAD ID, your subscription, and the Q&A service name from *step 1.*

STEP 2   ### Connect your QnA service to your KB.

After you create an Azure QnA service, refresh this page and then select your Azure service using the options below

Figure 2.39 – Connecting your Q&A to a KB

3. Name your KB:

STEP 3   ### Name your KB.

The knowledge base name is for your reference and you can change it at anytime.

Figure 2.40 – Name your KB

4. Populate your KB using any of the FAQ URLs out there; in this example, I am using `https://products.office.com/en-au/microsoft-office-for-home-and-school-faq`:

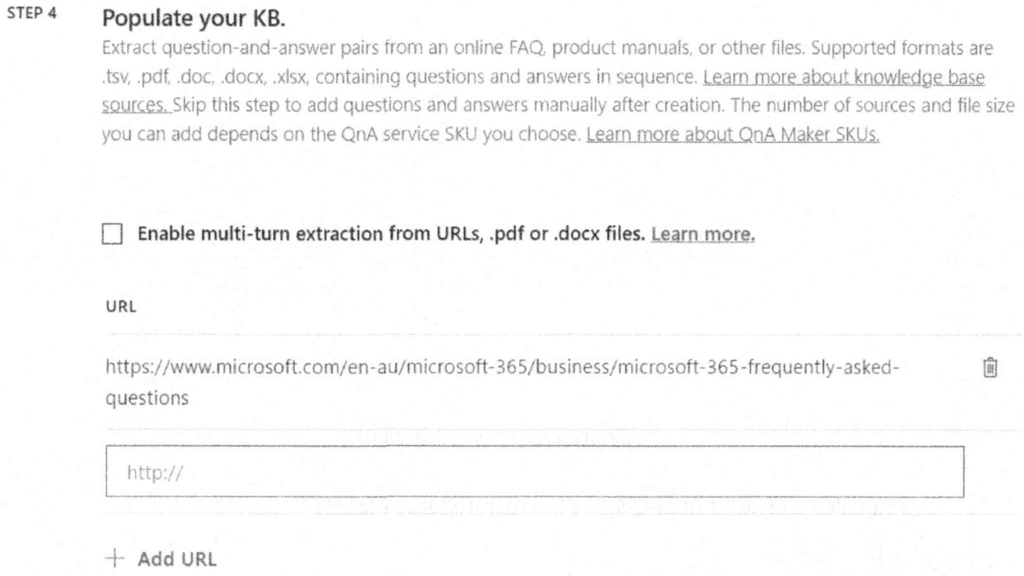

STEP 4   **Populate your KB.**

Extract question-and-answer pairs from an online FAQ, product manuals, or other files. Supported formats are .tsv, .pdf, .doc, .docx, .xlsx, containing questions and answers in sequence. Learn more about knowledge base sources. Skip this step to add questions and answers manually after creation. The number of sources and file size you can add depends on the QnA service SKU you choose. Learn more about QnA Maker SKUs.

☐ **Enable multi-turn extraction from URLs, .pdf or .docx files. Learn more.**

URL

https://www.microsoft.com/en-au/microsoft-365/business/microsoft-365-frequently-asked-questions   🗑

http://

+ **Add URL**

Figure 2.41 – Populating the Office 365 FAQ KB

5. Create your KB for the Q&A:

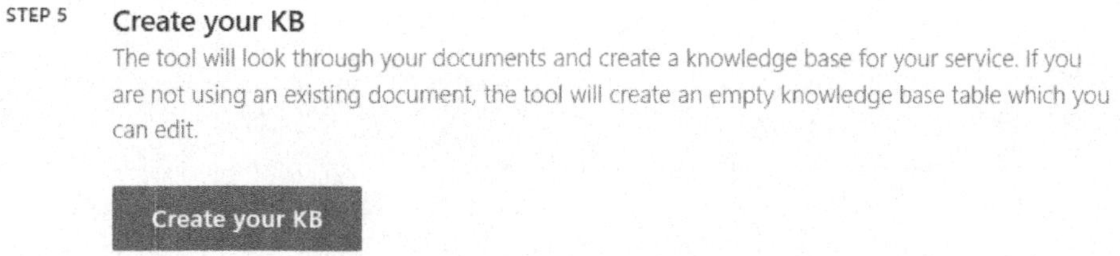

STEP 5   **Create your KB**

The tool will look through your documents and create a knowledge base for your service. If you are not using an existing document, the tool will create an empty knowledge base table which you can edit.

Figure 2.42 – Create your KB

6. Once the KB has been generated, click **Save and train**:

Figure 2.43 – Save and train

7. You can also add additional Q&As directly into QnA Maker:

Knowledge base

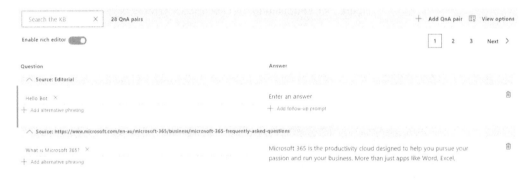

Figure 2.44 – Additional questions

8. Click **Test** – testing will help you to see whether QnA Maker is working correctly.

9. Click **Publish**.

After successfully testing the Q&A service, you can publish it to create a bot.

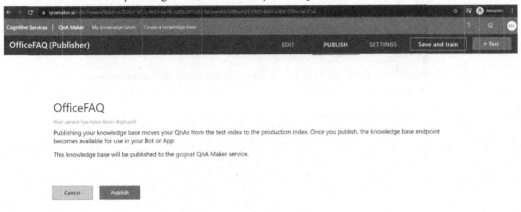

Figure 2.45 – Q&A service published

10. Click **Create Bot** after the QnA service has been published, which will take you back to Azure, and you can update the web app bot settings as required:

Success! Your service has been deployed. What's next?

You can always find the deployment details in your service's settings.

Create Bot

View all your bots on the Azure Portal.

Use the below HTTP request to call your Knowledgebase. Learn more.

Postman   Curl

```
POST /knowledgebases/ce722fc5-d51c-4c03-ba79-c685b36133b1/generateAnswer
Host: https://gcqnat.azurewebsites.net/qnamaker
Authorization: EndpointKey 56f07c71-a48e-4d15-9974-d881170403b8
Content-Type: application/json
{"question":"<Your question>"}
```

Need to fine-tune and refine? Go back and keep editing your service.

Edit Service

Figure 2.46 – Create Bot

11. Clicking on **Create Bot** on the preceding screen will take you to the Azure portal, and you can create a web app bot. Update the **Web App Bot** settings as required and click **Create**.

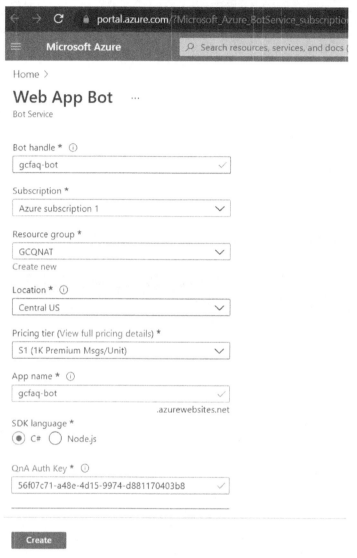

Figure 2.47 – Updating Web App Bot settings as required and clicking Create

After successfully creating the web app bot, you will see the following screen.

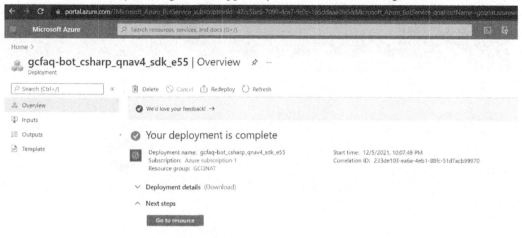

Figure 2.48 – Going to the resource group and opening the web app bot

12. Click **Go to resource** on the screen, and open the web app bot just created. From there, go to **Channels**, as shown in the following screenshot:

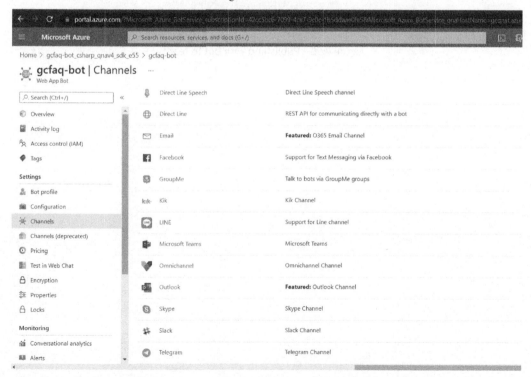

Figure 2.49 – Clicking Channels and going to Microsoft Teams

As we want this bot to be available through Microsoft Teams, click on **Microsoft Teams** as shown in the previous screenshot. You may be prompted to accept the terms of service; click **Agree** and **Save**.

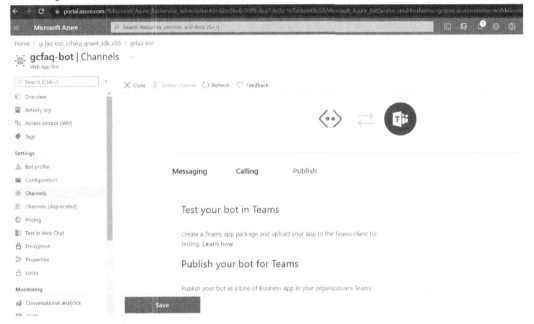

Figure 2.50 – Publishing your bot to Teams

13. After adding this bot to the Teams channels, click on **Microsoft Teams**:

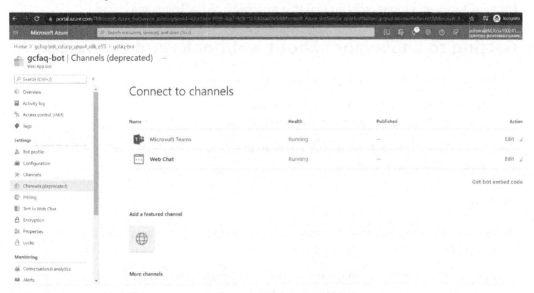

Figure 2.51 – Microsoft Teams in Channels

14. Now, **gcfaq-bot**, as shown in the preceding figure, has been published to Teams; you can add the bot to Teams by using Teams App Studio (or Developer Portal), or you can also directly access it from the search bar using the bot's GUID. The following screenshot demonstrates the user experience of interacting with the FAQ bot we have built.

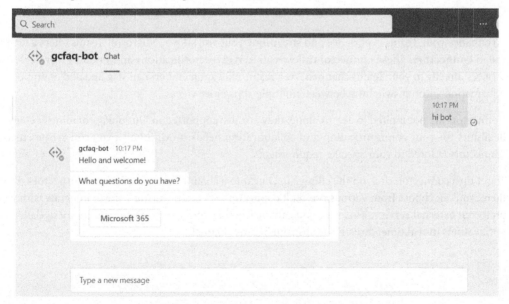

Figure 2.52 – FAQ bot

In this section, we built an FAQ bot with no code by using QnA Maker. Now, we will go through a few more topics on various other options that we could build as Teams apps.

Getting to know more about webhooks and connectors

The key role of webhooks and connectors is to integrate external services with channels and teams.

Webhooks are custom-built HTTP callbacks that can notify users about any actions in a Teams channel or, with an HTTPS endpoint, insert messages into a Teams channel.

Connectors allow channels to set up subscriptions to receive messages. We will explore more about them in the following sub-sections.

Webhooks

Webhooks in Microsoft Teams enable integration with external apps and web services. There are two types of webhooks available: outgoing and incoming.

Outgoing webhooks enable sending text messages from a Teams channel to external web services. This can be useful for passing alerts or notifications from company systems to relevant Teams channels.

On the other hand, incoming webhooks enable sending messages from external apps to Teams. This is done by exposing an HTTPS endpoint and inserting formatted JSON into the Teams channel where incoming webhooks have been enabled. This can be useful for creating webhooks for specific tasks, such as alerting a channel about orders in a queue.

Connectors

To enhance your Teams experience and streamline your workflows, Microsoft Teams offers a feature called **connectors**. These connectors allow you to receive notifications and updates from external services directly in your Teams channels. As a result, all team members can stay updated on important information without switching between multiple apps or services.

Connectors are not limited to Teams alone; they are also supported in Outlook, providing even more flexibility for your communication and collaboration needs. Additionally, you can create custom connectors tailored to your specific requirements.

To set up a connector, click on the ellipses (…) next to a channel name and select **Connectors**. From there, you can choose from various pre-built connectors or create a custom one to integrate with your preferred external service. This way, you can ensure that you receive all the necessary updates and notifications in real time, directly within your Teams channel.

The following figure shows you various connectors out there:

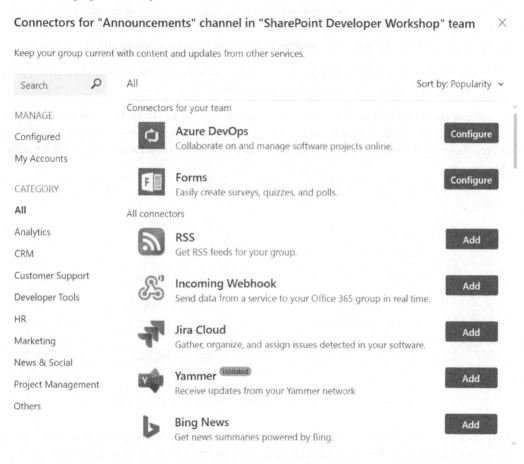

Figure 2.53 – Connectors to add/configure

Creating an Incoming Webhook connector

When you create an incoming webhook for a Teams channel, it sets up an HTTP REST endpoint that can be used to post messages to the webhook. This powerful way to bring external data and notifications directly into Teams allows users to stay informed without switching between different tools and platforms.

With an incoming webhook, you can configure external apps and services to send alerts and updates to your Teams channels, ensuring that everyone on the team has access to the information they need in a timely and organized manner. This can help streamline workflows and improve collaboration, as team members can quickly and efficiently respond to incoming messages and stay on top of important tasks.

Taking advantage of incoming webhooks allows you to create a more integrated and efficient Teams experience, improving communication across your organization.

To create an **Incoming Webhook** connector, navigate to the desired channel and select **Connectors** from the ellipsis menu. This will allow you to configure and set up the webhook to receive notifications and messages from external apps and services, enabling seamless integration and collaboration within Teams.

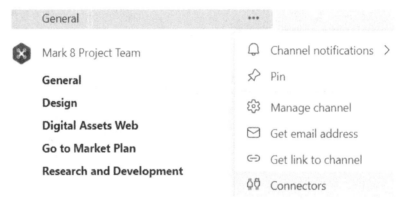

Figure 2.54 – Creating an incoming webhook using Connectors

After clicking on the **Connectors** option shown in the preceding figure, you will be directed to a connector gallery. From there, you can search for the Incoming Webhook option and add it, as shown here.

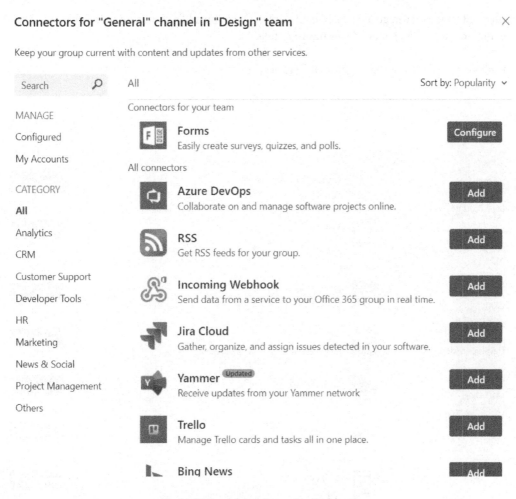

Figure 2.55 – Adding Incoming Webhook

After adding it, you can go ahead and configure it. Once you add a connector to the channel, the **Add** option next to it will change to **Configure** as follows:

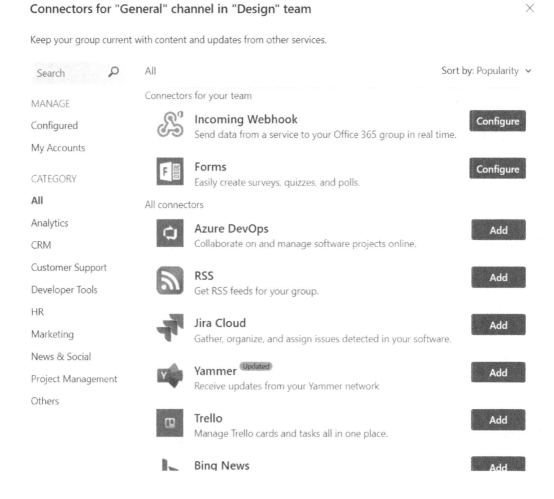

Figure 2.56 – Configuring Incoming Webhook

Then, you can give the webhook a name and customize the settings as needed, including selecting an icon and configuring security options.

At the bottom of the configuration page, as shown in the following figure, you will find the webhook URL provided by Teams. You can simply copy this URL and configure your external application or service to send messages to the Teams channel, ensuring your team members receive all the relevant information in real time.

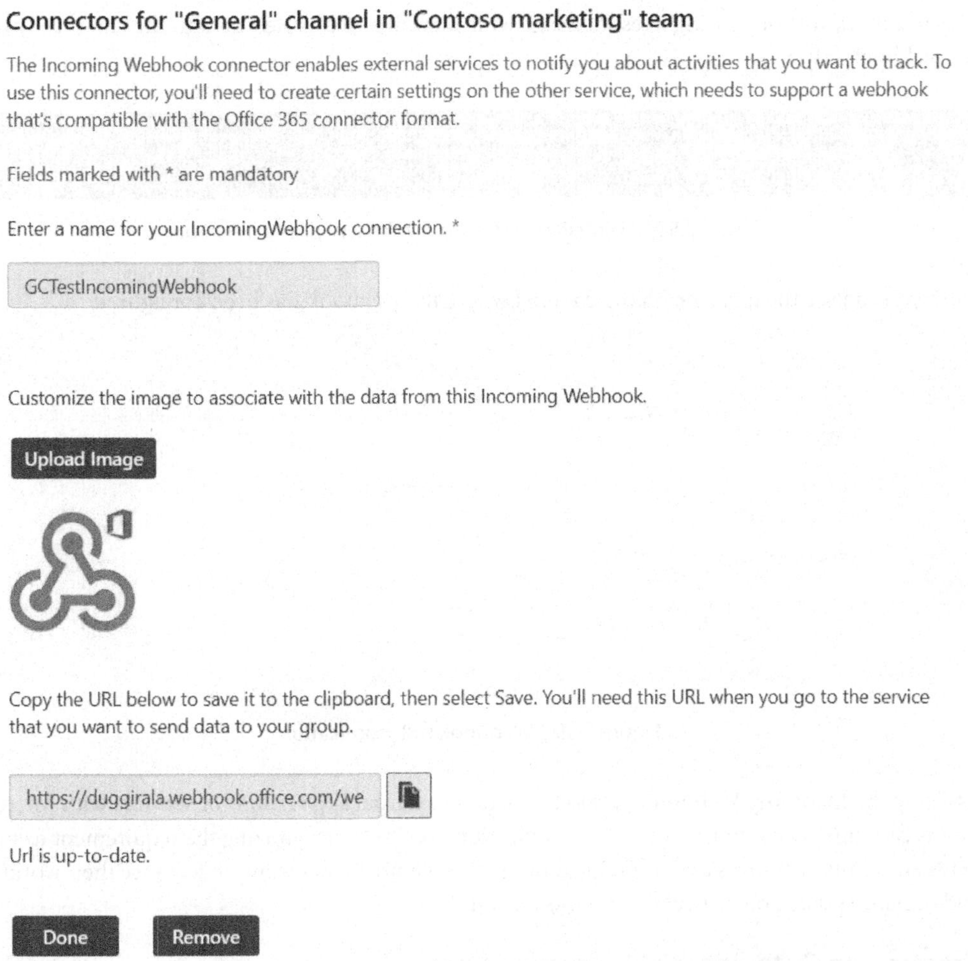

Connectors for "General" channel in "Contoso marketing" team

The Incoming Webhook connector enables external services to notify you about activities that you want to track. To use this connector, you'll need to create certain settings on the other service, which needs to support a webhook that's compatible with the Office 365 connector format.

Fields marked with * are mandatory

Enter a name for your IncomingWebhook connection. *

GCTestIncomingWebhook

Customize the image to associate with the data from this Incoming Webhook.

Upload Image

Copy the URL below to save it to the clipboard, then select Save. You'll need this URL when you go to the service that you want to send data to your group.

https://duggirala.webhook.office.com/we

Url is up-to-date.

Done   Remove

Figure 2.57 – Incoming webhook created

Once created, the webhook URL is unique to the Teams channel and cannot be shared with other channels. In addition, after setting up the webhook, any messages sent to the Teams channel will be displayed as posts on the channel and will include the sender's name and profile picture.

You can test this feature with `Invoke-RestMethod` in PowerShell or by using Postman and posting a message to the webhook URL that was created.

This is a quick way of sending a test message with `Invoke-RestMethod` to the channel by using the webhook URL:

Figure 2.58 – Using PowerShell to invoke and post a message

Now, you can see the message on the channel where the webhook has been configured:

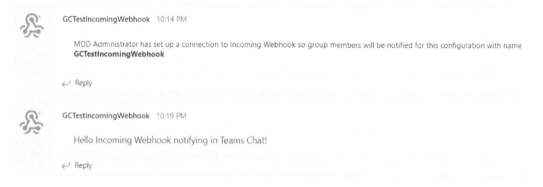

Figure 2.59 – Webhook URL notification

Utilizing the **Incoming Webhook** option to integrate external applications or services with Microsoft Teams can simplify communication and notification processes, minimizing the requirement to switch between various platforms and tools. In addition, this feature allows teams to enhance their workflows and remain updated on critical information instantly.

Creating an Outgoing Webhook connector

An outgoing webhook provides a way to send messages to your web service hosted externally without going through the entire process of creating bots. Instead, you can call a webhook to send messages from a Teams channel to a web service.

Teams only supports HTTPS-based URLs within its apps, so we use a tool called *ngrok* to expose locally hosted apps to the internet. For example, in the following screenshot, you can see `localhost:8080` mapped to one of the public URLs with HTTPS, which can be accessed over the web:

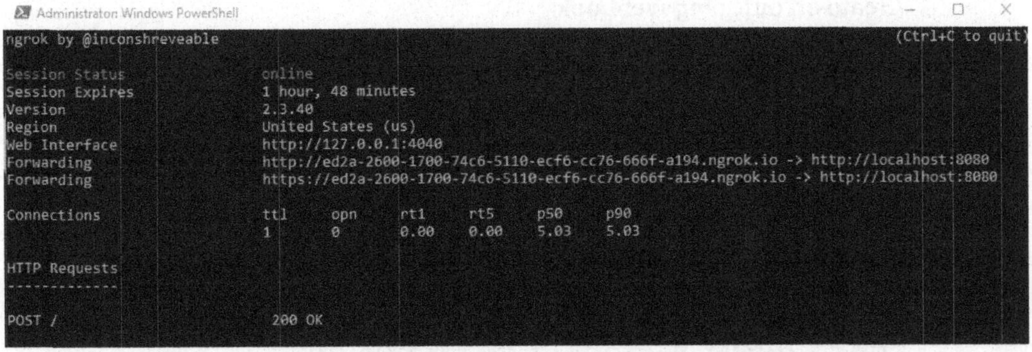

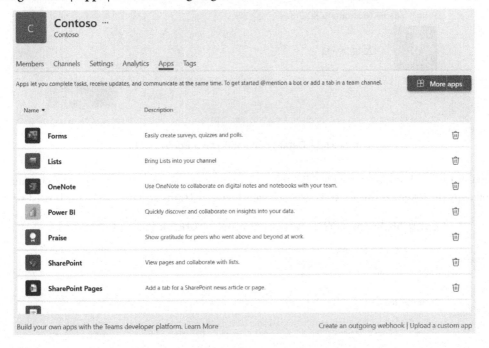

Figure 2.60 – ngrok public URL

An outgoing webhook for any team can be created by clicking on the ellipses next to **Team** and then **Manage Teams | Apps | Create an outgoing webhook** at the bottom of the screen:

Figure 2.61 – Create an outgoing webhook

When creating an outgoing webhook in Microsoft Teams, you can specify the name of the webhook and the external web service that will receive messages from Teams. This can be done by clicking on the **Create an outgoing webhook** option, as shown in the previous screenshot. Once you have accessed the webhook creation page, as shown in the following figure, you can customize the webhook settings, such as its name and the URL of the external service.

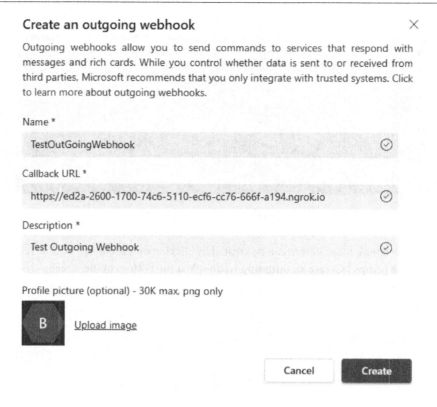

Figure 2.62 – Details of creating an outgoing webhook

Finally, the webhook is created by clicking on **Create**, and a security token is provided. Make sure you copy the token, as this token is used for calls between Teams and the externally hosted service.

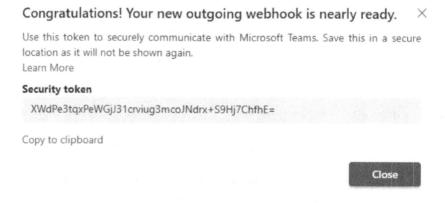

Figure 2.63 – Token for a handshake

If you host the service (locally as a public URL mapped with `ngrok` in development scenarios), an outgoing webhook is created with the token; you will add the token to your service so that the token authenticates calls.

Now, you can call the outgoing webhook from Teams with `@mention` (using the name of the webhook – in this example, `TestOutGoingWebhook`), and the webhook responds in the same thread. In this example, we echoed the same message sent to the callback URL, as follows:

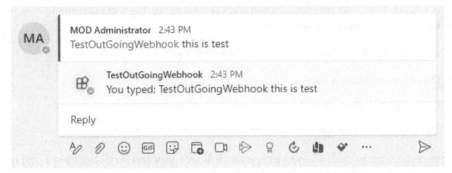

Figure 2.64 – Calling an outgoing webhook from Teams

This concludes our discussion of creating an outgoing webhook and being able to send messages from a channel in Teams. A limitation of outgoing webhooks in Microsoft Teams is that messages can only be sent from a public channel. Despite this limitation, outgoing webhooks can be a valuable tool for integrating Teams with other applications or systems, such as a custom CRM or ticketing system, or for automating workflows based on Teams events. By leveraging the flexibility and power of outgoing webhooks, developers can build custom integrations that extend Teams' functionality, helping users work more efficiently and effectively.

Messaging extensions

Message extensions, also called *compose extensions*, allow you to share rich cards in any conversation. This can be simple text or complex, formatted rich text with graphics.

There are a few built-in messaging extensions, which appear at the bottom of the compose box – for example, **Emoji**, **Giphy**, and **Sticker**:

Figure 2.65 – Messaging extensions

Messaging extensions are a powerful feature in Microsoft Teams that allows users to easily share information and perform actions within a chat or channel using custom-built interfaces. Developers can create these extensions using Developer Portal, which offers a range of tools and resources to help build and publish custom integrations. Users can simply click on the extension button in the message composer toolbar to access messaging extensions.

This opens up a list of available extensions, which can be used to search for information, create new items, or trigger other actions. With messaging extensions, Teams users can streamline workflows and collaborate more effectively with colleagues.

Users can invoke messaging extensions from the following places:

- The command/search bar
- The composed message area
- From a specific message

Messaging extensions provide a way to interact with Teams apps and services within a chat or channel and can be used in a wide range of scenarios.

Adaptive cards

Adaptive cards are rich UI containers authored in JSON and can be interactive between apps and teams. Users can take quick actions such as commenting, selecting options, setting a date, and so on.

You can use these cards in connectors, bots, and messaging extensions. Instead of creating the adaptive cards from scratch, you can use the Adaptive Cards Designer at `https://adaptivecards.io/designer/`. This online tool lets you create the required JSON data, and you can use Power Automate with the JSON to replace dynamic values and post in the Teams channel.

The following figure shows the Adaptive Cards Designer, which offers a rich designing experience for authoring adaptive cards.

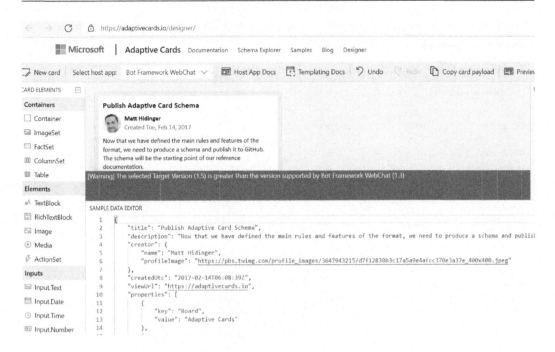

Figure 2.66 – The Adaptive Cards Designer

You can also create adaptive cards with **App Studio | Card editor**, and you can copy the JSON that you have built at `adaptivecards.io`:

Figure 2.67 – Going to Card editor from App Studio

Like App Studio, we have the same option to create cards through the new Developer Portal. Either you can build cards here or copy the JSON.

The following figure shows the options for creating adaptive cards with JSON.

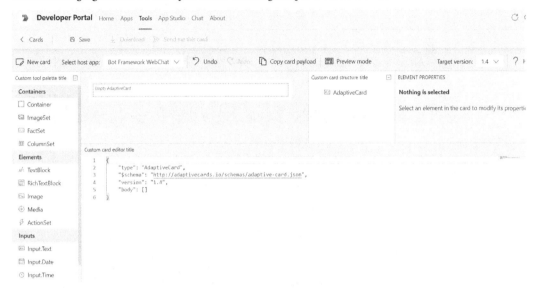

Figure 2.68 – An adaptive card in Developer Portal

The preceding figure is a schema explorer for defining the layout and various building blocks of adaptive cards such as **Containers**, **Elements**, and **Inputs**.

Containers will define the layout of an adaptive card's body. You can add various elements, such as **TextBlock** or **Image**, into a container. Inputs are used to collect information when the user submits it.

Adaptive cards are a key feature of Developer Portal for Microsoft Teams. Adaptive cards are a type of user interface component that allows developers to create rich, interactive, and adaptive card-based interfaces for their Teams apps.

Adaptive cards in Developer Portal can be used in a variety of ways, such as for displaying information, collecting user input, or triggering actions. They provide a powerful and flexible way for developers to create engaging and dynamic user interfaces for their Teams apps.

Summary

We now understand the architecture and composition of Teams apps/bots. We also gained firsthand experience in building Microsoft Teams apps for upcoming projects.

Microsoft Teams apps and bots can provide a powerful and flexible set of tools for improving teamwork and streamlining workflows in Teams. They can be used to automate repetitive tasks, provide access to critical information, and help teams stay organized and connected.

In the next chapter, we will explore the Graph API in greater depth, specifically focusing on how to use the Microsoft Graph API to interact with Microsoft Teams. We will cover various aspects of the Graph API and provide examples of how to use it to enhance the functionality and capabilities of Teams.

Part 2: Microsoft Teams Customization with Tools and Techniques

This part covers a wide range of topics related to Microsoft Teams, providing you with a comprehensive understanding of the platform and its capabilities. The chapters delve into topics such as the Microsoft Graph API and how it can be leveraged to work with Teams and the PowerShell module for provisioning and managing teams. The book also covers customization using the SharePoint Framework, a modern development model for SharePoint that can be used to customize Microsoft Teams. Finally, you will gain insights into the authentication and authorization options for creating custom tabs in Teams, including SSO and related topics. These chapters provide you with practical insights and a comprehensive guide to utilizing Microsoft Teams effectively and efficiently.

This section includes the following chapters:

- *Chapter 3, Microsoft Graph API*
- *Chapter 4, Microsoft Teams PowerShell*
- *Chapter 5, Microsoft Teams Customization Using the SharePoint Framework (SPFx)*
- *Chapter 6, Microsoft Teams Authentication*

3
Microsoft Graph API

In this chapter, we will start with a basic introduction to the Graph API and then dive deeper into understanding it and topics around it, but with more of a focus on Teams.

The Graph API is used in customizations (apps and bots) if they require you to interact with Office 365 services and manage the Microsoft Teams life cycle.

Some organizations do not like to enable their users with team creation and follow a customized provisioning process with a few approvals. They use the Graph API to create teams within the custom process and automate various actions, such as adding and removing channels and adding and removing members to and from teams.

The Graph API leverages Microsoft 365 data insights and relationships between various data elements. In this chapter, we are going to cover the following topics:

- What is the Graph API?
- Getting started with the Graph API
- Graph Explorer – a tool for trying the Graph API
- Authentication and authorization of the Graph API
- Microsoft Teams automation with the Graph API
- Best practices when consuming the Graph API

By the end of this chapter, you should be able to understand what the Graph API is and how to start using the Graph API in your applications with appropriate authentication and authorizations. You'll also learn about general best practices for working with the Graph API with large workloads and sensitive applications.

What is the Graph API?

There are several services that are a part of Microsoft 365, such as SharePoint, Exchange, OneDrive, Teams, and so on. Each service has REST endpoints. For any application development purpose, if we need to connect more than one service, then we need to connect individual REST service endpoints and perform authentication with each endpoint. So, as a developer, you need to discover and understand various aspects of each service, such as its endpoints, authentication mechanism, permission models, and data formats.

Microsoft Graph is a unique gateway to access data with one single endpoint to access all Microsoft 365 services. Additionally, with the Azure AD authentication mechanism, you can provide access to application users that consume the Graph API.

Microsoft Graph offers three interfaces for developers to consume in their applications:

- **A REST API**: A REST-based API through which you can perform CRUD operations using a single endpoint, `https://graph.microsoft.com`, on any Office 365 services that support the Graph API. You can use Azure Web Apps, Microsoft Teams apps, bots, Power Automate, or any background applications.

- **Microsoft Graph Data Connect**: This service can be used to move or copy Microsoft 365 data to your Azure Data Factory application's storage at configurable intervals. You can then build applications using this data to derive insights.

- **Adding Custom Data to Graph**: You can inject custom data into MS Graph.

In this book, we mainly focus on the REST API-based interface of the Graph API based on REST, OData, and OAuth standards, allowing access to various Microsoft 365 services with just one token and one API.

Interestingly, the Graph API is not just for third-party developers to consume Microsoft 365 data or relations of various objects in their applications. Microsoft also uses the Graph API in various first-party (apps built by Microsoft) applications. The most famous example is the People Picker web control, which offers a consistent experience and behavior on all applications, such as Outlook, Teams, SharePoint, Office applications, the Teams PowerShell module, and much more.

The People Picker control makes Graph API calls behind the scenes to pull users' information based on the search. The following figures show a few real-world usages of the Graph API by first-party applications.

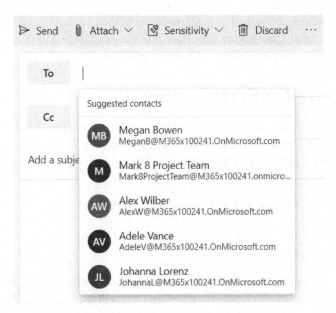

Figure 3.1 – Outlook new message for Graph API calls

In Microsoft Teams, whatever you search will make Graph API calls to provide results; this is another real-world example where Microsoft uses the Graph API.

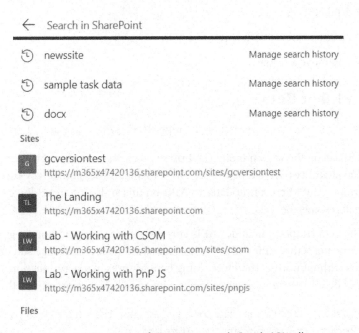

Figure 3.2 – Microsoft Teams to search Graph API calls

In the preceding section, you gained an understanding of the Graph API and the various interfaces that you can connect via. Also, you saw how Microsoft uses the Graph API in its tools. The following section talks about how to start working with the Graph API.

Getting started with the Graph API

Now that we have understood the Graph API and its core purpose of providing `https://graph.microsoft.com` as the single endpoint to access all Microsoft 365 services, we can move ahead and learn how to use it in our applications to access Microsoft 365 data or events to modify them in this section.

If you want to access the Graph API, all calls will follow this pattern:

```
https://graph.microsoft.com/{version}/{resource}/{id}/
{property}?{query-parameters}
```

The following HTTP methods (or verbs) are used to request the Graph API. With the Graph API, we can do all CRUD operations on Microsoft 365 data. We will use a verb based on the operation we are trying to do:

- GET: Read data from a resource
- POST: Create a new resource
- PATCH: Update a resource
- PUT: Replace a resource with a new one
- DELETE: Remove a resource

Version – v1.0 or Beta

Currently, there are two versions of Microsoft Graph REST APIs – they are V1.0 and Beta:

- **V1.0**: APIs set on the v1.0 endpoint (`https://graph.microsoft.com/v1.0`) have the **general availability** (**GA**) status. We recommend this API version for any customer production applications. Any Microsoft updates to APIs on this endpoint are additive and do not break existing app scenarios.

- **Beta**: The beta endpoint includes APIs currently in preview and not yet generally available. The assumption is that APIs with a preview status are subject to change and may break existing scenarios without notice. Therefore, using beta features in any production application is not recommended. To see more details about versions and beta support, review the following URLs:

  - `https://docs.microsoft.com/en-us/graph/use-the-api?context=graph/api/1.0#version`

- `https://docs.microsoft.com/en-us/graph/versioning-and-support#versions`

Resources – users, groups, sites, drives, devices, and more

The top-level endpoint directs the underlying services that your request interacts with to get the resources, members, and properties:

- **Member from the collection**: `users/James` (`https://graph.microsoft.com/v1.0/users/james`)

- **Property**: `users/James/department` (`https://graph.microsoft.com/v1.0/users/james/department`)

- **Traverse to related resources via navigation**: `users/James/meetings`

You can specify a member of the collection, James, as a member in the Users collection and properties of the resources (the department is a property of the member James). Also, you can apply various filters to the responses.

Query parameters

From the previous resources, you may want to customize responses for your application based on your needs. We have various OData query parameters to filter, select, or customize Graph API responses. Please see the following for some examples:

- **Query parameters**: `/users/James/messages?$select=Title?$top=5`

- **Format results**: `$select | $orderby /users/James/messages?$select=Title`

- **Control results**: `$filter | $expand /me/messages?$filter=emailAddress eq 'james@contoso.com'`

- **Paging**: `$top | $skip | $skiptoken /me/messages?$top=10`

To find more OData query options, you can review the following URL: `https://docs.microsoft.com/en-us/graph/query-parameters`

The preceding section helped you understand the Graph API and how to use the Graph API. The following section will help you start using the Graph API quickly.

Graph Explorer

Graph Explorer is a tool that allows you to make or test your queries to fine-tune your Graph API calls. Graph Explorer was developed and is maintained by Microsoft. You can access the tool by going to `https://aka.ms/ge`.

With Graph Explorer, you can make requests (GET, POST, PUT, PATCH, and DELETE) and see various responses.

You can sign into Graph Explorer using your tenant's Azure AD credentials; however, your tenant administrator should consent to delegated permissions to use Graph Explorer. We will discuss delegate permissions in more detail later, in the chapter's *Getting Graph API access without the user* section.

Based on the verb you are using, you can also include the request body and request header in your query, as shown here:

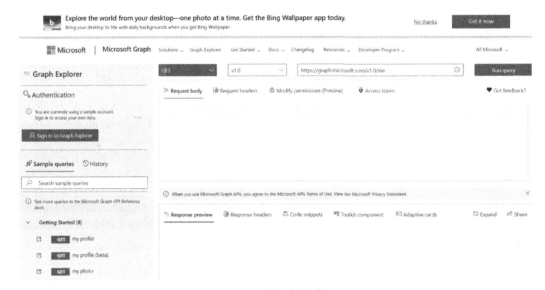

Figure 3.3 – Graph Explorer

On the left side of Graph Explorer, we have some sample queries for different services in Microsoft Graph; this will help you jump-start with a few Graph API queries. For example, look at the following screenshot with these sample queries organized under various categories. Then, you can click on a variety of options to review more details.

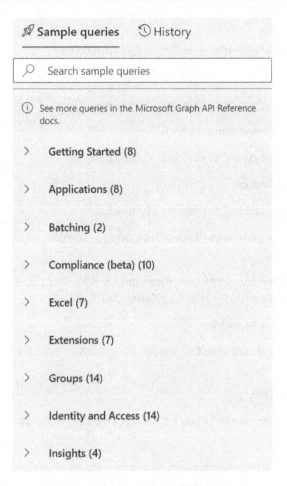

Figure 3.4 – Sample Graph API queries

Sample Graph API calls

After reviewing Graph Explorer, try a few basic Graph calls in Graph Explorer, such as the following, to understand the syntax of using resource and query parameters.

Get your profile:

```
https://graph.microsoft.com/v1.0/me
```

Get your files:

```
https://graph.microsoft.com/v1.0/me/drive/root/children
```

Get your job title:

```
https://graph.microsoft.com/v1.0/me/JobTitle
```

Get your manager:

```
https://graph.microsoft.com/v1.0/me/manager
```

Get people that you are communicating with:

```
https://graph.microsoft.com/v1.0/me/people
```

Get users in your organization:

```
https://graph.microsoft.com/v1.0/users
```

Get the top 10 users in your organization: `https://graph.microsoft.com/v1.0/users?$top=10`

Get users in your organization (only their name and job title): `https://graph.microsoft.com/v1.0/users?$select=displayName,jobTitle`

Get users whose names start with J:

```
https://graph.microsoft.com/v1.0/users?$filter=startswith(displayName,'J')
```

Get users whose state is CA:

```
https://graph.microsoft.com/v1.0/microsoft.com/users?&$filter=state eq 'CA'
```

Search in sites:

```
https://graph.microsoft.com/v1.0/sites?search=Test
```

This book is all about Teams, so you can click on Microsoft Teams to see various sample Graph API queries for consuming the Graph API with Microsoft Teams. The following screenshot shows some samples; if you click on any sample, it will open the query on the endpoint bar in Graph Explorer:

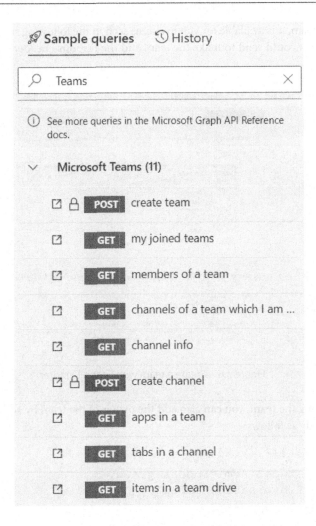

Figure 3.5 – Graph API queries for Microsoft Teams

For a quick example of creating a team using the Graph API, follow these steps:

1. Click on the first sample to create a team, as shown in the preceding screenshot.

   This will give a sample query for creating a team where you can customize the request body based on your needs.

2. In the following screenshot, you can see that **create team** is a **POST** call, and in the body, you provide the required JSON representation of a team.

   Also, the user who is running this query needs to have appropriate delegate permissions. If the request is successful, you will see it in the response as 202 Accepted.

After creating the team, it is available for you to use, as seen in the following screenshot. It also shows the request body you could send to make the team and the response header to show the successful team creation.

Figure 3.6 – Create a team with Graph Explorer

3. When creating the team, you can also add the owner of the team by adding members to the response body as follows:

```
"members":[{
"@odata.type":"#microsoft.graph.
aadUserConversationMember",
"roles":["owner"],
"user@odata.bind":"https://graph.microsoft.com/v1.0/
users('0040b377-61d8-43db-94f5-81374122dc7e')"
    }]
```

Graph Explorer is a playground for building sample graph queries or testing them. You will have the option to sign in for authentication and, based on your level of access, you can also adjust the permissions, but for other custom applications that you are going to make Graph API calls in, you need to prepare for authentication and authorization, which we will be discussing in the next section.

Authentication and authorization of the Graph API

As you noticed in Graph Explorer, the Graph API is not for anonymous users; you need to get authenticated and authorized to make any Graph API call. Looking back at Graph Explorer (*Figure 3.6*), we have an **Access token** area generated based on the user that's logged in.

Access tokens let your application call APIs protected by the Microsoft identity platform. These access tokens are also called **JSON Web Tokens (JWTs)**. These tokens include the expiry time and scopes that are valid.

The following screenshot shows an example of an access token:

Figure 3.7 – Access token

If you are more interested in decoding the access token, go to the URL `http://jwt.ms/` and paste the access token. In the next screenshot, we will look at this JWT using `jwt.m`.

Also, you can see the permissions that are required to create the team that we ran in the previous scenario, which is the authorization part of it:

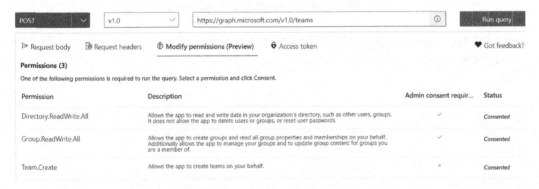

Figure 3.8 – Graph Explorer permissions

The key of any Graph API call is the access token. So you need to generate an access token and, of course, the access token needs to have the appropriate permission on the resource for accessing the actual resource through this Graph API call.

Registering an application in Azure Active Directory

You can register an application (app) by logging into `https://portal.azure.com`, going into your **Azure Active Directory (AD)** component, clicking on **App registrations** in the left menu, and then clicking on **New registration** as follows:

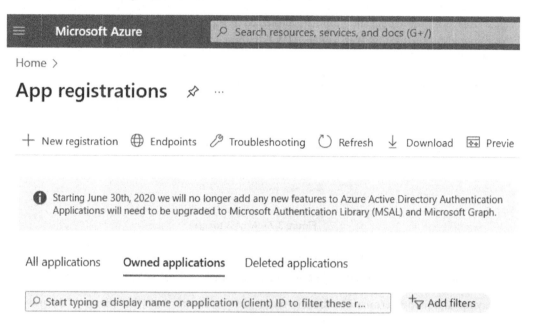

Figure 3.9 – Azure AD App registrations

From the **App registrations** screen, clicking **New registration** will bring up the screen that follows to register a new app:

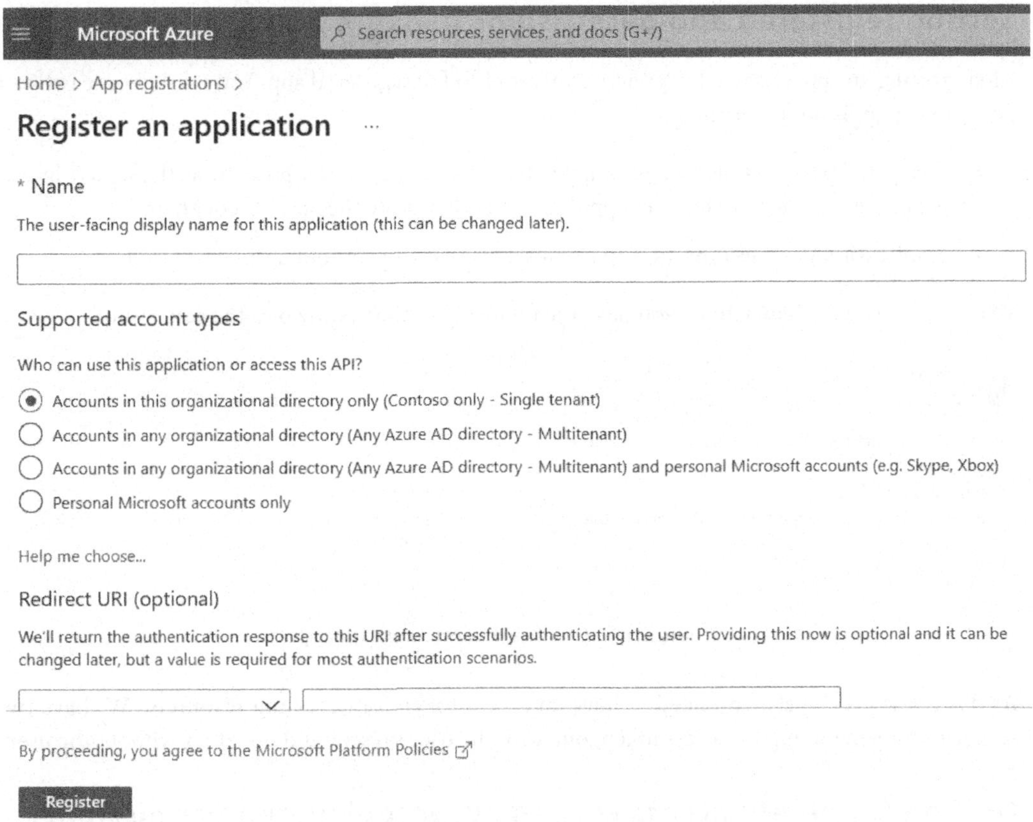

Figure 3.10 – New app registration

Registration includes the following vital details:

- **Application (client) ID**: The application ID is generated when registering the application in Azure AD

- **Client Secret**: A password or a certificate you can generate during application registration in Azure AD, used to authenticate with the Microsoft identity platform

The application ID and client secret generate an authorization code or token in Azure AD during authentication.

For more information on app registration, visit the following link: `https://docs.microsoft.com/en-us/azure/active-directory/develop/quickstart-register-app`

Setting registered app permissions in Azure AD

After creating an app, you need to grant permissions to the registered app. You must choose between delegated or application permissions:

- **Delegated permissions** mean the app will have a signed-in user present. As the signed-in user is present, you need to have an app that will authenticate the user's credentials.

- **Application permissions** are app permissions that run without a signed-in user.

When you click on **Permissions**, you have the following options, shown in the screenshot.

Microsoft Graph
https://graph.microsoft.com/ Docs

What type of permissions does your application require?

Delegated permissions	Application permissions
Your application needs to access the API as the signed-in user.	Your application runs as a background service or daemon without a signed-in user.

Figure 3.11 – Graph API permissions for app

As discussed previously, you need to have an access token for accessing resources. We have two scenarios for generating the access token, one with the user present and the other without the user.

Getting Graph API access with the user (delegated permissions)

To get an access token with a user present, the OAuth flow redirects the user to the Microsoft identity platform authorized endpoint (`https://login.microsoftonline.com/{tenant}/oauth2/v2.0/authorize`). After the user signs in and consents to the permissions that are required by the app, Azure AD will return an authorization code. You then need to make another `Post` request to the Microsoft identity platform token endpoint.

The following examples will give you various options to get an access token.

authorize

Check out the following `authorize` endpoint:

```
https://login.microsoftonline.com/{tenant}/oauth2/
v2.0/authorize?client_id=xxxxxxxx-xxxx-xxxx-
xxxx-xxxxxxxxxxxxandresponse_type=code&redirect_
uri=http%3A%2F%2Flocalhost%2Fmyapp%2F&response_
mode=query&scope=offline_access%20user.read%20mail.
read&state=54321
```

This endpoint has various query parameters; let's review each one:

- `tenant`: Tenant ID or tenant value

- `Client_id`: Application ID registered

- `response_type`: code : This is what you use for an access token

- `redirect_uri`: Where the authentication response can be sent and received from your app

- `scope`: Microsoft Graph API permissions that you want your user to consent to

- `response mode`: Query or form-post – the way that you get the token back to your app.

- `state`: A unique value typically used for preventing cross-site request forgery attacks. (Cross-site request forgery means an end user is executing an unwanted action on the application.)

Authorization code

A successful authorization response will look as follows:

```
https://localhost/app/?code=Mxxxxxx-b6fd-df08-87dc-
2cxxxxxxx&state=54321
```

Token Post request

With the authorization with user (delegated permissions code from the previous step, you can request an access token with a POST request to the token endpoint as follows:

```
POST /{tenant}/oauth2/v2.0/token HTTP/1.1
Host: https://login.microsoftonline.com
Content-Type: application/x-www-form-urlencoded
client_id=xxxxxxxx-xxxx-xxxx-xxxx-
xxxxxxxxxxxx&scope=user.read%20mail.read&code=
Mxxxxxx-b6fd-df08-87dc2cxxxxxxx&redirect_
uri=http%3A%2F%2Flocalhost%2Fapp%2F&grant_type=authorization_
code&client_secret=sxxxxx...
// NOTE: Only required for web apps
```

The preceding token request endpoint has various query parameters; let's review each one as follows:

- `Client_id`: The application ID registered

- `scope`: The Microsoft Graph API permissions that you want your user to consent to

- `redirect_uri`: Where the authentication response can be sent and received from by your app

- `grant_type`: `authorization_code` : This is for when you are using the authorization code flow

- `client_secret`: The application secret is created in the app registration and is required only with with user (delegated permissions web apps or web APIs.

Token Post Response

See the following response to the preceding token `Post` request. If you notice that you get an access token, you can use it for calling resources:

```
{
"token_type": "Bearer",
"scope": "user.read%20Fmail.read",
"expires_in": 3600,
"access_token":"d23sdfsdfsbwerwedsfsdrewMgsdfsdwCDSDF...",
refresh_token":
"d2dsfsdxdfdfswerewlrEqdFSBzjqfTGAMxZGUTdM0t4B4..."
}
```

Once you have the access token, you can call the Graph API with the authorization header, as follows:

```
"Authorization" = "Bearer" {AccessToken}
"Content-Type" = "application/JSON"
```

Getting Graph API access without the user (application permissions)

There are other scenarios where you want to call the Graph API in your custom solutions and may not have a user present to sign in to the applications, for example, background services, or you may have a situation where you want to elevate the privileges of the signed-in user.

Token request

You can send a POST request to the token endpoint as follows:

```
POST https://login.microsoftonline.com/{tenant}/oauth2/v2.0/
token HTTP/1.1
Host: login.microsoftonline.com
Content-Type: application/x-www-form-urlencoded
client_id=111111-1111-1111-1111-11111111&scope=htt
ps%3A%2F%2Fgraph.microsoft.com%2F.default&client_
secret=qMdcsdfsfdsSEDDxzzzX&grant_type=client_credentials
```

The preceding token request endpoint has various query parameters; let's review each one:

- `Client_id`: Application ID registered

- `scope`: The Microsoft Graph API permissions that you want your user to consent to

- `client_secret`: The application secret is created in the app registration and is required only with web apps or web APIs.

- `grant_type`: You must set `grant_type` as `client_credentials`, as you pass the client ID and client secret.

Token response

A successful response will be like the following:

```
{
    "token_type": "Bearer",
    "expires_in": 3600,
    "access_token":"d23sdfsdfsbwerwedsfsdrewMgsdfsdwCDSDF..."
}
```

In the *Getting Graph API access with the user and Getting Graph API access without the user* section, you reviewed the option to get access tokens from token responses. In the next section, you'll see how we can use these tokens to access Graph API resources through PowerShell.

Consuming the Graph API in PowerShell

You can consume the Graph API directly in PowerShell. In this section, we will review various steps required for reading all the groups in your tenant.

The first step is that you need to register an app in Azure AD and provide appropriate application permissions for the registered app with a `group member.Read.All`, `Group.Read.All`, `Directory.Read.All`.

You should always refer to the documentation for the required permissions to access any resources. Always follow the least privilege method and only provide the minimum required permissions.

If you look at the screen shown in the following figure, for `Directory.Read.All`, the permissions are in the format of Resource, Operation, and Constraint:

- **Resource**: User/Mail/Directory/Group, and so on

- **Operation**: Read, ReadWrite, Send, and so on

- **Constraint**: All, Shared, and so on

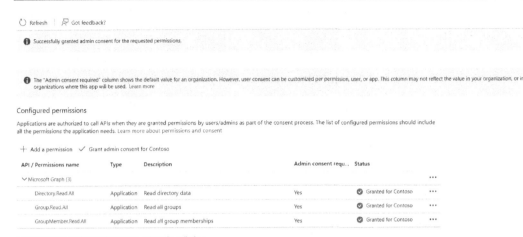

Figure 3.12 – Graph API permissions for the registered app

Here is the sample PowerShell code to call the Graph API to get the list of teams in your tenant:

```
#This is the ClientID
$ClientID = "7e7a32eb-289c-4467-abd3-b9a2bcfcdca2"
#This is the Client Secret
$ClientSecret = "NfK7Q~o~r4JHB6nuBCs~~bpsjaI8moPuEMuWR"
#This is your Office 365 Tenant Domain Name or Tenant Id
$TenantId = "0886a4dd-9300-44fd-b004-97f6e7a537a2"
#Note: Replace ClientId, ClientSecret and TenantId with your
actual values
$Body = @{client_id=$ClientID;client_
secret=$ClientSecret;grant_type="client_
credentials";scope="https://graph.microsoft.com/.default";}
$OAuthReq = Invoke-RestMethod -Method Post -Uri https://login.
microsoftonline.com/$TenantId/oauth2/v2.0/token -Body $Body
$TokenType = $OAuthReq.token_type
$AccessToken = $OAuthReq.access_token
$apiUrl = "https://graph.microsoft.com/v1.0/
groups?$filter=resourceProvisioningOptions/Any(x:x eq 'Team')"
$TeamsRequest = Invoke-RestMethod -Headers @{Authorization =
"Bearer $AccessToken"} -Uri $apiUrl -Method Get
$Teams = $TeamsRequest.Value
$Teams | select id, mailNickName,description, displayName, mail
| ft
```

Here is the sample output from the preceding PowerShell Script, which only shows the selected values of the teams:

```
>> $Teams | select id, mailNickName,description, displayName, mail | ft

id                                    mailNickname              description
--                                    ------------              -----------
015a62a9-f309-421b-bb43-1b91133bb3b0  GCTEST                    GCTEST
0e75721e-5ba4-44f1-9921-0d2e5f0d9645  leadership                Share what's on your mind and get important announcements fro
3f3d2b91-8e15-4efd-8ca9-af5792d67104  Mark8ProjectTeam          Mark 8 Project Team
1a9b35ea-e5be-40d1-8476-3a5a75b1fa10  Contoso                   Contoso
1aab0659-85da-413f-8ff8-7116d06fc53a  operations                Share what's on your mind and get important operations announ
201b4e66-9a05-4336-955e-01670a55bdcb  ArchitectureTeam509       The team for those in architecture design.
2e6e4535-fe5b-493d-89bb-b501360e519f  sgEngineering             All engineering personnel
2ff51ca4-a542-42f0-b7d0-95e45b3037e2  SSPRSecurityGroupUsers    Self-service password reset enabled users
384b69a1-dab8-47e5-ae35-c61c8f87f1e5  salesbestpractices        Sales Best Practices
40ee399f-7d14-42de-8fd9-b712a193c7c4  Falcon
45a39554-7bd8-4ce8-a9dc-497ed50481d6  DigitalInitiativePublicRelations Digital Initiative Public Relations
45e0fa72-0346-4102-ac8d-ad7387a7e7c5  Communications            Communications Team
4960bf63-fd8a-462e-9746-c1c968f19d04  ssgBugBashers             Self-service group of employees who wish to provide feedback
5334b395-6e65-418b-b0e6-0a9a3aa9ebeb  allcompany                This is the default group for everyone in the network
57e4c1b7-ffc9-4df0-9a7a-d348cdbf03b2  SOCTeam                   SOC Team
5866a908-acca-4998-93b9-556429b611e2  sgIT                      All IT personnel
506cf00e-5d4d-4745-b230-1b9e8045106e  sgHR                      All HR personnel
568349d5-4e91-49e8-a253-428faa624f55  Executives
783dec32-9faf-42e0-abb2-b15ec2707a79  ArchitectureTeam          The team for those in architecture design.
79dbc902-209d-432d-abf5-35f5e856e9ad  contosolife               Contoso Life
7c8e8a90-1608-4995-9eb2-d206f29e0c61  SalesTeam
3470a491-5bd4-44a6-ae9c-54c2bec92ae9  opertationteam            opertation team
```

Figure 3.13 – Output of the teams

With this PowerShell script, you have successfully gotten all the teams using the Graph API. The following section will review how you can automate the Microsoft Team's life cycle with the Graph API.

Microsoft Teams automation with the Graph API

You can use the Microsoft Graph API to automate the provisioning of teams based on business needs, assign the owner, add the right people to the team, and configure the team with channels, tabs, and apps.

You can automate the following actions:

- You can create teams, channels, and threads and update and delete them
- You can add and remove team owners and members
- You can add files to teams, which will add them to the team's document library of the SharePoint site
- You can add and publish tabs and apps
- You can manage various team settings

Team automation cycle

The following diagram is the life cycle of a Microsoft Teams team, starting from creation; modification by adding users or owners; configuring various settings, channels, tabs, and apps; and finally, archiving or deleting when required:

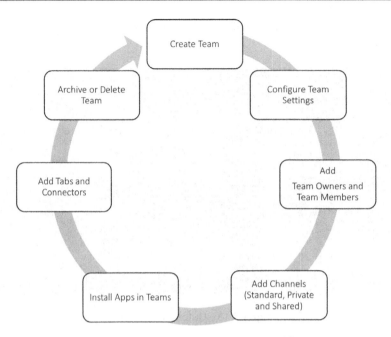

Figure 3.14 – Graph automation of the team life cycle

With the Graph API, you can automate various actions in the life cycle of a team on Microsoft Teams, as shown in the preceding figure. There are various Graph API functions for all the steps in the team life cycle. You can also create a large number of teams and populate them with users and channels.

Best practices with the Graph API

If you are using the Graph API in your scenario, you must follow some best practices so that you don't encounter performance issues, making your applications more reliable. In this section, we will talk about a few of them.

Pagination

You may have scenarios that require a Microsoft Graph API call to return multiple pages of data when you issue a query that may require pagination. This could happen either due to server-side paging or the query using the $top query parameter (client-driven pagination) to restrict the number of returned records.

You can review the following link for more details on understanding how you can manage pagination:

```
https://docs.microsoft.com/en-us/graph/paging
```

Batching

With batching, you can optimize queries to MS Graph by combining multiple requests into a single request. Batching reduces network latency significantly and consumes lower bandwidth.

You can review the following link for more details on batching:

Combine multiple requests in one HTTP call using JSON batching - Microsoft Graph | Microsoft Docs at `https://learn.microsoft.com/en-us/graph/json-batching`

Throttling

Throttling a service limits the number of requests to the service, preventing the service from going down. When a system has too many requests, Microsoft Graph returns an error with HTTP status 429 (which means too many requests) and a retry after interval value (suggesting waiting and trying the request again).

The following are best practices for handling throttling:

- First, reduce the number of operations per request.
- Reduce the frequency of calls.
- Avoid immediate retries because all requests accrue against your usage limits.

You can review the following link for more details on throttling:

Microsoft Graph throttling guidance - Microsoft Graph | Microsoft Docs at `https://learn.microsoft.com/en-us/graph/json-batching`

Summary

This chapter has discussed the Graph API as a gateway to data and intelligence in Microsoft 365. This REST-based API allows access to Teams and other Microsoft 365 services. You can use the Graph API in any custom apps that require you to consume Microsoft 365 services and automate a team's life cycle to manage team settings and members. We have discussed authentication and authorization in making Graph calls. In authentication, you must see whether any signed-in user is present or authenticated by an app. After authentication, authorization will determine whether the user or the app has permission to make the required Graph call.

In the next chapter, you will learn about the PowerShell Microsoft Teams module and options for managing Microsoft Teams and creating teams within it.

4

Microsoft Teams PowerShell

This chapter will help you understand the PowerShell module used to provision and manage teams and their backing groups. Here, you will find all the Microsoft Teams PowerShell topics.

Microsoft Teams PowerShell is a PowerShell module for managing Teams outside the **Graphic User Interface (GUI)**. These commands have features for managing your Teams workload. In this chapter, we are going to talk about the following topics:

- **Microsoft Teams PowerShell Module (TPM)**

- CLI for Microsoft 365:

  - CLI for Microsoft 365 is a handy and valuable open source project from the **Patterns and Practices (PnP)** team that allows Microsoft 365 administrators to perform administrative tasks on a Microsoft 365 tenant

> **Note**
>
> PnP is a community-driven initiative from Microsoft that provides guidance, tools, and open source projects to help developers and IT admins build rapid solutions on Microsoft platforms. The PnP team works closely with Microsoft engineers and partners to identify common patterns and best practices, and then shares this knowledge and experience with the community.

Upon completion of this chapter, you will be able to understand the PowerShell module to manage Teams administration, including users, teams, policies, and configuration. You don't need any additional modules for authentication or access tokens. In addition to Microsoft Teams PowerShell, you can manage Teams through PowerShell using the Microsoft Graph PowerShell SDK. This SDK acts as a wrapper for Graph API functions. However, in this chapter, we will focus on Microsoft Teams PowerShell.

Microsoft Teams PowerShell Module

Microsoft **Teams PowerShell Module (TPM)** is a PowerShell module with several cmdlets, used to manage and administrate various scenarios of Microsoft Teams in the command line.

First, you need to install this module to start trying a few scenarios in the command line. Also, you can use the following link to go to the latest version of TPM: `https://www.powershellgallery.com/packages/MicrosoftTeams`. It's always ideal to get the latest version of the module. Here, you can see whether any version of TPM has been retired, and you can update it if required.

Installing Microsoft TPM

You can install TPM on all supported Windows platforms. For macOS and Linux, we might have to use CLI for Microsoft 365 (we will talk more about CLI for Microsoft 365 in the next section).

To install TPM, you must make sure that you have PowerShell 5.1 or later installed on your Windows Platform. As such, your machine satisfies the prerequisites for installing TPM. Then, the `install-Module` cmdlet is used to install TPM. In the case of TPM, we need to use the `MicrosoftTeams` module.

> **Note**
>
> If you look at the following figure, you will see that we have also used the `-Force` and `-AllowClobber` parameters, which will overwrite the warnings. Make sure you open the PowerShell Command line under **Run as Administrator** to run the following command:
>
> ```
> Install-Module -Name MicrosoftTeams -Force -AllowClobber
> ```

The preceding command will download and install TPM from the PowerShell Gallery.

Updating Microsoft TPM

As you know, Microsoft keeps undertaking new development work on TPM from time to time with new functions, so you need to stay up to date with the latest version to take advantage of these changes. Updating TPM is extremely easy. Just use the `update-module` cmdlet, as shown here:

```
Install-Module -Name MicrosoftTeams -Force -AllowClobber
```

Figure 4.1 – Updating TPM

Now that you have installed or updated Microsoft TPM on your local machine, you can check whether this module has been installed successfully or even verify the version of the module you have. First, use `Get-Module`, as shown here:

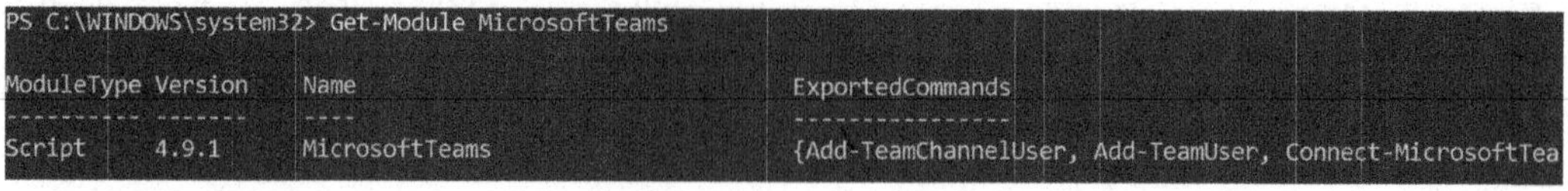

```
PS C:\WINDOWS\system32> Get-Module MicrosoftTeams

ModuleType Version    Name                    ExportedCommands
---------- -------    ----                    ----------------
Script     4.9.1      MicrosoftTeams          {Add-TeamChannelUser, Add-TeamUser, Connect-MicrosoftTea
```

Figure 4.2 – Verifying TPM

Connecting to Microsoft TPM

So far, you have installed, updated, and verified TPM so that you can start using it and the cmdlets that it provides. For example, if you use the `connect-MicrosoftTeams` cmdlet, it prompts you to provide credentials. Then, based on the role of the user connected, they get permissions to manage Teams, as shown in the following figure.

If your permissions are limited to the Team level, the cmdlets you can use are limited to the teams.

Figure 4.3 – Connecting to Microsoft Teams with TPM

From the preceding figure, you can sign with the appropriate credentials.

If you log in as a Global Administrator or a Teams Administrator, you can control various options, such as Team settings, Teams policies, and Teams Voice with TPM.

PowerShell commands are in the format of verb-noun syntax, also called the cmdlet naming convention. The verb part of the command is the action that performs, and the noun part is the entity on which the action will be performed – for example, `Get-Team`, where `Get` is a verb and `Team` is an entity as a noun.

Creating a new team with TPM

You can start with a simple scenario of provisioning a Microsoft Teams team with TPM. To get familiar with Teams TPM, go to the PowerShell command line and use `Get-Command *-Team`, which will show all the commands available with a suffix matching `-team`, as shown here:

```
PS C:\WINDOWS\system32> Get-Command *-team

CommandType     Name                                    Version    Source
-----------     ----                                    -------    ------
Cmdlet          Get-Team                                4.9.1      MicrosoftTeams
Cmdlet          New-Team                                4.9.1      MicrosoftTeams
Cmdlet          Remove-Team                             4.9.1      MicrosoftTeams
Cmdlet          Set-Team                                4.9.1      MicrosoftTeams
```

Figure 4.4 – Teams commands

Get, New, Remove, and Set are simple commands to manage Teams.

> **Note**
>
> The New-Team command lets you create a new team.

You don't need to remember the syntax of any PowerShell commands; all you need to do is use get-help and add -examples, as shown here:

```
PS C:\WINDOWS\system32> get-help new-team -examples

NAME
    New-Team

SYNOPSIS
    This cmdlet lets you provision a new Team for use in Microsoft Teams and will create an O365 Unified Group to
    back the team.  Groups created through teams cmdlets, APIs, or clients will not show up in Outlook by default.

    If you want these groups to appear in Outlook clients, you can use the Set-UnifiedGroup
    (https://learn.microsoft.com/powershell/module/exchange/set-unifiedgroup) cmdlet in the Exchange Powershell
    Module to disable the switch parameter `HiddenFromExchangeClientsEnabled`
    (-HiddenFromExchangeClientsEnabled:$false).


    Note: The Teams application may need to be open by an Owner for up to two hours before changes are reflected.



    -------------------------- Example 1 --------------------------

    New-Team -DisplayName "Tech Reads"

    This example creates a team with all parameters with their default values.
    -------------------------- Example 2 --------------------------

    New-Team -DisplayName "Tech Reads" -Description "Team to post technical articles and blogs" -Visibility Public

    This example creates a team with a specific description and public visibility.
    -------------------------- Example 3 --------------------------

    $group = New-Team -MailNickname "TestTeam" -displayname "Test Teams" -Visibility "private"
    Add-TeamUser -GroupId $group.GroupId -User "fred@example.com"
    Add-TeamUser -GroupId $group.GroupId -User "john@example.com"
    Add-TeamUser -GroupId $group.GroupId -User "wilma@example.com"
    New-TeamChannel -GroupId $group.GroupId -DisplayName "Q4 planning"
    New-TeamChannel -GroupId $group.GroupId -DisplayName "Exec status"
    New-TeamChannel -GroupId $group.GroupId -DisplayName "Contracts"

    This example creates a team, adds three members to it, and creates three channels within it.
```

Figure 4.5 – A new team PowerShell example

Following the new-team example from *Figure 4.6*, you can create a simple team, as shown here:

Figure 4.6 – A new team creation

As shown in the previous figure, you created a team through TPM. Similarly, you can use set-Team to change various properties and settings of the team, such as DisplayName, Description, and Visibility.

CLI for Microsoft 365

In the previous section, we discussed TPM, and you learned about the prerequisites of PowerShell Version 5.1 and later, and how it only works on Windows machines. However, platform independence is the new mantra, and whatever you can build should work beyond the Windows operating system. Therefore, we need a way to build scripts to administer Microsoft 365 through non-Windows platforms.

CLI for Microsoft 365 is a PnP-based initiative between Microsoft employees and community-based SMEs.

We have several other initiatives built on the PnP model, and a few of them are as follows:

- **PnPJS**: This is a collection of JavaScript libraries for Microsoft Graph REST APIs
- **Generator-spfx**: This is an open source generator that extends the Microsoft SPFx generator capabilities
- **PnP PowerShell**: This is a cross-platform-based PowerShell module to connect Microsoft 365, running on any platform that supports .NET Core.

CLI for Microsoft 365 is another important PnP-based project, managed on GitHub at https://github.com/pnp/cli-microsoft365. It is an excellent resource for administrators using non-Windows platforms to manage and administrate their Microsoft 365 tenant.

Now, you have had a quick introduction to CLI. But first, you must install the CLI component to see it in action. So, in the next section, you will learn to install CLI for Microsoft 365.

Installing CLI for Microsoft 365

To start using CLI for Microsoft 365, like TPM, you must install CLI on your computer. CLI is a distributable package hosted by **Node Package Manager** (**npm**). npm is a package manager for JavaScript components. Therefore, installing Node.js and npm is required to install CLI for Microsoft 365.

You can download the Node.js installer from the official Node.js website at https://nodejs.org. When you install Node.js, npm is installed automatically.

You can use the npm command, as shown here, to install CLI for Microsoft 365:

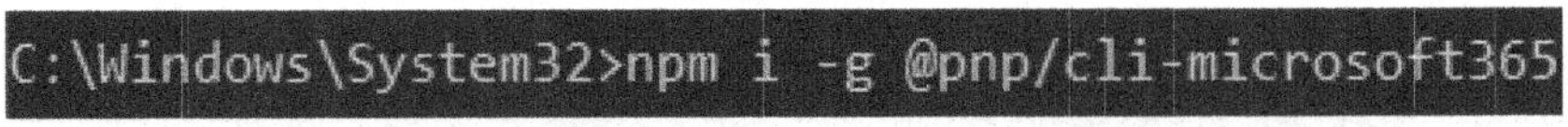

```
C:\Windows\System32>npm i -g @pnp/cli-microsoft365
```

Figure 4.7 – Installing CLI for Microsoft 365 using the npm command

After running the previous command, you will have CLI for Microsoft 365 successfully installed on your machine, as shown in *Figure 4.8*. Later, you can also run this command with @latest as npm install -g @pnp/cli-microsoft365@latest to update CLI for Microsoft 365 to the latest version.

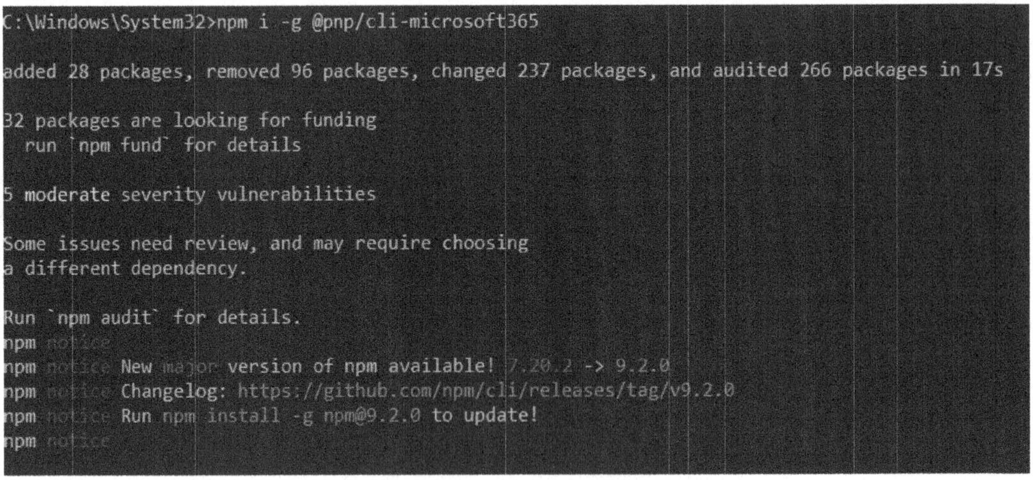

```
C:\Windows\System32>npm i -g @pnp/cli-microsoft365

added 28 packages, removed 96 packages, changed 237 packages, and audited 266 packages in 17s

32 packages are looking for funding
  run `npm fund` for details

5 moderate severity vulnerabilities

Some issues need review, and may require choosing
a different dependency.

Run `npm audit` for details.
npm notice
npm notice    New major version of npm available! 7.20.2 -> 9.2.0
npm notice    Changelog: https://github.com/npm/cli/releases/tag/v9.2.0
npm notice    Run npm install -g npm@9.2.0 to update!
npm notice
```

Figure 4.8 – Installing CLI for Microsoft 365 using the npm command

As shown here, you have successfully installed the CLI using the npm package. Now, you can start using CLI commands and manage your Microsoft 365 tenant.

If you want to remove CLI for Microsoft 365 from your computer for any reason, all you require is the npm command with uninstall, as shown here:

```
npm uninstall -g @pnp/CLI-microsoft365
```

Now that we have installed CLI for Microsoft 365, we will talk about connecting to our Microsoft 365 tenant and running a few commands in the next section.

Connecting to CLI for Microsoft 365

After installing CLI for Microsoft 365, you should know what commands are available and review them to get your scripts to manage your Microsoft 365 tenant. As shown in the following figure, you start with m365 help:

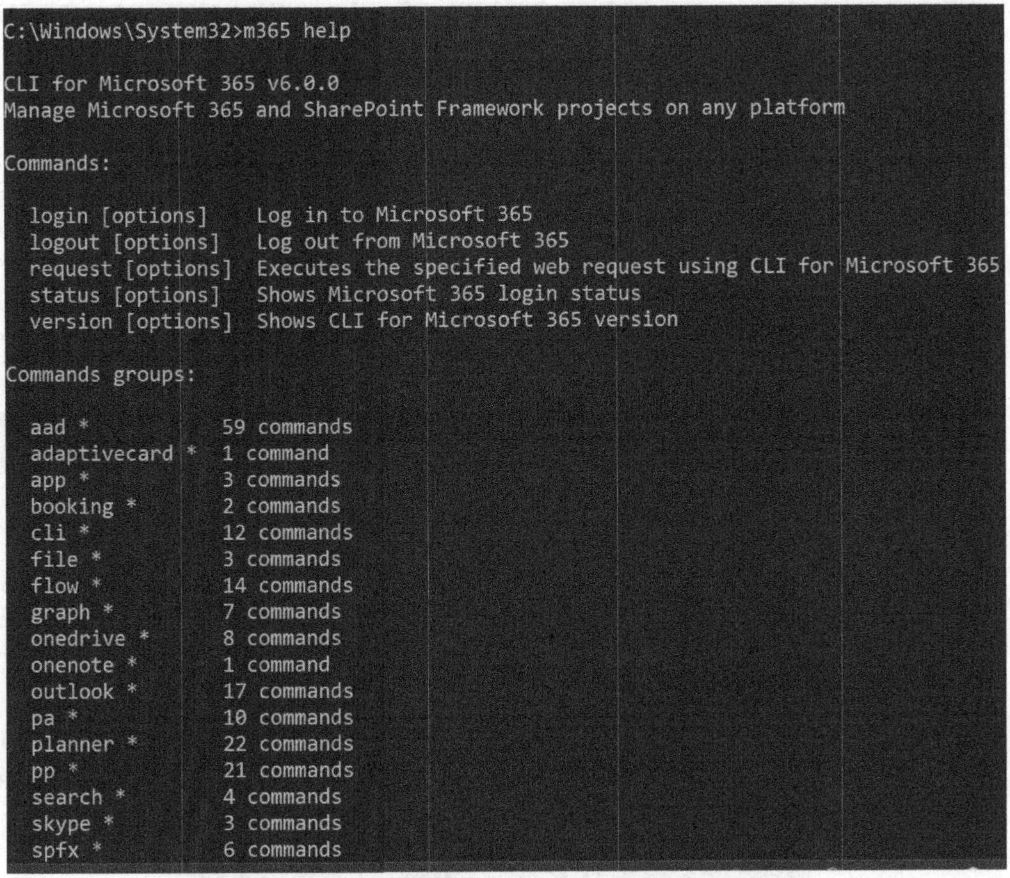

```
C:\Windows\System32>m365 help

CLI for Microsoft 365 v6.0.0
Manage Microsoft 365 and SharePoint Framework projects on any platform

Commands:

  login [options]    Log in to Microsoft 365
  logout [options]   Log out from Microsoft 365
  request [options]  Executes the specified web request using CLI for Microsoft 365
  status [options]   Shows Microsoft 365 login status
  version [options]  Shows CLI for Microsoft 365 version

Commands groups:

  aad *              59 commands
  adaptivecard *     1 command
  app *              3 commands
  booking *          2 commands
  cli *              12 commands
  file *             3 commands
  flow *             14 commands
  graph *            7 commands
  onedrive *         8 commands
  onenote *          1 command
  outlook *          17 commands
  pa *               10 commands
  planner *          22 commands
  pp *               21 commands
  search *           4 commands
  skype *            3 commands
  spfx *             6 commands
```

Figure 4.9 – The m365 help CLI command

With m365 help, you can see the various command options (login, logout, request, status, and version) for Microsoft 365. Also, you can see the command groups (aad, app, graph, OneDrive, spo, and teams). If you note all the commands that are required to manage Microsoft Teams, start with teams and go ahead from there. Again, starting your connection with your Microsoft 365 tenant is the most important step, and this can be done with a device code flow authorization. On the device (your computer), go to the https://microsoft.com/devicelogin web page.

As shown in the following figure, if you run the m365 login command, you will get a code, and then go to the aforementioned web page. After signing in, you are prompted to authenticate the PnP Microsoft 365 Management Shell application to access your tenant.

Figure 4.10 – m365 login for CLI authentication

As discussed, you can also log in by providing a username and password instead of a device code flow. Using a username and password would help in scenarios where you do not have a user interactively providing the code on the web page. In addition to the username and password, you also have various options using the certificate and client secret.

After logging in with the CLI, it persists the connection information. Therefore, if you want to find out what the connection in the session is and whether the session still exists, you need to use the m365 status command, as shown here:

```
PS C:\WINDOWS\system32> m365 status
{
   "connectedAs": "admin@M365x47420136.onmicrosoft.com",
   "authType": "DeviceCode",
   "appId": "31359c7f-bd7e-475c-86db-fdb8c937548e",
   "appTenant": "common"
}
```

Figure 4.11 – The m365 status of the session connected to your tenant

And it is always a clever idea to log out if you have finished the required scripting work by running the m365 logout command:

```
PS C:\WINDOWS\system32> m365 logout
PS C:\WINDOWS\system32> m365 status
"Logged out"
PS C:\WINDOWS\system32>
```

Figure 4.12 – m365 logout

If you rerun the m365 status command after the m365 logout command, it will show you clearly that you have logged out of the CLI session.

Therefore, it is always a good idea to check your script to see whether the Microsoft 365 session is still there; if the status is Logged Out, you need to log in again, as shown in the following code:

```
$mstatus = m365 status --output text
if ($mstatus -eq "Logged Out")
    {
    m365 login
    }
```

Adding a new Microsoft team with CLI for Microsoft 365

After trying to createa Microsoft Teams team with TPM in the previous section, you can try the same with CLI for Microsoft 365 using the following command:

```
m365 teams team add --name "First CLE Team" --description "My
First CLE Team."
```

You can try teams team add after authenticating with login. As we discussed, all Microsoft Teams commands start with teams, and if we want to add a new team, team add with the command name and description will let you create a new team with the name First CLE Team in your Microsoft 365 tenant. If your command is successful, you will see the following output:

```
C:\Windows\System32>m365 login
"To sign in, use a web browser to open the page https://microsoft.com/devicelogin and enter the code DMYHF8Y44 to authenticate."

C:\Windows\System32>m365 teams team add --name "First CLE Team" --description "My First CLE Team"
{
  "@odata.context": "https://graph.microsoft.com/v1.0/$metadata#teams('e2982f3a-d226-46d7-aedc-dc41247085ba')/operations/$entity",
  "id": "8999ef43-07b7-4d7e-80f3-4f653c3b6b6c",
  "operationType": "createTeam",
  "createdDateTime": "2022-12-19T05:04:52.3914195Z",
  "status": "notStarted",
  "lastActionDateTime": "2022-12-19T05:04:52.3914195Z",
  "attemptsCount": 1,
  "targetResourceId": "e2982f3a-d226-46d7-aedc-dc41247085ba",
  "targetResourceLocation": "/teams('e2982f3a-d226-46d7-aedc-dc41247085ba')",
  "Value": "{\"apps\":[],\"channels\":[],\"WorkflowId\":\"northcentralus.5731affb-cf5e-40a2-bf7b-9eab3c9084ad\"}",
  "error": null
}
```

Figure 4.13 – Creating the First Microsoft Teams team with CLI for Microsoft 365

Now that we have successfully created a team through CLI, let's add a channel. You can extend the CLI commands as follows:

```
m365 teams channel add --teamName "First CLE Team" --name
CLIChannel --description CLIChannelTesting
```

If you run this command, it will add the CLIChannel channel to your First CLE Team team; the output is as follows:

```
PS C:\WINDOWS\system32> m365 teams channel add --teamName "First CLE Team" --name CLIChannel --description CLIChannelTesting
{
    "id": "19:5970290b34894eb4b6247aaf95725b46@thread.tacv2",
    "createdDateTime": "2022-12-20T03:32:34.4650927Z",
    "displayName": "CLIChannel",
    "description": null,
    "isFavoriteByDefault": false,
    "email": "",
    "webUrl": "https://teams.microsoft.com/l/channel/19%3a5970290b34894eb4b6247aaf95725b46%40thread.tacv2/CLIChannel?groupId=e298
5-46d7-aedc-dc41247085ba&tenantId=98245402-7e72-44c0-ac44-3930d9d28a43",
    "membershipType": "standard"
```

Figure 4.14 – Adding CLIChannel through CLI for Microsoft 365

As you can see in the preceding figure, you have added a new channel; take this example to the next level by adding a user to the Microsoft Teams team. In the following sample code, you are adding a user, alexw@duggirala.onmicrosoft.com, to the First CLE Team team you created earlier. For that, we need to use the m365 teams user add CLI command, which needs to pass the team ID and the username. So, to get the team ID, we use the m365 teams got CLI command, pass the team name, and convert the output to JSON to read the team ID:

```
$team = m365 teams team get --name "First CLE Team" --output
JSON | convertFrom-JSON
$teamid = $team.id
m365 teams user add --teamId  $teamid --userName 'alexw@
duggirala.onmicrosoft.com'
```

This code added the user to your Microsoft Teams team. You can log in to the Microsoft Teams team and verify the member.

Summary

This chapter gave you a quick jumpstart on scripting Teams for various activities such as administration, including users, teams, policies, and configuration. First, we reviewed Microsoft TPM with which TPM administrators can manage teams, channels, meetings, policies, and other components of Microsoft Teams. TPM provides a comprehensive set of cmdlets to automate tasks and manage Teams more efficiently. Next, we discussed CLI for Microsoft 365 as a cross-platform CLI for managing Microsoft 365 services and applications. It allows you to perform various tasks, such as creating and managing SharePoint sites, managing Microsoft Teams, and managing Power Platform environments. CLI for Microsoft 365 is available on Windows, macOS, and Linux. You can tap into this knowledge and create your scripts for any customization or automation needs.

In the next chapter, we will learn how to use **SharePoint Framework** (**SPFX**), a development framework used to build customizations for Microsoft Teams. SPFx provides a robust framework to build custom Teams apps with which you can provide a more customized user experience.

Microsoft Teams Customization Using the SharePoint Framework (SPFx)

In this chapter, we will introduce you to the **SharePoint Framework** (**SPFx**), a modern development model for SharePoint. We will also cover how you can bring the customizations built for SharePoint to Microsoft Teams. First, we will start with a history of SharePoint development just to set the context and understand what it is. Then, we will cover the open source tools we need to develop the SharePoint Framework components and how to install and configure them.

These are the main topics we'll cover in this chapter:

- SharePoint development history
- Setting up an SPFx development environment.
- Developing your first Teams tab using the SPFx
- Leveraging the SPFx for Teams

This book is about customization on Teams, so we will focus on building customizations with the SPFx for Teams. If you want to explore the SPFx further, you can learn more about web parts, extensions, and the library components of the SPFx. However, this book is limited to the simple web parts, but you can find several books that focus only on SPFx development. Hosting these SPFx components in App Catalog (also called Add-in Catalog) is another topic we don't cover in this book.

SPFx solutions can benefit organizations, whether due to improved productivity, collaboration, or better decision-making. With the power of Microsoft Teams and the SPFx, you can create custom solutions that meet your business needs and streamline processes. Scalability and security are all included in the platform and are easily applied to Microsoft Teams.

Here are a few examples of SPFx solutions that can be deployed and used in Microsoft Teams.

You can build **Custom Forms** as an SPFx solution that permits organizations to create customized business forms to access within Microsoft Teams. These are used for employee onboarding, vacation submissions, tickets, project kick-offs, supplies records, resource booking, and so on and these forms can consume different services and SharePoint sites as repositories. It simplifies access to forms by making them available in Microsoft Teams.

The SPFx offers a **Knowledge Sharing** solution that provides a centralized location for organizational knowledge, including articles, FAQs, policies, announcements, news, and other relevant resources. In addition, this SPFx solution allows members to access this information quickly within Microsoft Teams.

The SPFx-based **Task Management** solution for Microsoft Teams streamlines task tracking, improves collaboration and productivity, and provides a centralized location for managing tasks. It can include task creation, assignment, progress tracking, setting deadlines, and various insights. As a result, this solution helps improve resource control, avoids duplication of efforts, and provides a unified interface for managing tasks and project activities. In addition, integrating with Microsoft Teams facilitates collaboration between team members, simplifies task tracking across multiple projects, and reduces the time spent on administrative tasks. Overall, an SPFx-based task management solution efficiently increases productivity and streamlines organizational project management.

SharePoint development history

It is good to know the history of SharePoint development; a few options are available for developing in SharePoint, so let's see how it has changed over the years. In addition, learning about the history will help us better understand the latest trends in SharePoint development and contextualize what we are doing and why we are doing it this way. For example, SharePoint development started with a farm solution on the version of 2007, also called MOSS 2007.

Here is a list of various development strategies in SharePoint:

- Farm solutions: These full-trust code solutions need to be deployed on SharePoint Server. This option is unavailable with SharePoint Online as we cannot access SharePoint Server.

- Sandbox solutions: This was introduced with the 2010 version of SharePoint and could be deployed on site collection, which did not require any code on SharePoint Server. Sandbox solutions with server-side code have been deprecated and removed from SharePoint Online.

- CSOM/JSOM: The **Client-Side Object Model** (CSOM) with server-side code and **JavaScript Object Model** (JSOM) communicate with SharePoint for client-side or browser customizations.

- A **Representative State Transfer** (REST) API: SharePoint REST is another popular option for interacting with the SharePoint API in custom applications through a browser or server-side code.

- An add-in model: The add-in model introduced in SharePoint 2013 took the sandbox solutions to a new level. A SharePoint add-in enabled the development of custom solutions to run in an isolated domain and host server-side code outside SharePoint. SharePoint Online supports this model.

- The SPFx: Microsoft introduced the SPFx in 2017 as a new development model through which you can do client-side development to deliver customized capabilities with SharePoint. Microsoft built this for first-party (Microsoft Product Group) and third-party developers to create customizations on SharePoint Online and On-Premises SharePoint 2016, 2019, and Subscription Edition at various levels. The toolchain required to build these SPFx components is entirely new to Microsoft developers and is based on open source tools.

Microsoft released SPFx version 1.0 as generally available, and from then, every 3 to 4 months, it has released the latest version with more features. So, with version **SPFx v1.7**, you can create a Microsoft Teams tab using the SPFx, which is a significant step toward customizing Teams. In this chapter, you will prepare your machine by installing all the open source tools for developing the SPFx components, specifically Microsoft Teams Tab and personal apps.

Setting up an SPFx development environment

The tools required for building SPFx components are open source Node.js-based toolchains and embrace all web frameworks and code editors. This section will discuss how to install them on your development machine:

1. **Install Node.js**: The first step is installing Node.js (`https://nodejs.org/`). Next, make sure you install a version of Node.js that supports SPFx development; currently, the recommended version is LTS V14. However, Node.js periodically releases new versions, so you will need to check the Microsoft documentation for the supportability of the node version with the SPFx.

2. Install **Node Package Manager** (**npm**): npm (`https://www.npmjs.com`) is a package manager for Node.js solutions. So, when you install Node.js, npm also gets installed. The npm registry has become a center to host various JavaScript code repositories. npm itself is also just a package, so if you want to update it, run the following command:

   ```
   npm install -g npm
   ```

3. **Development toolchain prerequisites**: The next set of tools you need to install is Gulp and Yeoman:

   - **Gulp**: Gulp (`https://gulpjs.com`) is a task runner to automate SPFx built-in tasks, such as compiling, packaging, starting, testing, and so on.

   - **Yeoman**: (`https://yeoman.io`) Any project scaffolding generator helps to create new projects. In addition, SharePoint tools include a Yeoman generator, which provides standard build tools and common boilerplate code.

- **SharePoint Framework Generator**: This Yeoman generator helps quickly generate SPFx solutions. Please see the following command to install the SPFx generator:

```
npm install @microsoft/generator-SharePoint -g
```

Alternatively, you can install all three tools mentioned earlier with the following command:

```
npm install gulp-cli yo @microsoft/generator-SharePoint
--global
```

Because these three tools are npm packages, you can install them using npm. -g means it will be available globally on your machine, so every project can use it.

- **TypeScript**: TypeScript is a superset of JavaScript; you can write your code in TypeScript, but it compiles to plain JavaScript so the browser can understand it. TypeScript is the primary development language on which the SPFx project base templates are built (`https://www.typescriptlang.org`).

- Visual Studio Code: Visual Studio Code is a lightweight source code editor for building SPFx components (`https://code.visualstudio.com`).

After following these steps, you have the tools to develop solutions with the SPFx. In the next section, you will create your first Teams tab with the SPFx.

Developing your first Teams tab or app using the SPFx

As discussed earlier, you can build components such as client-side web parts and extensions with the SPFx. However, this book will not cover the SPFx in further depth than this chapter:

- **Client-side web parts**: These are the controls built with client-side technologies and hosted on a SharePoint page. You can also make these controls available on Microsoft Teams.

- **Extensions**: Extensions are also built with client-side technology to enhance the modern page experience and modern lists. Modern lists are the new list experience available with SharePoint Online.

This chapter aims to bring the web parts built for SharePoint to Microsoft Teams as an app or tab, but before that, let us understand the difference between a Teams app and a tab.

What is the difference between a Teams app and a Teams tab?

Tabs are specific to a Microsoft Teams team, so you can add them to any Teams channel, whereas Teams apps are not specific to a Microsoft Teams team; you can add them to the left rail of the Teams client.

The first step is creating an SPFx solution with the following command:

```
Yo @microsoft/SharePoint
```

The following screen shows you the initiation of creating a solution and leads to the following steps:

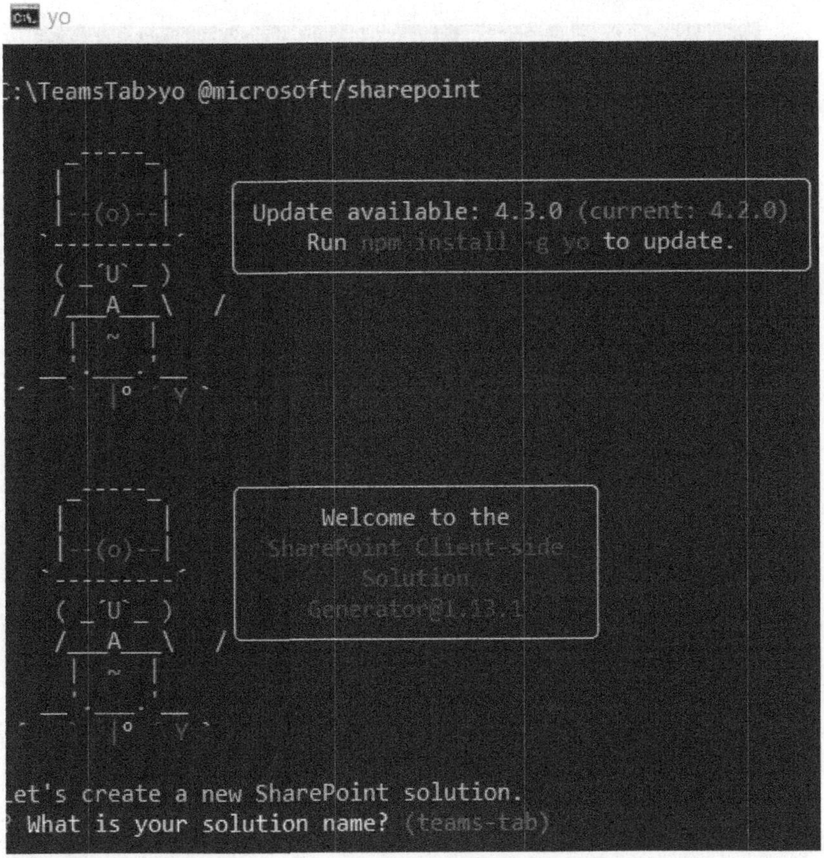

Figure 5.1 – Creating an SPFx solution using Yeoman

The Yeoman generator prompts developers with questions to generate projects and to project scaffolding with the required folders and files, as shown in the following figure:

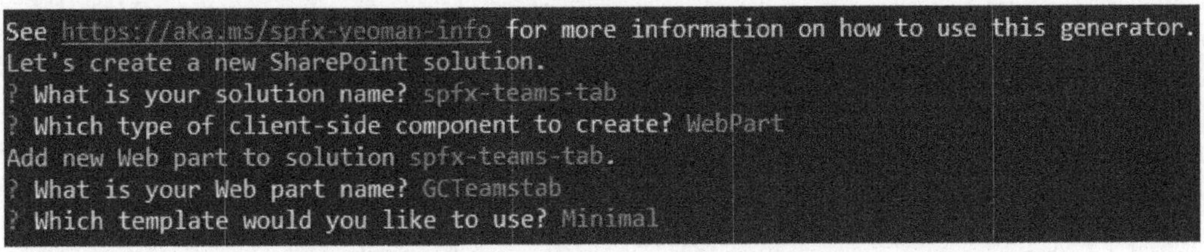

Figure 5.2 – Yeoman-generated questions

To open and customize the SPFx components generated by the Yeoman generator, you can use Visual Studio Code, as shown in *Figure 5.2*.

```
slint/issues/4534 for more information.

dded 2342 packages, and audited 2343 packages in 2m

16 packages are looking for funding
  run `npm fund` for details

27 vulnerabilities (12 low, 86 moderate, 26 high, 3 critical)

o address issues that do not require attention, run:
  npm audit fix

o address all issues (including breaking changes), run:
  npm audit fix --force

un `npm audit` for details.

    _=+#####!
  ##########|
  ###/    (##|(@)        .----------------------------------------.
  ### ######|    \       |           Congratulations!             |
  ###/   /###|    (@)    |  Solution spfx-teams-tab is created.   |
  ####### ##|    /       |    Run gulp serve to play with it!      |
  ###    /##|(@)          '----------------------------------------'
  ##########|
    **=+####!

:\TeamsTab>
```

Figure 5.3: SPFx solution created

Your first SPFx solution has been created, as shown in *Figure 5.3*. Next, this is the solution you can open in Visual Studio code for customizing. To open the solution in Visual Studio Code, type `code .` into the same prompt where you created the solution, as shown in the following figure:

Figure 5.4 – Opening the SPFx solution in Visual Studio Code

After opening the solution in Visual Studio Code, explore the files by clicking on each one. For example, as you develop the Teams tab, go to `serve.json`, and change the Workbench pointing to your demo tenant's SharePoint site, which could be any site in your tenant.

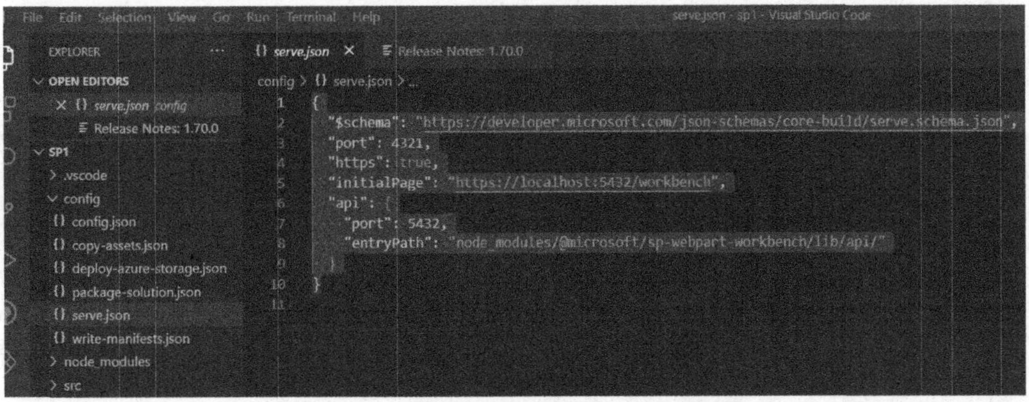

Figure 5.5 – The serve.json file

Developers can use the Workbench tool to evaluate or preview their client-side web part. You have a local Workbench automatically installed with the toolchain and an online Workbench accessible from any site with the `Layouts` folder. The online Workbench will execute the client-side web part in the context of the site where you are accessing Workbench. The URL is `HTTPS://[tenant].sharepoint.com/_layouts/workbench.aspx`.

As shown in the following figure, you update the `initialPage` section in `serve.json` with any site you want to use in your tenant:

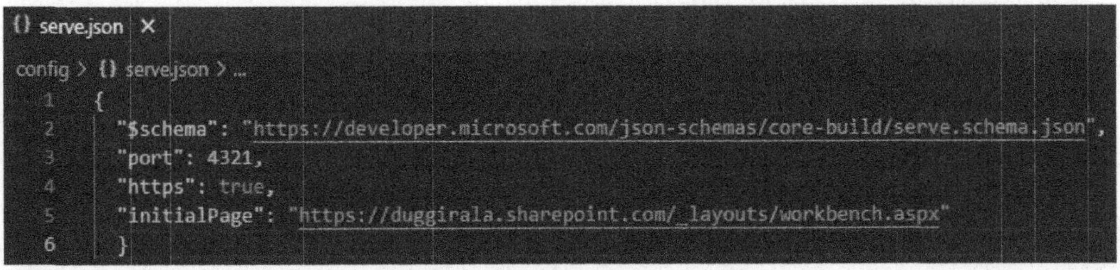

Figure 5.6 – Updating serve.json with your Microsoft 365 tenant site

Furthermore, in your solution, you may note that there is a `teams` folder in the project, which has the following two files:

- `[componentId]_color.png`: The default small picture for a tab
- `[componentId]_outline.png`: The default large picture for a tab

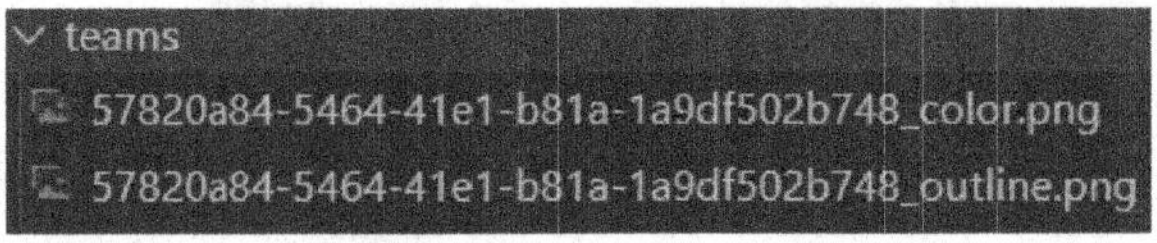

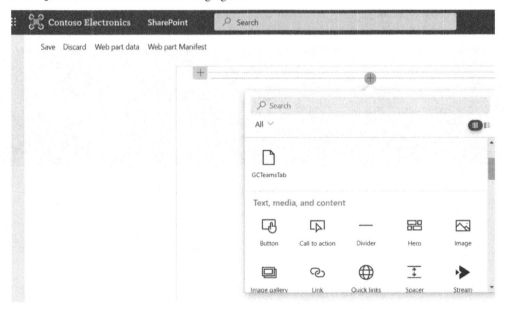

Figure 5.7 – Teams' default icons

These are the default icons used in the Microsoft Teams `color.png` and `outline.png`; you can replace these pictures with custom images. However, it helps if you used an exact name so that it packages without any issues when you plan to synchronize the solution to the Teams store.

Building and running the web part in Workbench

Now that you have reviewed the solution and made the minimal changes required to `serve.json` on your tenant's Workbench, you can build and run the web part. It would be best to use the `gulp` command, `gulp-serve`, which starts Node.js and hosts the project. It will then launch your default internet browser and open the page to the Workbench with the site you have already configured in `serve.json`, as shown in the following figure:

Figure 5.8 – Launching the URL with the SharePoint Workbench

You can add GCTeamsTab, as shown in *Figure 5.8*, to the Workbench, and then the GCTeamsTab web part will appear, as shown here:

Figure 5.9 – Web part on the SharePoint Workbench

What you have done here is ensured the web part works okay on Workbench so that you can package and deploy it to use in SharePoint or Microsoft Teams. So, to use this client-side web part on Teams, you need to ensure the web part's manifest (<project>.manifest.JSON) has the supported hosts present – TeamsPersonalApp and TeamsTab.

Now, you can package the solution to use this web part in sites or Teams.

Packaging the solution

You need to use a few gulp commands for packaging the web part to get an SPPKG file. An SPPKG is deployed to your **tenant's App Catalog**, also called **Add-In Catalog**.

Continuing the same command prompt, use gulp bundle --ship to build and minify the assets – --ship indicates the build process for production distribution.

The following figure shows a successful bundling solution for production shipping:

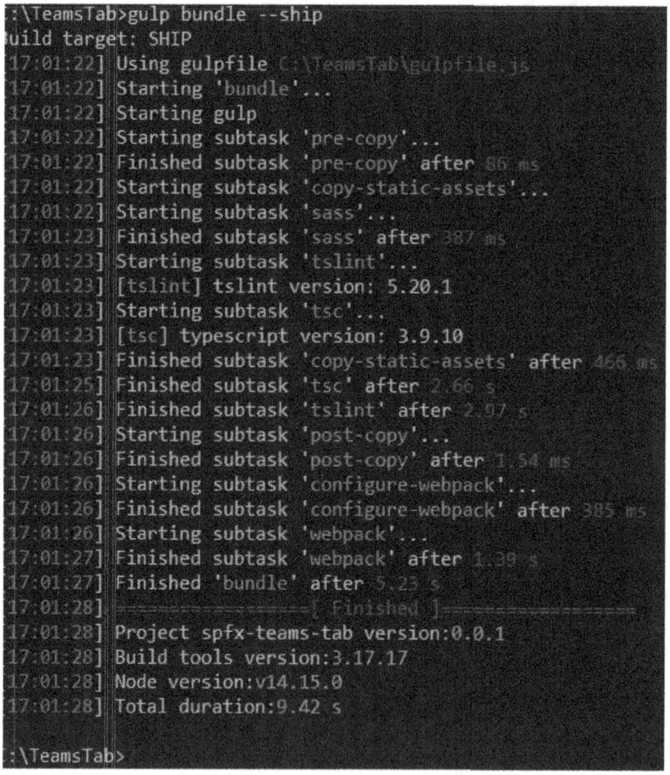

```
:\TeamsTab>gulp bundle --ship
uild target: SHIP
17:01:22] Using gulpfile C:\TeamsTab\gulpfile.js
17:01:22] Starting 'bundle'...
17:01:22] Starting gulp
17:01:22] Starting subtask 'pre-copy'...
17:01:22] Finished subtask 'pre-copy' after 86 ms
17:01:22] Starting subtask 'copy-static-assets'...
17:01:22] Starting subtask 'sass'...
17:01:23] Finished subtask 'sass' after 387 ms
17:01:23] Starting subtask 'tslint'...
17:01:23] [tslint] tslint version: 5.20.1
17:01:23] Starting subtask 'tsc'...
17:01:23] [tsc] typescript version: 3.9.10
17:01:23] Finished subtask 'copy-static-assets' after 466 ms
17:01:25] Finished subtask 'tsc' after 2.66 s
17:01:26] Finished subtask 'tslint' after 2.97 s
17:01:26] Starting subtask 'post-copy'...
17:01:26] Finished subtask 'post-copy' after 1.54 ms
17:01:26] Starting subtask 'configure-webpack'...
17:01:26] Finished subtask 'configure-webpack' after 385 ms
17:01:26] Starting subtask 'webpack'...
17:01:27] Finished subtask 'webpack' after 1.39 s
17:01:27] Finished 'bundle' after 5.23 s
17:01:28] ===============[ Finished ]===============
17:01:28] Project spfx-teams-tab version:0.0.1
17:01:28] Build tools version:3.17.17
17:01:28] Node version:v14.15.0
17:01:28] Total duration:9.42 s

:\TeamsTab>
```

Figure 5.10 – Successful build for an SPFx web part

If the build is successful, you can package the solution. See `package-solution.json` in the project if you want to change any values.

On the command prompt, type the `gulp` command as `gulp package-solution --ship`, which creates the successful package, the `SPFx-teams-tab.sppkg` file, as shown in the following figure:

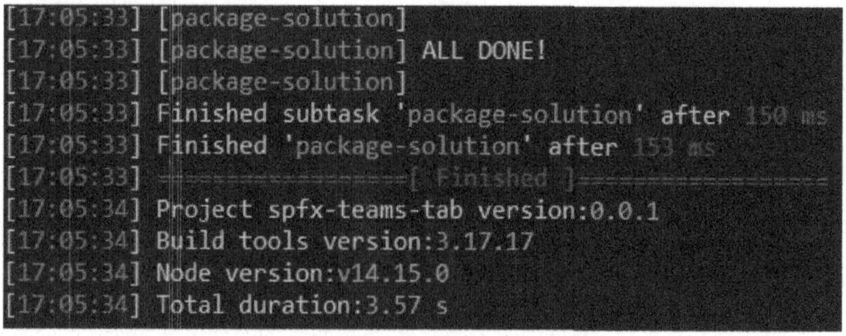

```
[17:05:33] [package-solution]
[17:05:33] [package-solution] ALL DONE!
[17:05:33] [package-solution]
[17:05:33] Finished subtask 'package-solution' after 150 ms
[17:05:33] Finished 'package-solution' after 153 ms
[17:05:33] ===============[ Finished ]===============
[17:05:34] Project spfx-teams-tab version:0.0.1
[17:05:34] Build tools version:3.17.17
[17:05:34] Node version:v14.15.0
[17:05:34] Total duration:3.57 s
```

Figure 5.11 – Successful package for the SPFx web part

Now the package has been built and is ready to go, in the next section, we will deploy this to your tenant App Catalog so that you can consume this web part on SharePoint sites or Microsoft Teams.

Deploying the SPFx package to the App Catalog

The App Catalog or Add-In Catalog is a site collection with the `AppCatalog#0` template, allowing you to host your add-ins and SPFx components. Each tenant has one app catalog at the tenant level but can activate app catalogs at the site collection level.

If you deploy the packages at the site collection level of an App Catalog, all the package components (web parts) will only be available to that site; if you want to make the web part available for all sites in your tenant, you need to deploy the package to the tenant-level app catalog. Unfortunately, each Microsoft 365 tenant has only one app catalog.

To deploy the app package (the SPPKG file), follow these steps:

1. Go to the App Catalog site and click on the **Apps for SharePoint** link on the left, as shown in the following figure:

Figure 5.12 – App Catalog

Drag and drop the package (SPPKG) created in the previous step, as shown in the following figure:

Figure 5.13 – Drag and drop the SPPKG file

2. Now, the package has been dropped onto the document library; it will prompt you to deploy. Check the checkbox (if you want to make the web part available to all the sites in your tenant) shown in the following figure to make this solution available for all sites in the tenant. This way, you do not need to add the app to sites that you need; it will be available automatically.

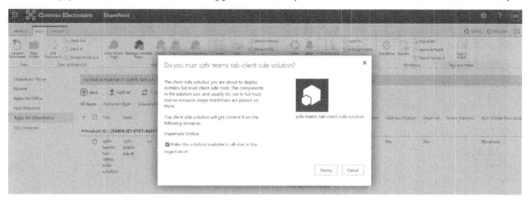

Figure 5.14 – Deploying the SPFx package

Now, the web part has been added to the App Catalog and deployed for all sites in the tenant. For a quick test to check this web part, go to any SharePoint site in your tenant and try to add a web part on any page. You should be able to find the web part that you just deployed. For example, the following figure shows the option of adding the web part to the SharePoint modern page:

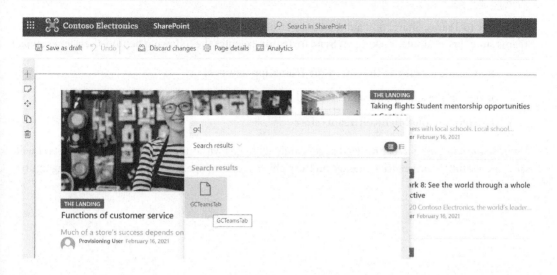

Figure 5.15 – Web part availability on the SharePoint Modern Page

Currently, you have the web part available to use on any SharePoint page. However, we want to bring this customization (the web part) to a Microsoft Teams team.

Syncing SharePoint web parts to Teams

In the previous section, we added SPFx web parts to a SharePoint page; now, we can bring these web parts to Teams by embedding this page as a Teams tab or app. Making the package available in the Microsoft Teams store would be best.

In the App Catalog, as shown in the following figure, you must click on the **Sync to Teams** ribbon action. After that, the solution will synchronize to the Microsoft Teams app store.

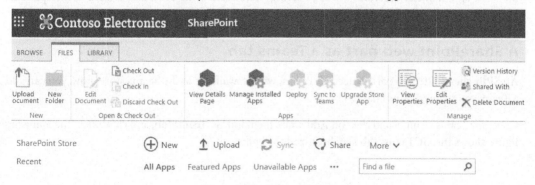

Figure 5.16 – Sync to Teams

With **Sync to Teams**, SharePoint automatically creates and deploys a Microsoft Teams manifest to the Teams store. For example, clicking on **Sync to Teams** executes the following behind-the-scenes steps:

- It dynamically creates the Microsoft Teams app manifest
- It zips up the app manifest created and the images in the solution
- It deploys to the Microsoft Teams store

Suppose the solution is synchronized successfully in Teams without any issues. In that case, you will see a successfully *synchronized message* on the right side of the page, as shown in the following figure:

Figure 5.17 – Successful sync to Teams

Sideloading app in Teams

While you have seen the option to deploy an app to the Team store from the App Catalog, you also have another option for uploading the app directly to the Team store. This option is called **sideloading**.

When an admin clicks on the **Sync to Teams** button, SharePoint Online will look for the `*.sppkg` file, dynamically create a Teams app, and deploy it to the tenant's Microsoft Teams app store.

Alternatively, you can manually create the Teams app manifest and the Teams app Package (`.zip` file). The app manifest describes the app's configuration and other attributes related to the app. This should be a JSON file called `manifest.json`.

A SharePoint web part as a Teams tab

An SPFx client-side web part, synced to Teams, will be available in the Teams store; now, you can add a Teams tab to any Teams channel.

Go to any Teams channel and click on **Add a tab**, then find **GCTeamsTab**, and click on it. The following figure shows the **GCTeamsTab** synchronized to Teams:

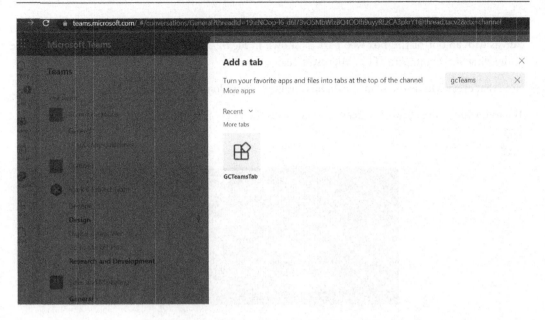

Figure 5.18 – GCTeamsTab synced in Microsoft Teams

Once you click on **GCTeamsTab**, it opens the following screen, and you can save it to the Teams channel you are on.

Figure 5.19 – Adding the tab to the Teams channel

Now that the custom Teams tab has been added to the channel, you will see the web part in the Teams canvas with an out-of-the-box web part, as shown in *Figure 5.20*, and this web part is hosted by the underlying SharePoint site of the Microsoft Teams team.

Note that every Microsoft Teams team has a unique SharePoint site supporting the team.

The following figure shows the Teams canvas with the web part added.

Figure 5.20: The SPFx Teams tab on the Teams channel

In the SPFx web part solution, we have a manifest file, `manifest.json`, which supports the hosts for the web part developed with the solution. Here, you have choices for a Teams tab, personal app, SharePoint web part, and full page. A Teams tab connects to a Teams channel, and a personal app is not connected to any Microsoft Teams team.

Here are the various supported hosted available in `manifest.json`:

```
supportedHosts": ["SharePointWebPart", "TeamsPersonalApp",
"TeamsTab", "SharePointFullPage"]
```

A SharePoint web part as a Teams personal app

Now, you can try adding the SPFx custom web part, **GCTeamsTab**, as an app to the Microsoft Teams client. First, you can search for the **GCTeamsTab** app on the App Store and select it to add it, as shown in the following figure:

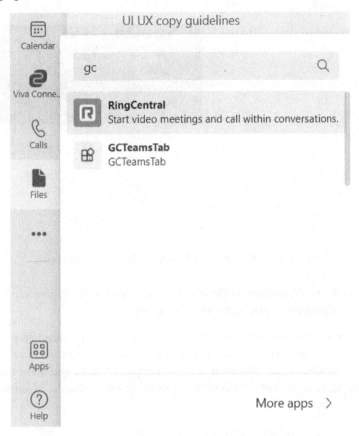

Figure 5.21 – Searching for GCTeamsTab in the Teams app store

Once you add the app, it will be available in Teams, as shown in this figure:

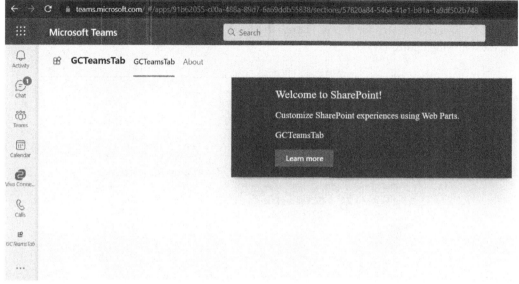

Figure 5.22 – GCTeamsTabs as a Teams personal app

After clicking on the **GCTeamsTab** on the left rail (also known as the Teams app bar), the web part opens in the Teams canvas without connecting to any team.

That concludes our section on building a simple SharePoint client-side web part and making it available to the Teams store as a tab or personal app. From here, you can create robust client-side web parts, which can make calls to various APIs or Graph API calls, and make them available in a Microsoft Teams team. In the last section of this chapter, we will review the advantages of using SPFx with Microsoft Teams.

Leveraging the SPFx for Microsoft Teams

There are several advantages of using SPFx with Teams tabs or Teams apps, as mentioned here:

- **Hosted with SharePoint**: You have the actual code hosted on a SharePoint site that relates to Teams, so you do not need to worry about seeing where you can host the code on Teams customizations. Also, it simplifies your deployment operations by deploying them in a SharePoint Online App Catalog and synchronizing to the Teams store from there.

- **Graph API support**: You can consume the Graph API easily with a web part using `GraphHTTPClient` or ADAL.JS and get the code running.

- **Reuse implementation**: You can quickly implement the same customization on SharePoint and Microsoft Teams, saving a lot of development time.

- **Seamless collaboration**: Combining the collaborative features of Microsoft Teams with the content management features of SharePoint, SPFx solutions enable seamless collaboration and communication among team members.

SPFx solutions deployed in Microsoft Teams can benefit organizations significantly, including improved collaboration, streamlined development, and increased efficiency. We will wrap up this chapter by discussing using **Application Lifecycle Management** (**ALM**) with DevOps to build SPFx solutions that enhance the development process, enabling teams to deliver high-quality solutions more quickly and efficiently.

ALM with Azure DevOps

Using ALM with Azure DevOps in building SPFx solutions is a modern software development approach that focuses on streamlining the development process, minimizing errors, and ensuring the timely delivery of high-quality software solutions. It combines the best practices of DevOps with the capabilities of the SPFx to provide a unified platform for development, testing, and deployment.

Streamlining SPFx development using Azure DevOps involves leveraging the various tools and services available within the Azure DevOps platform to automate the entire SPFx project life cycle, from its initial development to deployment and management.

Using Azure DevOps for SPFx development, you can work more efficiently, reduce the risk of errors, and deliver high-quality software solutions faster.

Let's look at the key benefits of this approach.

Azure DevOps provides a powerful version control system, which facilitates effective change management and collaboration for development teams on complex projects. With this system, teams can track changes to their code base, identify contributors, and roll back to earlier versions when needed. This streamlined process can help teams manage changes efficiently, ensuring high quality.

Continuous Integration/Continuous Delivery (**CI/CD**) using Azure DevOps for SPFx solutions involves a whole suite of features in CI/CD, which automates the build, testing, and deployment process for SPFx solution code changes.

Azure DevOps provides a comprehensive suite of project management tools that can help development teams easily manage their SPFx development projects. These tools include work item tracking, backlog management, and report creation features. Work item tracking enables teams to monitor the progress of individual tasks and identify any potential roadblocks, while backlog management helps teams prioritize and plan their work efficiently. Finally, report creation features allow teams to generate detailed reports on project progress, team performance, and other vital metrics. These powerful project management tools allow development teams to stay organized and focused, ultimately leading to more efficient and effective project delivery.

Automated testing with Azure DevOps for SPFx solutions leads to more efficient development, higher-quality solutions, and reduced risk of errors. It allows developers to quickly identify and fix any issues or bugs in their code, ensuring that the final product is reliable and functional. In addition, Azure DevOps provides powerful tools and features to streamline the testing process and ensure that SPFx solutions meet the given requirements and specifications.

By embracing ALM and leveraging the powerful features of Azure DevOps, development teams can optimize their SPFx development process, boost team productivity, minimize errors, and deliver top-notch software solutions on time. ALM and Azure DevOps provide a comprehensive approach to SPFx development, from version control and project management to automated testing and deployment, which can help organizations achieve their development goals efficiently and effectively.

Summary

In this chapter, we introduced the SPFx, starting with the history of SharePoint development. Then, we walked through how to set up our machine for SPFx development by installing all the required open source tools, such as Node.js, npm, Gulp Yeoman, TypeScript, and SharePoint Framework Generator.

Once the machine was ready, we built an SPFx web part and brought that customization (web part) to Microsoft Teams as a tab or an app.

This is a beautiful opportunity to bring your custom solutions under the wrapper of an SPFx web part to a Microsoft Teams team so that your business users don't need to leave the Microsoft Teams team to do their day-to-day tasks.

In the next chapter, we will learn more about authentication for Teams.

6

Microsoft Teams Authentication

In this chapter, you will learn about various authentication options available to developers for creating custom Microsoft Teams tabs. This chapter primarily focuses on the following topics:

- Authentication and authorization in Microsoft Teams apps
- **Single sign-on** (SSO) in Microsoft Teams tabs

Authentication and authorization are vital processes that are used in protecting data. Authentication verifies the user or service, and authorization verifies whether the user or service has appropriate permissions to access the resources or data.

So, both authentication and authorization are essential to keep data secure.

SSO is an authentication method that uses the Teams user's identity and provides access to the app. The idea is that the user who logs into Microsoft Teams doesn't need to log in again to use the app running in the Teams environment.

In this chapter, we'll look at implementing SSO with authentication and authorization with Azure Active Directory.

Various authentication options

Microsoft Teams is built on Microsoft 365 and leverages the authentication provided by the Microsoft 365 tenant, which could be Cloud Identity, Synchronized Identity, or Federated Identity, based on how the Microsoft 365 tenant is configured.

All three authentication models listed below authenticate Microsoft Teams, as Microsoft Teams supports SSO. This avoids the user being asked to log in multiple times. However, the crux of this chapter is the supporting mechanism of the Teams tab app created by developers to support authentication with SSO.

Here are the various authentication options:

- **Cloud Identity**: This is suitable for organizations with no on-premises Active Directory. Here, user identities are maintained with Azure Active Directory, so users are authenticated by Azure AD. You create user accounts in the Microsoft 365 admin center.

- **Synchronization Identity**: With this authentication, users use the same username and password as on their on-premises. We synchronize on-premises Active Directory objects to the Azure cloud. In this model, hashes of users' passwords are synchronized from your on-premises Active Directory to Azure AD. If password changes happen on-premises, the new hashes are synchronized to Azure AD.

- **Federated Identity**: This is more suitable for large organizations. In this authentication, users are authenticated by an Active Directory federation service or any third-party federation solutions against their on-premises Azure Directory.

This chapter mainly focuses on SSO-enabled Teams tabs in Microsoft Teams in the context of customizations.

Authentication and authorization in Microsoft Teams apps

Custom apps you built and deployed in Teams may consume numerous Microsoft 365 services within your tenant or external services such as DocuSign, Twitter, and so on. For example, it could be Azure AD, the Graph API, a REST API, and so on, of the tenant where the app is installed. All these services require authentication and authorization to access the required data in the custom app from these services. Therefore, you should choose the appropriate authentication methods suitable for your needs.

There are two authentication methods used in the Teams app:

- **Authentication using SSO in the Teams app**: With this approach, the Teams app uses the identity of the user who logged into Teams. And since it requires consent from the app user, it doesn't prompt the user to log in multiple times.

- **Authentication using a third-party OAuth provider in the Teams app**: With this approach, the Teams app uses an OAuth provider such as Azure AD, Google, GitHub, and so on. When the app user logs into the app, the identity provider who was registered will validate the user and provide access to the app.

You can use one of the above authentication methods to authenticate your Teams apps; we will review these concepts further.

Authentication using SSO in the Teams app

Authentication using SSO is crucial for the usability of an app so that it does not disrupt the user experience by having the user log in separately to each app. So, when you are building Teams tabs, make sure you have configured an SSO experience. We will review the required tasks to have the Teams tab app support SSO in your Teams app.

What is the Teams tab app?

The Teams tab app is a web page created using HTML and client scripts that allows you to render content in your Teams app as `<iframe>` and the web page can be hosted on any website with a well-known address. When you design the web page, ensure it is clean and engaging to users.

We also have restrictions on the website that hosts the Teams tab. If the website has conditional access policies in place, the web page will not render in the Teams desktop app but in Teams in a browser.

We have three steps to enable SSO for a Teams tab app:

1. Register and configure your app in the Azure AD application. The first thing is to create an Azure AD app and configure it to represent your Teams tab.

2. The code to handle the access token to your app's code validates the received access token.

3. Update the Teams client app manifest. This is where your app tells the Team that it is using SSO with the Azure AD application created in the first step.

Before registering an application, we need to use `ngrok.exe`, like in other chapters. With `ngrok`, you can use a public URL pointing to a local host running on your local computer. For example, in this Teams tab, we have the page running locally, and the Teams app will point to that local page using `ngrok`, which creates a tunnel to the local host.

Note that the usage of `ngrok.exe` is only for developmental purposes; here is the link to download ngrok: `https://ngrok.com/download`.

After downloading, run `ngrok.exe` in any folder on your local drive, open the folder in a prompt with `run as admin`, and use **ngrok** `http://localhost:3007`. With this, you are starting ngrok where you get a public URL that can be accessed from anywhere and the traffic is routed to the localhost as shown in the following figure.

```
ngrok

Check which logged users are accessing your tunnels in real time https://ngrok.com/s/app-users

Session Status            online
Account                   ▮▮▮▮▮▮▮▮▮▮▮▮▮▮ (Plan: Free)
Version                   3.1.0
Region                    United States (us)
Latency                   36ms
Web Interface             http://127.0.0.1:4040
Forwarding                https://df37-2600-1700-74c6-5110-a801-33b5-b7f6-8018.ngrok.io -> http://localhost:3007

Connections               ttl       opn       rt1       rt5       p50       p90
                          5         0         0.00      0.00      5.11      5.23
```

Figure 6.1: ngrok tunnel to localhost

Azure AD app registration

Let us explore the first step of creating an Azure AD application and configure it as follows. By this time, you have already registered Azure AD applications in previous chapters, so follow the same steps, log in to `https://portal.azure.com`, and search for `App Registrations`, or you can go to Azure Active Directory and navigate to **App Registrations**. Either way, you can go to **App Registrations**, click **+ New registration**, and **Register an application**, as shown in the following figure:

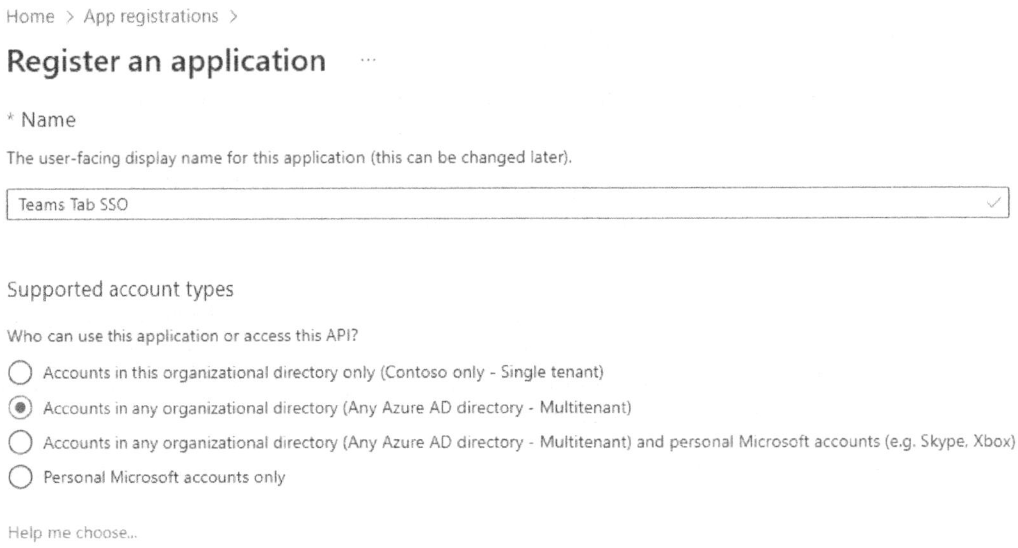

Home > App registrations >

Register an application   ···

* Name

The user-facing display name for this application (this can be changed later).

| Teams Tab SSO |

Supported account types

Who can use this application or access this API?

○ Accounts in this organizational directory only (Contoso only - Single tenant)

◉ Accounts in any organizational directory (Any Azure AD directory - Multitenant)

○ Accounts in any organizational directory (Any Azure AD directory - Multitenant) and personal Microsoft accounts (e.g. Skype, Xbox)

○ Personal Microsoft accounts only

Help me choose...

Figure 6.2: Teams tab SSO app registration

As shown in the preceding figure, all you need is the name of the app and the supported account types if your application is used only in the tenant that the app is registered for or if the app is planned to be used by many other tenants. For example, many customers use apps written by **independent software vendors (ISVs)**. Then, you need to pick the supported account type as multi-tenant.

Once you click **Register**, your app will be registered and redirected to the following screen.

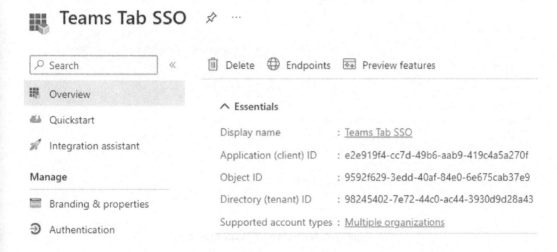

Figure 6.3: Teams tab SSO registered

As shown in the preceding figure, your app is registered, so you can note down the client ID to use in the next steps for the application. The next thing that you need to do is expose an API, as shown in the following figure. Then, under the **Manage** section on the left, click on **Expose an API**. Through this step, you can expose your web API through scopes and can provide permission for authorized users and client apps that access your app.

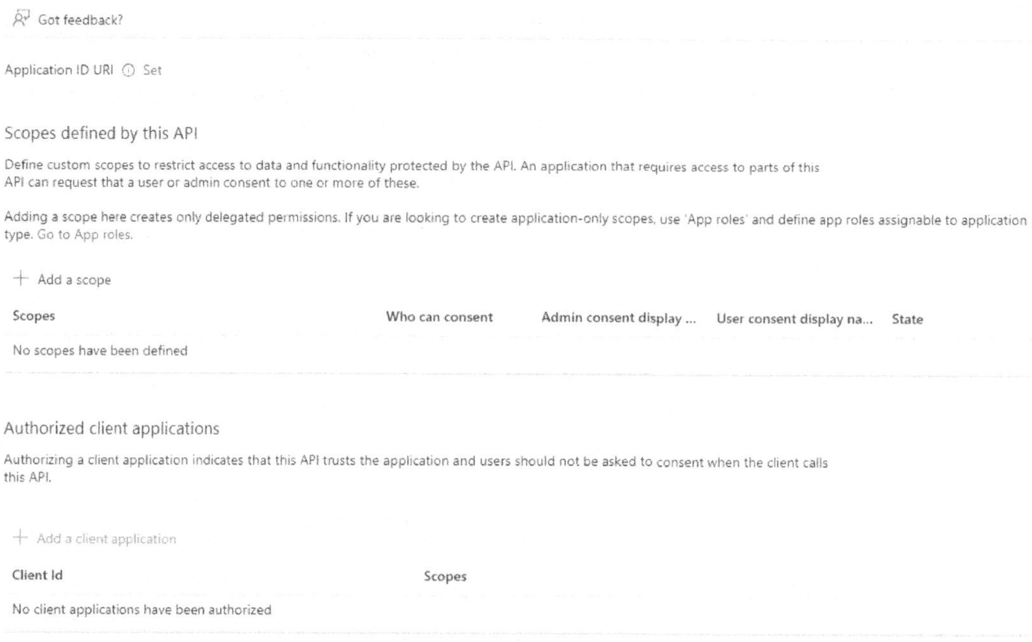

Got feedback?

Application ID URI ⓘ Set

Scopes defined by this API

Define custom scopes to restrict access to data and functionality protected by the API. An application that requires access to parts of this API can request that a user or admin consent to one or more of these.

Adding a scope here creates only delegated permissions. If you are looking to create application-only scopes, use 'App roles' and define app roles assignable to application type. Go to App roles.

+ Add a scope

Scopes	Who can consent	Admin consent display ...	User consent display na...	State

No scopes have been defined

Authorized client applications

Authorizing a client application indicates that this API trusts the application and users should not be asked to consent when the client calls this API.

+ Add a client application

Client Id	Scopes

No client applications have been authorized

Figure 6.4: Teams tab SSO Expose an API

In this step, you expose a web API to configure a few things such as the application ID URL, scopes for the API, and authorized client IDs that you want to pre-authorize.

First, you can set the application ID URL (in the format of API: //<fully qualified domain name>/< Application (Client) ID>), for example, api://contoso.com/e2e919f4-cc7d-49b6-aab9-419c4a5a270f, and this should be a valid one as verified at runtime. Then, you can add the API URL using the **Set** link from the preceding figure. To get the public URL for testing purposes, you can use ngrok, as discussed in the previous chapter. The URL that you can use with ngrok is api://%ngrokUniqueId%.ngrok.io/00000000-0000-0000-0000-000000000000. With a paid ngrok subscription, you could use custom ngrok domains.

After the application ID URL, the next step is to configure API scopes; these scopes restrict access to data and functionality provided by the API. The scope here only provides delegated permissions, so an active user must always use this app.

To add a scope, click + **Add a Scope**, as shown in *Figure 6.4*. Once you click **Scope**, you will see the following:

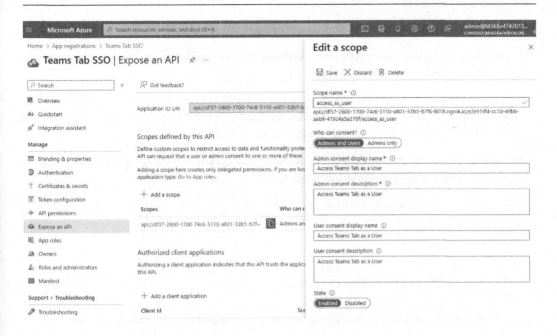

Figure 6.5: Expose an API

In the panel, you enter `access_as_user` for **Scope name**. As this API is called on behalf of the user, we need to hardcode the scope `access_as_user`.

For the **Who can consent?** option, select the **Admins and users** option.

Here are some options to understand from the preceding screenshot:

- **Admin consent display name**: Teams can access the user's profile
- **Admin consent description**: Allows Teams to call the app's web APIs as the current user
- **User consent display name**: Teams can access the user's profile and make requests on the user's behalf
- **User consent description**: Enable Teams to call this app's APIs with the same rights as the user

Finally, ensure **State** is set to **Enabled** and save the scope.

If you go back to the **Expose an API** page and look at the **Scopes** section, you will have something like this: `api://df37-2600-1700-74c6-5110-a801-33b5-b7f6-8018.ngrok.io/ e2e919f4-cc7d-49b6-aab9-419c4a5a270f/access_as_user`.

This is the application ID URL, and the scope name `access_as_user` is appended.

The final thing about **Expose an API** is the **Authorized client applications** section, where you want to pre-authorize your app's web application.

If you want the app to be used in Teams for desktop or mobile, add the ID `1fec8e78-bce4-4aaf-ab1b-5451cc387264`. In addition, if you want your app available in the Teams web application, add the ID `5e3ce6c0-2b1f-4285-8d4b-75ee78787346`.

After adding IDs in the **Authorized client applications** section of the **Expose an API** screen, you will see the client applications in the following figure.

$+$ Add a client application

Client Id	Scopes
1fec8e78-bce4-4aaf-ab1b-5451cc387264	1
5e3ce6c0-2b1f-4285-8d4b-75ee78787346	1

Figure 6.6: Authorized client applications for Teams for desktop and Teams for the web

Next, you set the appropriate API permissions to the registered application (client ID). In this case, we give the **User. Read** delegated permissions to Microsoft Graph. Also, ensure you have granted the admin consent for the required permissions. Once you set the permission, the screen looks like the following figure.

Configured permissions

Applications are authorized to call APIs when they are granted permissions by users/admins as part of the consent process. The list of configured permissions should include all the permissions the application needs. Learn more about permissions and consent

$+$ Add a permission $\checkmark$ Grant admin consent for Contoso

API / Permissions name	Type	Description	Admin consent requ...	Status	
∨ Microsoft Graph (1)					...
User.Read	Delegated	Sign in and read user profile	No	✔ Granted for Contoso	...

Figure 6.7: Graph API permissions for the registered application

With this, app registration is complete. Now we will build a Teams tab for a quick proof of concept using SSO, which displays the logged-in user without logging into the Teams tab app separately. For a user who logs into Microsoft Teams, when they click on the Teams tab app, it will show their username. If you want more functionality beyond displaying the logged-in user, add more permissions for the registered app ID and do the required Graph API calls.

Creating a Teams tab app

The next step is to create an actual Teams tab app that works with SSO. And for that, we can use Teams Toolkit. In *Chapter 5, Microsoft Teams Customization Using the SharePoint Framework (SPFx)*, you used a Yeoman generator to generate **SharePoint Framework** (**SPFx**) components. Similarly, you can use **Yo Teams** to build a Microsoft Teams application here. First, you create a folder and use the command shown in *Figure 6.8*. Before trying this, ensure you have the Teams generator installed on your computer. In *Chapter 5*, you used Gulp and Yeoman commands to create SharePoint Framework solutions. You should use those commands to create the Teams tab with Teams Toolkit.

In addition, you might need to install a Yeoman generator for Microsoft Teams. With this generator, you can build various Teams apps. To install a Teams generator, you need to run `npm I -g generator-teams` on a command prompt.

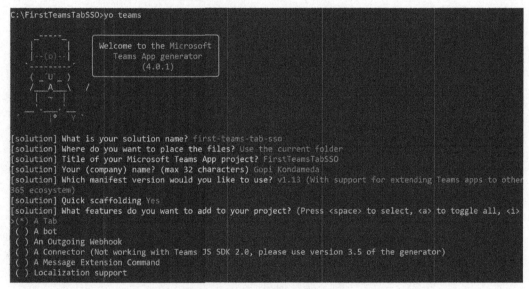

Figure 6.8: Create a Microsoft Teams application

With **Yo teams**, you can generate various types of Microsoft Teams apps, as it prompts a series of questions and, based on your answers, creates a project and structure shown as follows. In the feature options, you select **A Tab** as we want to create a Teams tab, but you can also create a bot, messaging extensions, and webhooks similarly.

The folder view of the generated app follows.

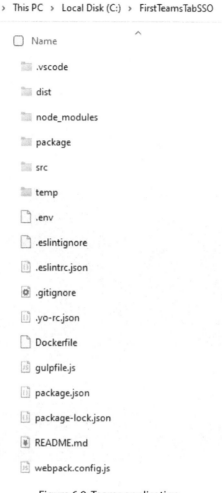

Figure 6.9: Teams application

Open the solution in Visual Studio Code or any code editor. First, make sure `manifest.json` from the `Src | manifest` folder has been modified with the appropriate information, as shown in *Figure 6.10*.

```json
"id": "65c09e20-8fdd-11ed-9b7d-ed8fa22d5c2a",
"version": "0.0.1",
"packageName": "firstteamstabsso",
"developer": {
  "name": "Gopi Kondameda",
  "websiteUrl": "https://df37-2600-1700-74c6-5110-a801-33b5-b7f6-8018.ngrok.io",
  "privacyUrl": "https://df37-2600-1700-74c6-5110-a801-33b5-b7f6-8018.ngrok.io/privacy.html",
  "termsOfUseUrl": "https://df37-2600-1700-74c6-5110-a801-33b5-b7f6-8018.ngrok.io/tou.html"
},
"name": {
  "short": "FirstTeamsTabSSO",
  "full": "FirstTeamsTabSSO"
},
"description": {
  "short": "TODO: add short description here",
  "full": "TODO: add full description here"
},
"icons": {
  "outline": "icon-outline.png",
  "color": "icon-color.png"
},
"accentColor": "#D85028",
"configurableTabs": [],
"staticTabs": [
    {
      "entityId": "bd2f5bad-ca1b-4317-a125-3353b5680f76",
      "name": "FirstTeamsTabSSO",
      "contentUrl": "https://df37-2600-1700-74c6-5110-a801-33b5-b7f6-8018.ngrok.io/firstTeamsTabSsoTab/index.html",
      "scopes": [
        "personal"
      ]
    }
],
"bots": [],
"connectors": [],
"composeExtensions": [],
"permissions": [
  "identity",
  "messageTeamMembers"
],
"validDomains": [
  "df37-2600-1700-74c6-5110-a801-33b5-b7f6-8018.ngrok.io"
],
"showLoadingIndicator": false,
"webApplicationInfo": {
  "id": "e2e919f4-cc7d-49b6-aab9-419c4a5a270f",
  "resource": "api://df37-2600-1700-74c6-5110-a801-33b5-b7f6-8018.ngrok.io/e2e919f4-cc7d-49b6-aab9-419c4a5a270f"
}
```

Figure 6.10: Manifest.json

If you look at the preceding figure, most sections have the `ngrok` URL where your content is hosted locally and mapped with an `ngrok` tunnel. Beyond that, you also use the Azure AD registered application ID in the `webApplication info` section. After you finish all the changes, go back to the same command prompt and run `gulp serve` so that the Teams tab pointed to `index.html` runs locally. You can also see it in the browser, as shown in the following figure.

Note that `gulp serve` is the command to test the solution locally by building the app and starting a local web server with port 3007, as shown in the following figure. This helps to test or debug applications.

This is your tab

Hello undefined

A sample button

(C) Copyright Gopi Kondameda

Figure 6.11: Local run of Teams tab SSO index.html

Everything is now ready to evaluate our Teams Tab for SSO. You must now package the app and load your app into Microsoft Teams without distributing it tenant-wide. The Packaging app will create a ZIP file, which you can upload to **Microsoft Teams | Apps | Managing Your Apps | Upload an App**. After uploading the packaged ZIP file through the Upload app, it will prompt you as in the following figure. As shown in the figure, you can click **Add** to add the app to Teams. As this is a personal app, you do not need to add a team.

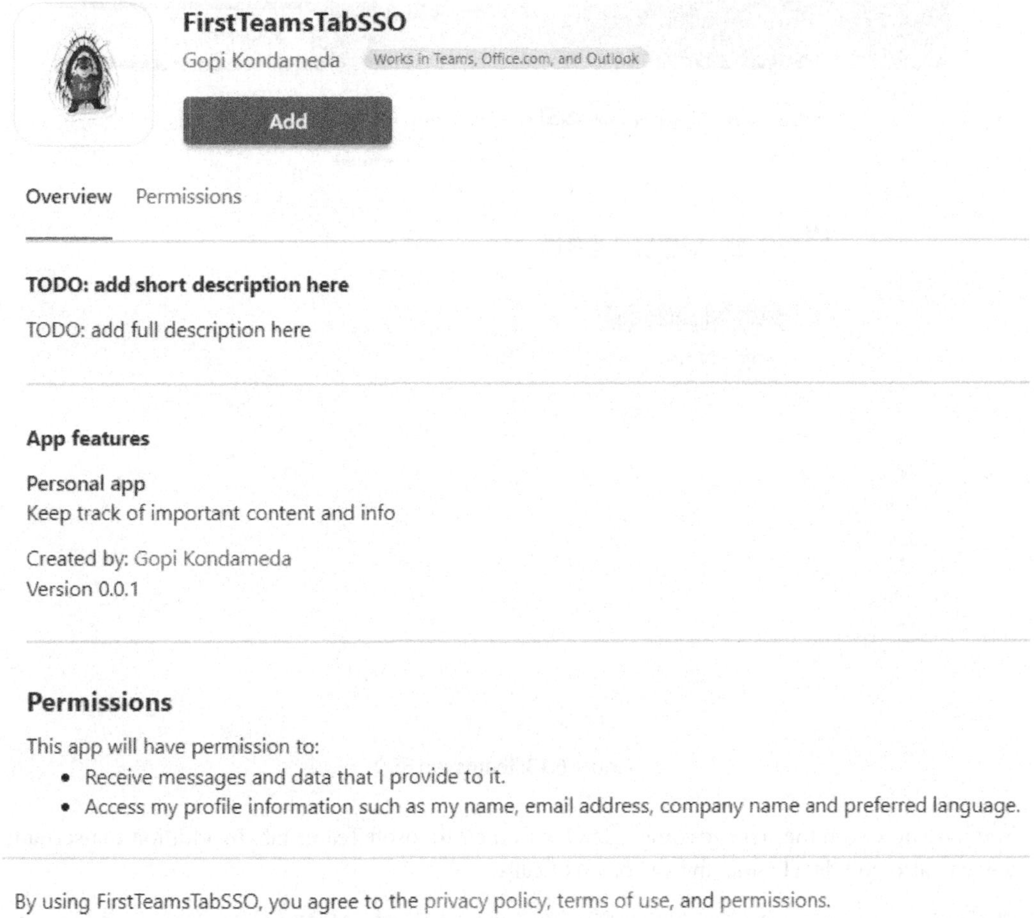

FirstTeamsTabSSO

Gopi Kondameda   Works in Teams, Office.com, and Outlook

Add

Overview   Permissions

TODO: add short description here

TODO: add full description here

App features

Personal app
Keep track of important content and info

Created by: Gopi Kondameda
Version 0.0.1

Permissions

This app will have permission to:
- Receive messages and data that I provide to it.
- Access my profile information such as my name, email address, company name and preferred language.

By using FirstTeamsTabSSO, you agree to the privacy policy, terms of use, and permissions.

Figure: 6.12 Adding the Teams app to the Teams client

After successfully adding the app to Teams, the Teams tab SSO is open, and this is the same index. html we saw locally. However, if you notice here, it will show the logged-in username with the same user that logged in to Microsoft Teams.

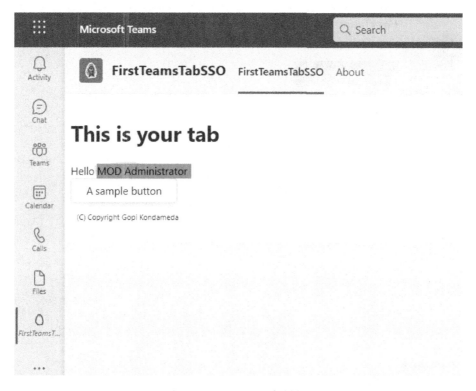

Figure 6.13: Teams tab SSO

You have now seen the steps to achieve SSO with the Microsoft Teams tab. In addition to username, you can also pull data by making various API calls.

There are various scenarios in which you can use these tabs. Here is just a couple of them:

- A meeting tab: We can surface all the information required for the meeting in a tab as one view so that participants will have the opportunity to review and access it easily

- About us and help page: if you are building a bot and need to provide information about the bot, you can have a web page with the details and you can surface this as a Teams tab.

Summary

In this chapter, you learned about the authentication options available to developers and created custom Microsoft Teams tabs that use **Single-Sign On (SSO)** authentication.

In the next chapter, we are going to talk about Microsoft Dataverse for Teams, a built-in platform for low-code apps for Microsoft Teams.

Part 3: Microsoft Teams Customization with Low-Code and No-Code

This part covers customizing Microsoft Teams with low-code platforms such as Microsoft Dataverse for Teams and Microsoft Teams app templates, a community-driven initiative providing ready-to-deploy app templates for common scenarios. Additionally, you will learn about Microsoft Viva, an integrated employee experience platform, and third-party app integration, including ISV-built Teams apps and Microsoft Dynamics 365 app integration.

This section includes the following chapters:

- *Chapter 7, Microsoft Dataverse for Teams*
- *Chapter 8, Microsoft Teams App Templates*
- *Chapter 9, Microsoft Viva*
- *Chapter 10, Microsoft Teams Third-Party Apps*

7
Microsoft Dataverse for Teams

In this chapter, I will introduce you to Microsoft Dataverse for Teams, which is a built-in, low-code data platform for Microsoft Teams. You can also look at this as a way of bringing Power Platform to Microsoft Teams. With this, you can build solutions using Power Apps, Power Automate, and Power Virtual Agents on Teams.

This chapter will cover the following main topics in detail:

- Introducing Microsoft Dataverse for Teams
- Microsoft Dataverse capabilities for Teams
- Power Platform capabilities for Teams:
  - Power Apps
  - Power Automate
  - Power Virtual Agents
- General administration, governance, and security for Microsoft Dataverse for Teams

After completing this chapter, you will be able to understand Microsoft Dataverse for Teams and its architecture and build solutions on this platform.

Introducing Microsoft Dataverse for Teams

Every Microsoft 365 tenant will have a default Microsoft Dataverse environment, and as per Microsoft's best practices, it is recommended to use the default environment for personal productivity. So, if you need to build business apps, business process automation is recommended to create new Microsoft Dataverse environments. You can accomplish this through Microsoft Dataverse for Teams if you need to build a small-scale scenario.

Microsoft Dataverse for Teams is a subset of the full-blown Microsoft Dataverse. Microsoft Dataverse is a robust data storage and the backend for Dynamics 365 and Power Platform. As mentioned in the introduction, Microsoft Dataverse for Teams delivers the features to build apps, flows, and chatbots and use them in the context of a Microsoft Teams team. These applications will have access to Dataverse within the Teams environment. Also note that these apps are only accessible via the Teams app, desktop, or mobile.

Here are a few other features that make Dataverse for Teams interesting:

- **No additional license**: Microsoft Dataverse is a premium feature for consuming with Power Platform, so any user building or using the apps and flows that require Microsoft Dataverse needs a premium license, such as Power Platform per user or per app. However, in the case of Microsoft Dataverse for Teams, it doesn't require any additional license to use Microsoft Dataverse. Dataverse for Teams is available for most Microsoft 365 subscriptions.

- **Guest users**: You can even have guests use these apps, flows, bots, and data within Dataverse for Teams.

- **Access to Dataverse for Teams**: Access to Dataverse for Teams is through the Microsoft 365 group associated with the team. Team members can create, update, and run the apps, whereas owners have full access to the Dataverse for Team environment. Therefore, access aligns with the core roles identified in that environment, such as owners, members, and guests.

Why do we need Microsoft Dataverse for Teams?

As discussed previously, organizations like to build business apps through Power Apps or business automation through Power Automate outside a tenant's default environment. Therefore, it would require you to create custom Microsoft Dataverse environments, but each Microsoft Dataverse environment requires 1 GB of free space from your Dataverse storage allocation. For some organizations, storage availability can be a challenge, so you can start business apps or automation through a Microsoft Dataverse for Teams environment, and the Dataverse storage in Dataverse for Teams is not counted against your tenant Dataverse storage allocation. Furthermore, if the solutions that you are building require more than 2 GB, then you can upgrade Dataverse for Teams to full-blown Microsoft Dataverse environments.

In this section, we discussed the Microsoft Dataverse environment and the context of Microsoft Dataverse for Teams and how, over the custom Microsoft Dataverse environments, organizations like to treat the Default tenant's environment. So, in the next section, we continue creating these Dataverse for Teams environments.

Creating a Dataverse for a Teams environment

In this section, we will discuss creating a Microsoft Dataverse environment for a Microsoft Teams team. You can create a new canvas app in each team or add an existing one to Microsoft Teams. Either of these processes initiates the creation of a Microsoft Dataverse for Teams environment.

On the left navigation bar of the Teams environment, go to the apps and search for `power`. Your screen should look like this:

Figure 7.1: Searching the Teams app catalog for Power Apps

Let's now initiate Microsoft Dataverse for Teams by creating a new canvas app. To do this, click on the **Power Apps** option, as shown in the preceding figure. It will take you to the **Power Apps** home page for Teams, as shown in the following figure:

Figure 7.2: The Power Apps homes screen

The **Recent apps** section will show up if you have any apps already. You can create a new app by clicking the **New app** option, as shown in the preceding figure, which leads to a screen where you can create an app in any team, as shown in the following figure. Here, all the teams that you have access to will be populated, and you can pick a team to create the app. Here, I am choosing **Contoso marketing**.

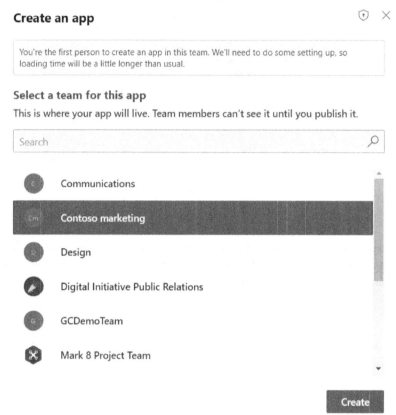

Figure 7.3: Creating an app in Contoso marketing

Once you create the app by clicking **Create**, as shown in the preceding figure, the app will be created while a **Getting things ready** screen appears.

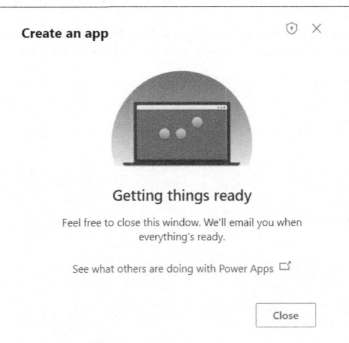

Figure 7.4: The process of creating an app in Contoso marketing

During the process of creating the app, Microsoft Dataverse for Teams will be created in the background. If you have access to the Power Platform environment, you can go to the Power Platform Admin center (aka.ms/ppac) to verify the environment, as shown in the following figure. Note that the type of environment is Microsoft Teams.

Figure 7.5: The Microsoft Dataverse for Teams Power Platform environment

Let's now move to discuss Power Apps for Teams

Power Apps for Teams

Steps from the preceding section will create a Microsoft Dataverse for Teams environment for the selected Microsoft Team, Contoso marketing, and also create a Power App, as shown in *Figure 7.6*.

Power Apps are low-code solutions to build apps in Power Platform. We will start with a blank canvas for building a contracts app. In the canvas, you can drag and drop components in any order to design a user interface.

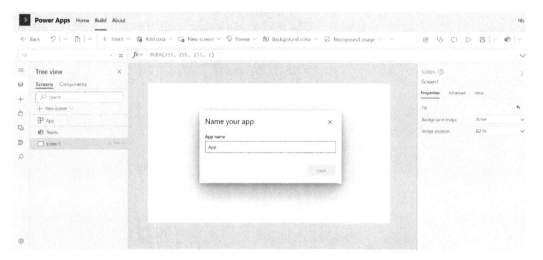

Figure 7.6: The first canvas app

Name your app `MyFirstApp` and click **Save** to create your first canvas app in Microsoft Teams:

Figure 7.7: Saving the canvas app

Figure 7.6 shows the Power App editor on the left pane, where we have various sections. But first, we will start creating a new table named `Contacts`, as shown in *Figure 7.8*.

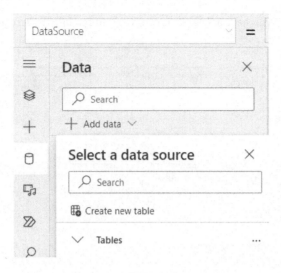

Figure 7.8: Creating a new table

When you click **Create new table**, as shown in the preceding figure, you will have the option to create a table in the Dataverse for Teams environment. You can create the **Contacts** table, as shown in the following figure, with a few columns such as **Name**, **Project Role**, and **Time Zone**, and you can also add some sample data.

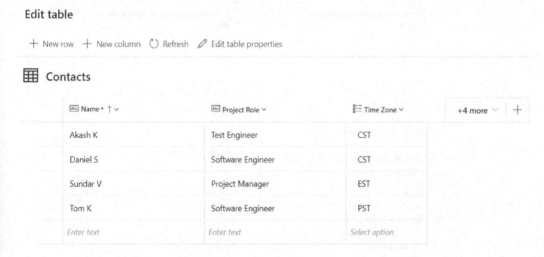

Figure 7.9: The Contacts table with Name, Project Role, and Time Zone

In the app you created, you have a default screen; you can rename the screen as shown here.

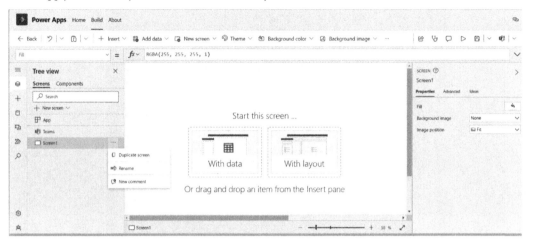

Figure 7.10: Renaming the screen in the app

Our goal is to create a contacts app for use in the team, so the next step is to add the **Contact** table to the screen using the **With data** option, as shown in the following screenshot.

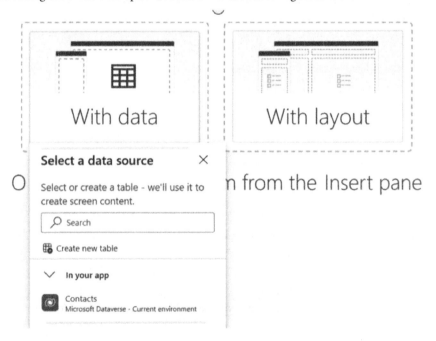

Figure 7.11: Adding the Contacts table to the canvas app

Now our **Contacts** app is ready for publishing; this is a simple process where we display contacts relevant to the Contoso business team through this app. To make this app available for all members of the team, publish it as shown in the following figure.

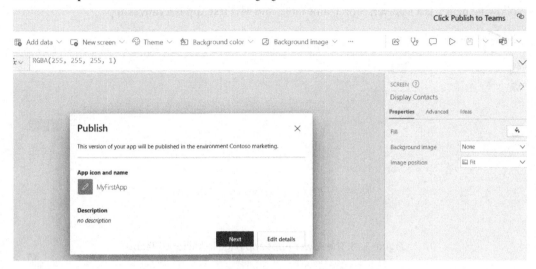

Figure 7.12: Publishing an app to Microsoft Teams

When you are publishing the app, you can pick the channel where you need to make this available. If you have multiple channels in your team, you can pick the required channel; here, we have only one.

In this scenario, I picked the **General** channel and added the app as a tab to the team.

Figure 7.13: MyFirstApp added the Teams General channel

If you go to the Power App's app, it will show all the teams with Dataverse for Teams environments added. The following screenshot shows two teams (**Communications** and **Contoso marketing**), and if you click on **Contoso marketing**, it will show you the resources created. **Contacts**, as shown in the following figure, is a Dataverse for Teams table, and **MyFirstApp** is a canvas app.

Figure 7.14: The Power Apps app page in Microsoft Teams

In this section, we created a simple contacts canvas Power App app to show how you can create a no-code app, publish it in Teams, and make it available for your users.

Power Automate for Teams

In this section, we will talk about Power Automate; whereas Power App lets you build apps with no code, Power Automates lets you build business automation.

Power Automate for Teams lets you build business process automation on Microsoft Dataverse for Teams. Some business scenarios might require business automation in addition to apps.

Power Apps and Power Automate flows can connect to various enterprise data sources using connectors. For process automation, these connectors will have various triggers that Power Automate flows can initiate the process, which, with actions, will execute the necessary steps.

If you go to the Microsoft Teams app catalog and click on the **Power Automate** app, you will be directed to the **Power Automate** home page, as shown in the following figure. If you already have Microsoft Team flows, they will show up here.

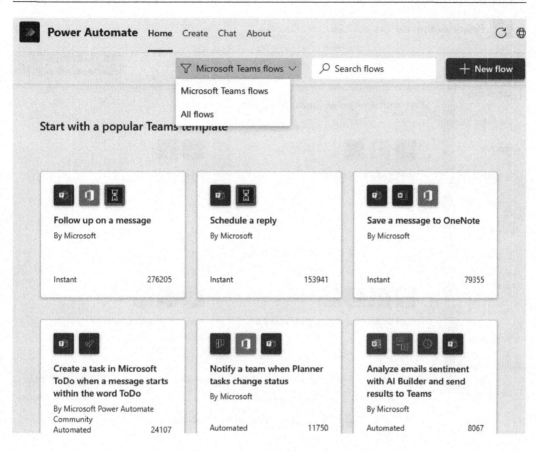

Figure 7.15: The Power Automate home page

On the **Power Automate** home page, you also have the option to create Power Automate flows; you can click **Create**, which will take you to the screen shown in the following screenshot with a few popular Power Automate templates. Here, you have two options to create Power Automate flows, either from an existing template or creating one from blank.

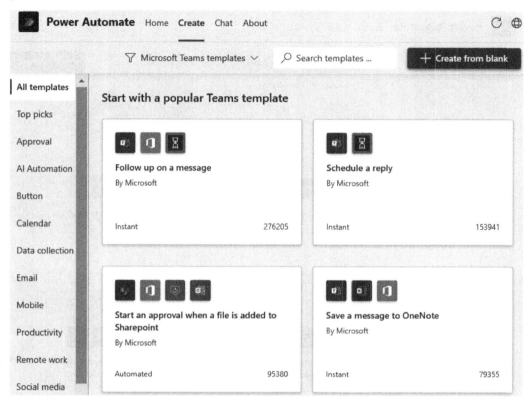

Figure 7.16: Power Automate templates

Let's next see how to create a flow on Power Automate.

Creating a Power Automate flow

As a quick example, you can create a flow by selecting the **Get notified when you're @mentioned email** template. This template can send you a notification when someone mentions you directly in an email, such as @Steve Manny.

The first step is to click on the selected template from *Figure 7.16*, and you will get a prompt like the one in the following figure so that you can choose a name. A general recommendation is to be as descriptive as possible so that it will be easier when you refer to it in the future to understand the purpose of this flow.

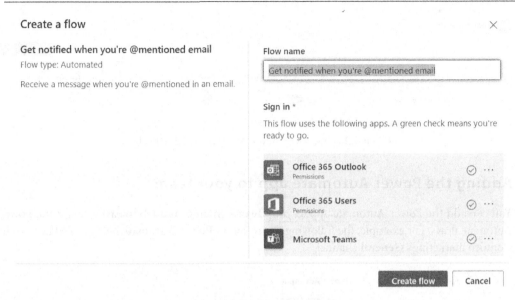

Figure 7.17: Creating a flow

If you look at the preceding figure for the selected template, you can see that it will populate all the connections required for it and prompt you to sign in to access these connections.

Click on **Create flow** to create the flow.

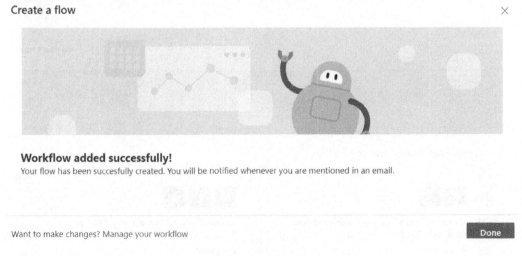

Figure 7.18: The flow added successfully

After successfully creating the flow, if you click **Done**, you will be taken to the Power Automate app home page. The following figure shows the details of the newly created flow. If, for some reason, you don't want to activate this flow, you can flip the status to **Off**.

Figure 7.19: The Power Automate app after the first flow

Adding the Power Automate app to your team

You can add the Power Automate app to your Teams channel as a tab to easily access the Power Automate flows. For example, the following figure shows **Power Automate** being added as a tab to Contoso marketing's **General** channel.

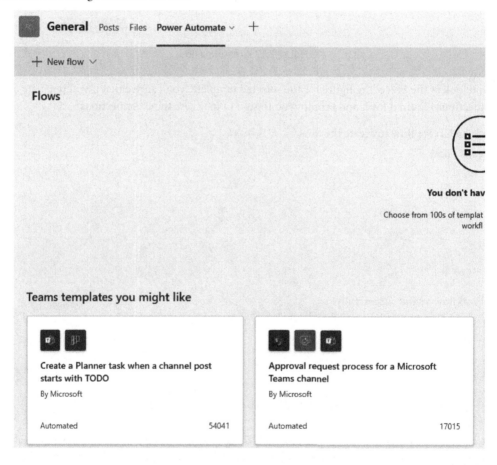

Figure 7.20: Power Automate as a tab

Let's create another example of Power Automate with the existing template, but we'll now configure the changes of the actions.

Select the **Approval request process for a Microsoft Teams Channel** template if you are a member of a Microsoft Teams team. If you want to build a system for your members to request new channels, this will be a simple no-code request, approval, and channel creation automated process. The following figure will show you the required connections for this automation.

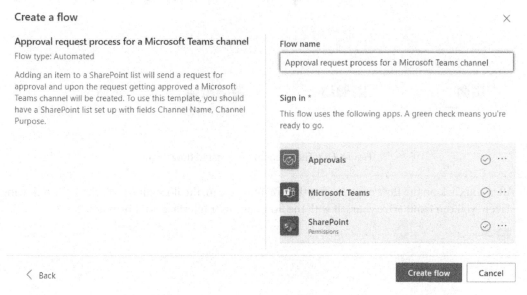

Figure 7.21: Creating a channel request process

When you click on **Create flow**, as shown in the preceding figure, it creates a flow. If you click the flow name, as shown in the following figure, it opens the flow in the flow editor, allowing you to make changes to the flow.

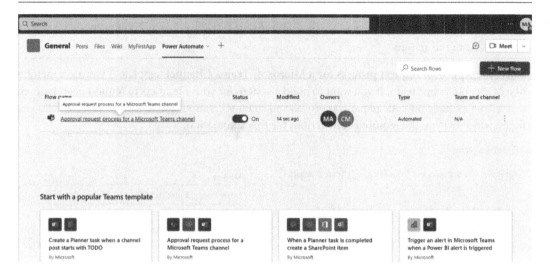

Figure 7.22: The channel's requested flow page

After you click on the flow name, as per the previous screen, the flow editor will show the following screen; you can familiarize yourself with the flow page user interface, as shown here:

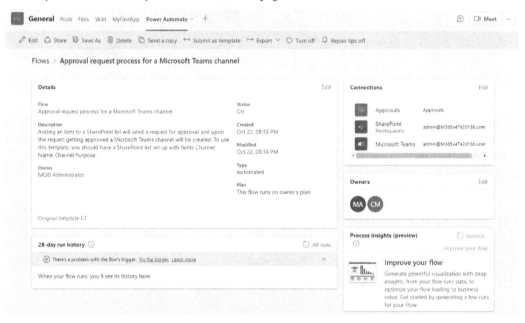

Figure 7.23: The flow page

You can click, edit, and review the flow and sequence of actions.

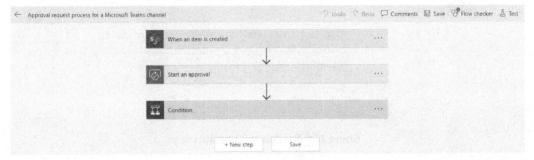

Figure 7.24: Flow details

As you know, every Microsoft Teams team has a SharePoint site; we can create a new request channel list on the Contoso marketing team's SharePoint site so that members can request a new channel. The preceding flow from Power Automate (**Approval request process for a Microsoft Teams channel**) will get triggered when a new request is made to the request channels list.

The following figure shows a custom list created on a SharePoint site. For this scenario, we have created a few additional columns, such as **Channel Name** and **Channel Purpose**.

Figure 7.25: The Request Channels list

Once the list is created, you can go back to Power Automate and update the values relevant to the details. For example, here, Power Automate is triggered by adding an item in SharePoint, as shown in the following figure.

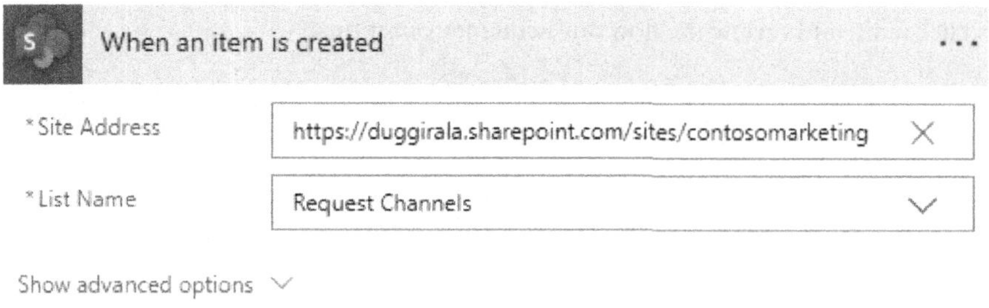

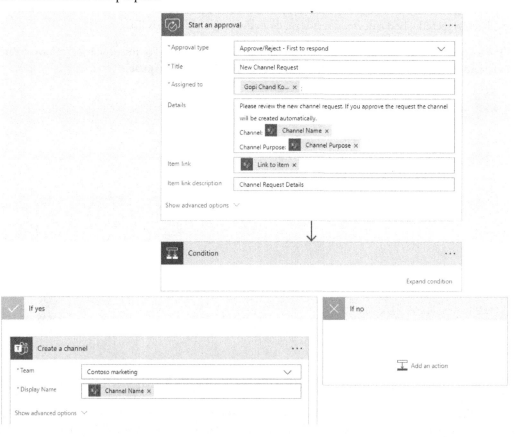

Figure 7.26: The Power Automate trigger

In addition to the trigger, you need to update the actual values for the approval step with a subject and assign them to the approver. This approval will be in the form of an email from the approver. It would be easier for the approver to make a decision if we include as many details as possible, such as the channel name and purpose.

Figure 7.27: Power Automate in edit mode

After you have made the necessary changes to the details, you can save the flow. Now that you are ready to test the flow, go to the SharePoint list request channels and add an item, as shown here.

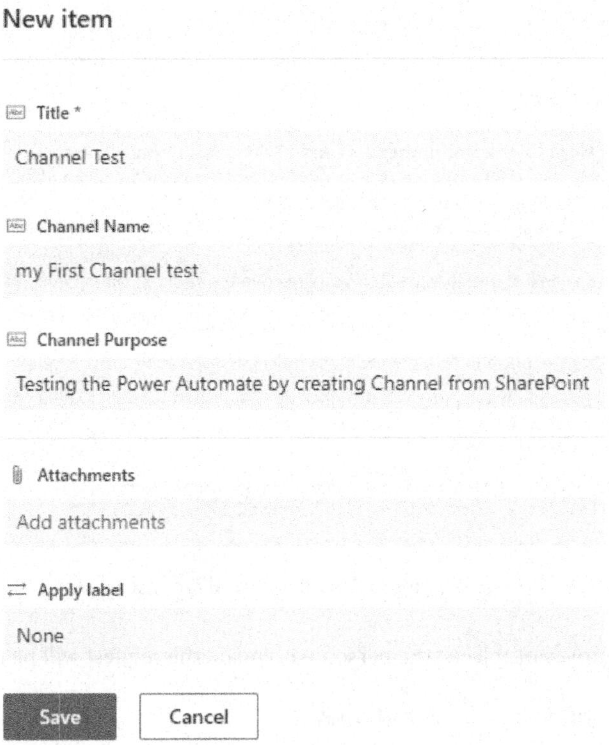

New item

Title *

Channel Test

Channel Name

my First Channel test

Channel Purpose

Testing the Power Automate by creating Channel from SharePoint

Attachments

Add attachments

Apply label

None

Save   Cancel

Figure 7.28: Adding a new request channel

Per our flow design, the approver will get an email to approve or reject the new channel request, as shown in the following screenshot.

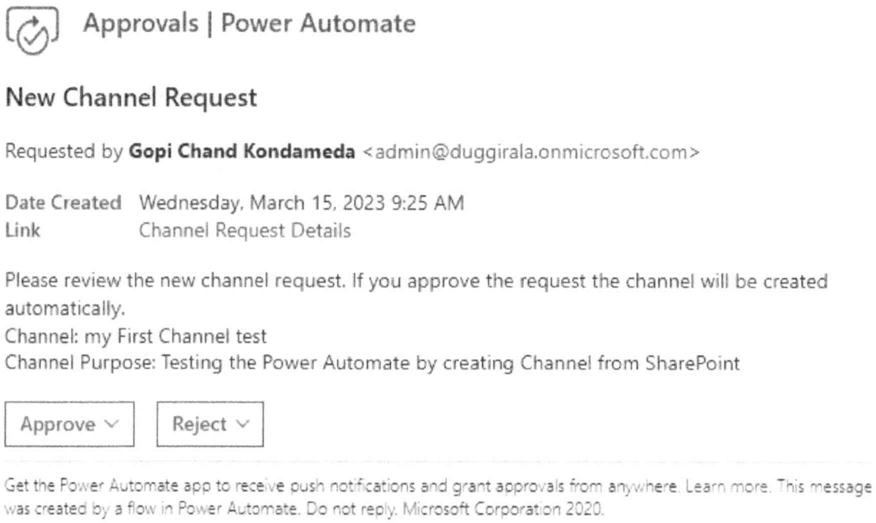

 Approvals | Power Automate

New Channel Request

Requested by **Gopi Chand Kondameda** <admin@duggirala.onmicrosoft.com>

Date Created   Wednesday, March 15, 2023 9:25 AM
Link   Channel Request Details

Please review the new channel request. If you approve the request the channel will be created automatically.
Channel: my First Channel test
Channel Purpose: Testing the Power Automate by creating Channel from SharePoint

| Approve ∨ | | Reject ∨ |

Get the Power Automate app to receive push notifications and grant approvals from anywhere. Learn more. This message was created by a flow in Power Automate. Do not reply. Microsoft Corporation 2020.

Figure 7.29: An approval request

If the approver approves or rejects, the person who made the request will be notified, like so:

 Approvals | Power Automate

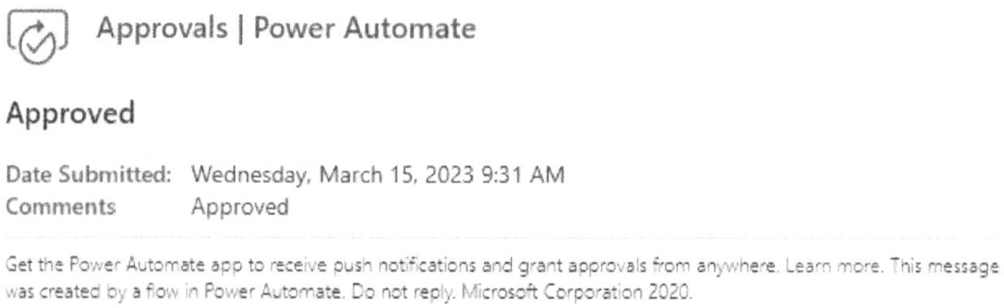

Approved

Date Submitted: Wednesday, March 15, 2023 9:31 AM
Comments   Approved

Get the Power Automate app to receive push notifications and grant approvals from anywhere. Learn more. This message was created by a flow in Power Automate. Do not reply. Microsoft Corporation 2020.

Figure 7.30: The approval notification

Once the request is approved, the `create the channel` action will create the requested and approved channel, as shown in the following figure.

Figure 7.31: The newly created channel

Now that you have successfully executed Power Automate to create new Teams channels through the Teams UI, you can explore creating Power Automate flows in Web UI. For example, you can directly go to the browser of the `https://flow.microsoft.com` site, or you can go to the **Power Automate** tab and click **Go to website**, as shown in the following figure.

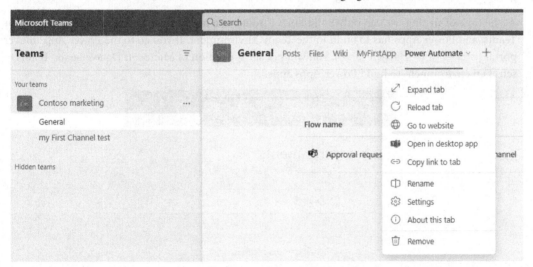

Figure 7.32: The Go to flow website

On the flow portal, if you go to **My flows** and then to the **Shared with me** section, you should be able to see the flow that you created in the preceding section. If you look in the top right, you'll see **Contoso (default)**, a default environment of this tenant; even though you created the flow from the Microsoft Teams team environment, the flow was created in the default environment.

Figure 7.33: Power Automate in the maker portal

Building flows in Microsoft Dataverse for Teams

In the Power Automate maker portal, you can click on **Environments** at the top right. It will open all the environments you can access, including Microsoft Dataverse for Teams. In our scenario, we are going to select **Contoso marketing**.

At the time of writing, we can only build flows through the maker portal in Microsoft Dataverse for Teams, and Power Apps has to build in the Teams environment. If you go to the Power Apps maker portal (`make.powerapps.com`), you will not see the option of Microsoft Dataverse for Teams to select an environment to build Power Apps apps.

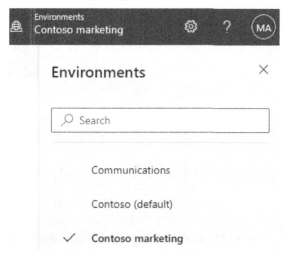

Figure 7.34: The Environments choices in the Power Automate maker portal

After you pick the **Contoso marketing** environment, you will see a portal like the one you saw in the Teams environment, with all the Power Automate templates and the option to create from blank:

Figure 7.35: The Power Automate maker portal

If you click **New flow** at the top left, as shown in the preceding figure, it will expand with various options, as shown here.

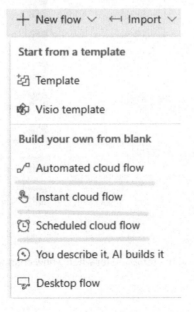

Figure 7.36: The New flow options

You have two options to create flows – by creating from blank or using an existing template. With the blank, we have a few options based on how our flow gets triggered; a trigger is a condition that kicks the flow. Here are those options:

- **Automated cloud flow**: Automated cloud flow is one that triggers based on various events happening, such as creating an item in the SharePoint list, a new email arriving, or a user submitting a form

- **Schedule cloud flow**: This flow type is scheduled to run regularly, so the flow triggers are recurrent

- **Instant cloud flow**: Instant cloud flow is the type of flow run by users manually on demand

Here, you can perform another quick example of using a team's template if you want to get notified when someone adds a message to one of your Teams channels. Most of what will be in the activity feed. However, you may have some channels that you need to monitor more closely.

The first step is to find the template closer to your requirement; in this scenario, we already have one, as shown in the following figure. Then, select the template and create a flow.

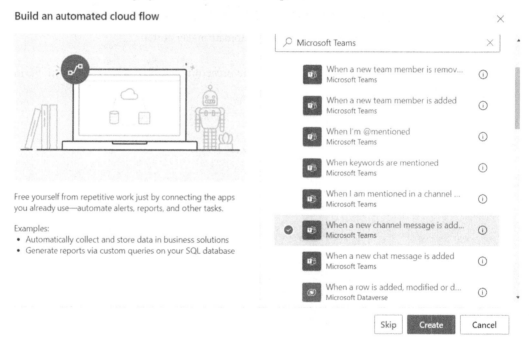

Figure 7.37: Finding the template for when a new channel message is added

When you click **Create**, as shown in the preceding figure, a flow will be created based on the selected template; now, you can edit the flow and change the values according to your needs.

In this scenario, we will pick **Contoso marketing** and the channel we created from the previous Power Automate in automation. So, if any user posts a new message on this channel, you want to get notified through push notification.

In the following figure, the first action is a trigger that kicks the flow when a new message is added to a channel, and the second action is a push notification that specifies the subject. The body is the actual message that you posted on the channel.

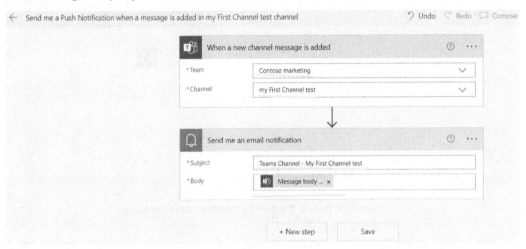

Figure 7.38: Editing Power Automate

After configuring the values in edit mode, you can save the flow by using the **Save** option at the bottom. This flow will turn on automatically. Now, you can quickly test this by posting a message in the channel, as shown in the following screenshot.

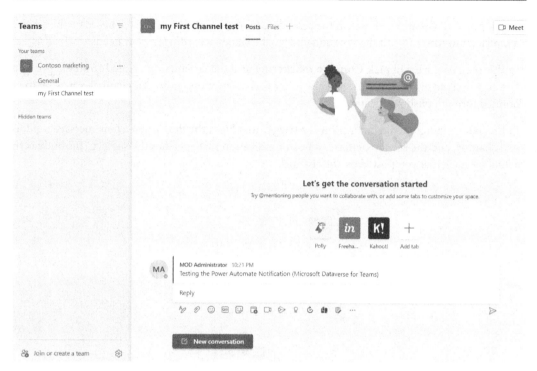

Figure 7.39: Testing the flow by posting a new message

As shown the preceding figure, you posted the message in the Teams channel and got a notification, as shown in the following figure. If you are a member of several teams and your team has lots of activities, this will become very handy in monitoring several channels for important messages.

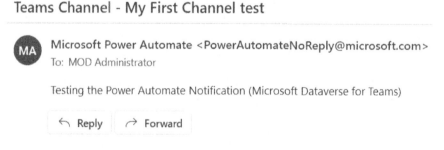

Figure 7.40: Push notification for the channel message

You can automate very advanced scenarios with Power Automate flows by using Microsoft Dataverse for Teams, an excellent tool for no-code or low-code automation at your fingertips.

In the next section, we will talk about another important tool that can be used as a chatbot in Microsoft Teams.

Power Virtual Agents for Teams

Team's users can create, build, and publish custom chatbots in Microsoft Teams. Chatbots automatically empower business users to solve internal-facing issues, freeing staff to focus on complex requests and high-value interactions.

This makes Teams integration better by offering the following:

- A fully embedded bot-building experience in Teams
- A configuration-free way to authenticate Teams users
- A seamless way to make bots available to end users

To access the Power Virtual Agent app, go to the Microsoft Teams app catalog and search for `Power`. You will see all the Power Platform apps, one of which is the Power Virtual Agent.

Figure 7.41: Power Platform apps in the Microsoft Teams app catalog

Like Power Apps and Power Automate, the Power Virtual Agent app can be found in the Microsoft Teams catalog. Once you select the app, you will be taken to the home page of the Power Virtual Agent, as shown in the following figure.

Figure 7.42: The Power Virtual Agents chatbot home page

Power Virtual Agents makes creating a virtual agent straightforward to do. First, go to **Chatbots**, as shown in the preceding figure. This screen will show the chatbot home page of your tenant and any existing chatbots you have access to, which can be seen by selecting a team. You also have the option to create a new chatbot. . Like in Power Apps, you will be prompted to pick a team where you want to have a chatbot created, as shown in the following figure.

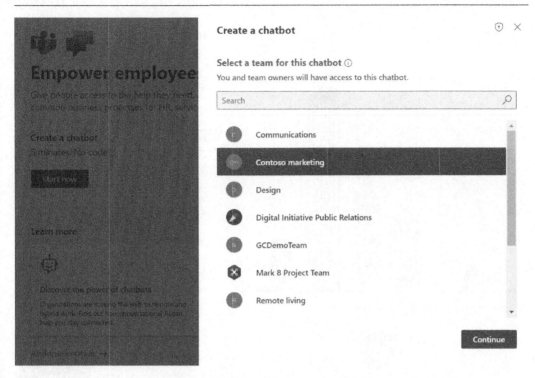

Figure 7.43: Creating a chatbot for the Contoso marketing Microsoft Teams team

Here, we select **Contoso marketing**, a test Microsoft Teams team, and click **Continue**. Next, you will be asked for a name for the chatbot and the language it needs to speak, as shown in the following figure.

Figure 7.44: Naming the chatbot and giving it a language

After naming your bot as First Chat bot on Teams and setting the language as **English (US)**, click on **Create** to create the chatbot.

Figure 7.45: Creating a chatbot

You will be briefly shown a screen that says **Working on it...**, as shown in the preceding figure, and you will be finally redirected to the newly created chatbot, as shown in the following figure.

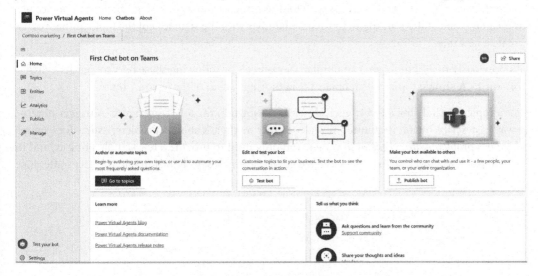

Figure 7.46: Your first chatbot

As shown in the preceding figure, a chatbot was created for the **Contoso marketing / First chatbot on Teams** team. If you look at the preceding figure, you can see the options of **Go to topics**, **Test bot**, and **Publish bot** options.

First, look at the topics, click on **Go to Topics** and you will be redirected, as shown in the following figure.

Figure 7.47: The user/system topics of the chatbot

When you create your chatbot, you must decide what business scenarios you want your chatbot needs to address. Then, you can create a topic for each scenario/question you want the bot to address. For example, you can see that a bot comes with four user topics and eight system topics; as a novice user, you can use one of the four topics to become familiar with the structure of the topic so that you can create a new one.

As previously mentioned, you can familiarize yourself by following these user topics; let's click on **Lesson 1 - A simple topic**, which opens the authoring canvas of the lesson 1 topic.

For a topic, you'll define a few trigger phrases, as shown in the following figure. A trigger phrase is a way to describe intent; it captures how a customer might ask about a problem/issue – for example, *there is a problem with weeds in the lawn*. You only need to provide a few sample phrases, and the AI will parse whatever the user says and trigger the topic closest in meaning to the user's utterance.

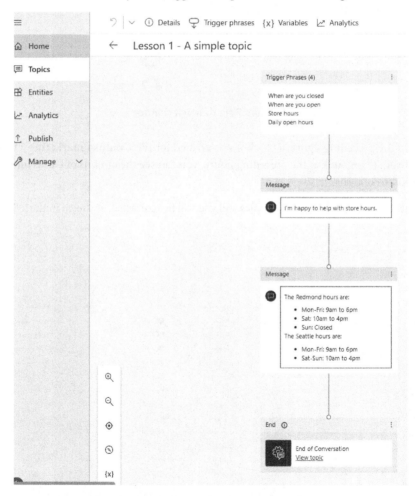

Figure 7.48: Authoring the canvas of the lesson 1 topic

As shown in the preceding figure, you will see the trigger phrases at the top, and then you can edit the conversation tree by adding questions that you want your chatbot to ask, what the bot should say, and so on.

As suggested previously, to understand the topic, open lesson 1 and review the trigger and conservation. Similarly, you learn this by testing what you have with lesson 1 by clicking on the test bot (at the bottom left) to expand the test window.

As shown in the following figure, we triggered the conversations by asking about store hours.

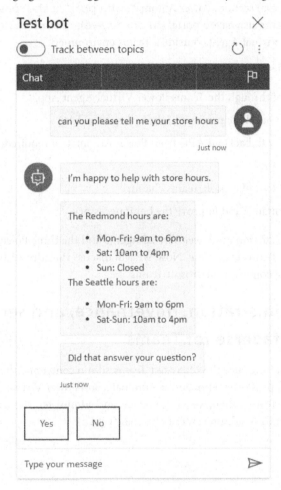

Figure 7.49: Test bot

After testing the bot, you will understand how the conversation takes place through the chatbot; this will help you to create a custom topic for your bot. Once you are ready, you can publish the bot to various channels.

Power Virtual Agent life cycle

In the preceding section, you saw how the Power Virtual Agents chatbot acted like an AI-powered chat bots and let you create from Microsoft Teams. As we discussed in the Power Apps (`https://web.powerapps.com`) section, Power Automate (`https://make.powerautomate.com/`) and Power Virtual Agents also have a portal (`https://web.powerva.microsoft.com`)from which you can access Virtual Agents outside a Teams environment.

Let's quickly review the steps in the life cycle of Power Virtual Agents:

1. Create a chatbot through the Teams Power Virtual Agent App.
2. Create topics to build the purpose of the bot, such as FAQ.
3. Extend the bot with backend APIs from Power Automate if required.
4. Test the bot.
5. Publish the bot to a Microsoft Teams channel.
6. Monitor performance and improve the bot if necessary.

This concludes our discussion on Power Virtual Agents and the three Power Platform apps that are part of the Microsoft Teams Dataverse. Now, we will discuss the administration, governance, and security of these in the context of Microsoft Teams.

General administration, governance, and security for Microsoft Dataverse for Teams

In this section, we will introduce the Microsoft Teams admin center and the things required to have the Power Platform Apps (Power App, Power Automate, and Power Virtual Agents) available for use throughout Microsoft Teams. Then, we will go review and administer Microsoft Dataverse for Teams through the Power Platform admin center (`aka.ms/ppac`).

Manage apps

We had a lengthy discussion in *Chapter 1* about managing apps in the Microsoft Teams admin center. This is the first step you need to take to make sure that the following Power Platform apps are allowed in your tenant. A global admin or Teams admin role is required to manage these apps to make sure they are allowed in your tenant.

Figure 7.50: Managing apps

Permission policies

After allowing Power Platform apps in your tenant, you need to ensure that users can use these apps. For example, if your tenant has custom permission policies, admins need to ensure these Power Platform apps are allowed for use, as shown in the following figure.

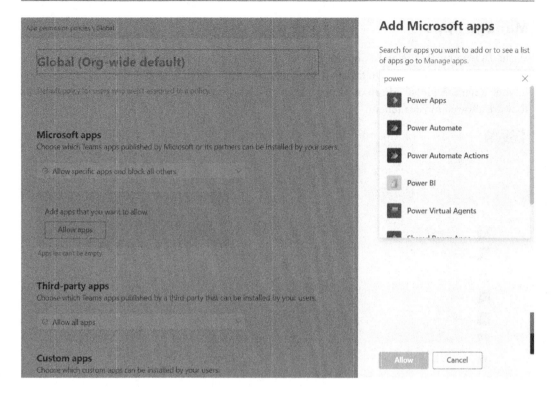

Figure 7.51: Permission policies

Setup policies

Teams app setup policies let you pin apps to Team clients; this will help a user easily access the Power Platform apps from a Teams client. The following figure shows the pinning of these apps in the Teams admin center. As with the preceding policies, you must have a minimum Teams admin role.

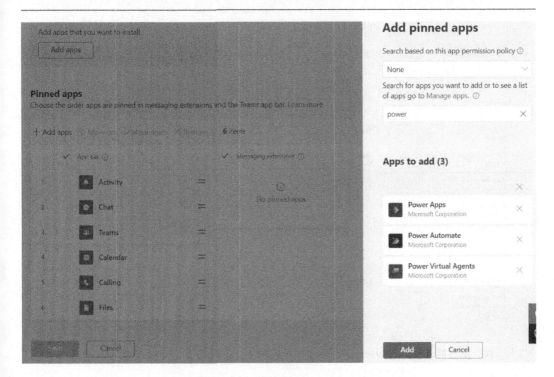

Figure 7.52: Pinning apps through setup policies

Power Platform admin center

As discussed earlier in the chapter, after you add a new or existing app to a team, you will create a Microsoft Dataverse for Teams environment. Again, you can view this through Power Platform admin center.

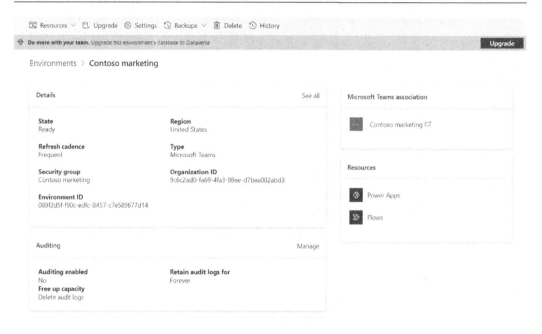

Figure 7.53: A Microsoft Dataverse for Teams Environment overview in Power Platform admin center

From the preceding figure, you can see the team associated with the Dataverse environment and also the resources created in this environment. In addition, we discussed the capacity limitations of a Dataverse for Teams environment as being 2 GB for database and file storage, with a portion of that amount reserved for system users. Therefore, you could review the Microsoft Teams Dataverse capacity from the admin center.

Capacity

Summary   Dataverse   **Microsoft Teams**   Add-ons   Trial

See how your org's Microsoft Teams environments are using storage capacity. Their usage doesn't count toward your org's Dataverse usage. Learn more

↓ Download   ⌕ Search

Environment	Capacity used	
Contoso marketing	605.16 MBs of 2 GBs	30% used

Figure 7.54: The capacity of the Contoso marketing team's Dataverse

As you can see in the preceding figure, the Dataverse for Teams capacity is at 30%, and we have spare capacity. If your capacity doesn't match this, you can upgrade this to the full Dataverse package, as there is no option to increase Dataverse for Teams storage. Fortunately, we don't need to depend on just admins to notify users about the storage situation. At 80% of the storage limit, the Microsoft Teams maker section will receive a message indicating that the capacity limit is about to be reached so that the maker can reduce the usage or reach admins to upgrade. At a 100% storage limit, users can't create new apps. However, the existing apps work.

A Data Loss Prevention (DLP) policy for Microsoft Dataverse

Power Platform DLP policies allow you to control the data flow between various data sources within Power Apps and Power Automate. These DLP policies act as a guardrail for data leaks between business and non-business systems.

Power Platform admin can create and apply these DLP policies for Dataverse environments; these policies segregate systems (or connectors) by business, non-business, and blocks. Based on these groups, only systems (or connectors) in the same group can co-exist within a given app or flow, and the blocked connectors can't be added to any app or flow.

In addition to admin, the environment administrators (Microsoft Dataverse for Teams and the the team owners) can also create these DLP policies. However, global-level DLP policies always take precedence over environment DLP policies.

You can create/edit and view the DLPs, as shown here:

Figure 7.55: Viewing DLP policies through Power Platform admin

Security

Microsoft Dataverse for Teams security aligns with Microsoft Teams roles; if you are a team owner, you have complete access to Microsoft Dataverse for Teams and can manage environmental administration, such as backup and restoring. If a team owner deletes a team, the Microsoft Dataverse for Teams environment will also be deleted. The team owner also can create Microsoft Dataverse for Teams through Power Platform admin center.

Team members can view Dataverse for Teams and resources such as created apps, flows, and chatbots, as they have access to Dataverse data, and they can also create new resources of these types.

Finally, Teams guests are the people outside your tenant who have access to all the resources and the data they create.

Summary

In this chapter, we have introduced Microsoft Dataverse for Teams and the resources you can build as a no-code and low-code solution in it. You can create a Microsoft Dataverse for Teams environment to empower a Microsoft Teams team. This includes users building apps, automations, and chatbots. You can even upgrade Microsoft Dataverse for Teams to a full-blown Dataverse environment if more resources are required for the environment.

The next chapter will be a continuation of this chapter, where we will talk about the various available app templates, review a few of the apps, and see how to integrate them into Microsoft Teams.

8

Microsoft Teams App Templates

In the previous chapter, we learned how to build low-code/no-code apps per your business requirements and publish them on Microsoft Teams so that your Teams users can use them. Though we have seen how easy it is to develop and deploy these Power Apps from scratch, it would be much easier if we had templates to start from. Along these lines, Microsoft initiated a community-driven App templates initiative to build App templates for common use case scenarios.

These App Templates are open source and ready to deploy for production usage, and you can get them through GitHub. Each app template has instructions for deploying and installing that app for your organization and an app you can install and start using immediately.

The core principles of these app templates are that they enable community-driven, open source, production-ready apps for Microsoft Teams, designed and developed under the following principles:

- **Plug-and-play experience**: App templates will have a clear deployment script and allow you to host all essential services in Microsoft 365, Microsoft Azure, or Power Platform.

- **Production-ready code**: All the app templates follow the best practices in terms of security and hosting.

- **Customizable and extensible**: If the base template does not satisfy your requirements, you can easily customize it for your needs; all the source code is available.

- **Detailed documentation and support**: All app templates have detailed documentation on GitHub, covering deployment, configuration, and solution architecture.

In this chapter, we will discuss and guide you on how you can find the App Template that is close to your business needs and how you can deploy it by using the documentation provided with the App Template.

In this chapter, we will cover the following topics:

- **Catalog:** In this section, we will review the prerequisites for deploying the App templates and the core usage of a few templates from the full catalog found here: `https://aka.ms/TeamsAppTemplates`

- **Deployment of App Templates:** Here, we will take one App Template, *Icebreaker*, and walk you through deploying it in your demo tenant

- **Extensibility in Microsoft Teams:** Here, we will talk about a few customizations you can make to the app template you got from GitHub

Let's get started with the catalog!

The catalog

In this section, we'll talk about the available App Templates and review a few of the templates from GitHub. You can also visit `https://aka.ms/apptemplates` for information about the latest App Templates. First, however, I will provide a quick overview of some of these so you can learn a bit more about them.

Most of the templates included in this app catalog require Azure resources, so you must have an Azure subscription.

So, you need to make sure you can create a resource as defined in the following list with your Azure subscription:

- App Service
- App Service plan
- Bot Channels Registration
- Azure Functions
- Logic Apps
- An Azure storage account
- Service Bus
- Application Insights
- Azure Key vault
- Azure Web Apps and Bot Service
- Azure Cognitive Search

- QnA Maker

- Azure Blob Storage and Azure Table storage

- App Insight (optional)

- Cosmos DB

In addition to an Azure subscription, some of the templates might need a Microsoft 365 license with the following apps required for the users of the templates:

- Power Apps

- Power Automate

- SharePoint Online

- Teams

- Exchange Mailbox

In some scenarios, you might need to execute a script requiring Global Admin rights, so you need to work with a global administrator.

Before deploying any of these app templates, I suggest you thoroughly read the documentation and the architecture and deployment guide.

How to sign up for a Developer Tenant with the Microsoft 365 Developer Program

The Microsoft 365 Developer Program offers a free developer subscription to Microsoft 365, providing a sandbox environment for testing and developing Microsoft 365 apps and services. To sign up for a developer tenant, visit the Microsoft 365 Developer Program website (`https://aka.ms/M365DevProgram`) and click the **Join now** button. From there, you will be prompted to sign in with your Microsoft account or create a new one and then fill out a registration form with your personal and contact information. You must also choose a unique tenant name for the developer environment, and accept the terms and conditions of the Microsoft 365 Developer Program.

A few app templates

Here are some of the most popular Microsoft Teams App Templates. Please review them and find the documentation through the App Templates catalog URL as provided previously.

Book-a-room is a Microsoft Teams bot designed to simplify reserving a meeting room. With Book-a-room, users can quickly find and book a meeting room for a default duration of 30 minutes from the current time, selecting from a list of available rooms by location or building. In addition, to streamline future bookings, the bot allows users to mark frequently booked rooms as favorites.

If the user's preferred room is unavailable or if a new location is required, Book-a-room offers the option to book any other available room for a longer duration of up to 90 minutes. This feature enables users to find the best available room to meet their needs without the hassle of searching for rooms individually.

The Book-a-room bot operates within the personal scope and can be customized to meet organizational needs, providing a starting point for organizations to build custom room booking solutions.

Organizations can use the **Building Access** app to safely bring employees back into the office facilities as economies and businesses reopen and organizations plan to gradually reopen their office facilities.

Microsoft Teams **FAQ Plus** chatbots are an excellent way to quickly answer frequently asked questions. However, many bots need human intervention to provide a personalized and engaging user experience.

That's where FAQ Plus comes in. It's a friendly **question-and-answer** (**Q&A**) bot that involves human experts when it cannot provide an answer. Users can ask a question, and if the answer is in the bot's knowledge base, it will respond immediately. If not, the bot will offer the option to **Ask an expert**, which routes the query to a pre-configured team of experts for further assistance.

Once an expert is assigned to the question, they can chat directly with the user to better understand their query and add the question to the knowledge base using a messaging extension. This continuous feedback loop ensures that the bot's knowledge base remains up to date and can provide future users with more accurate and relevant information.

Request-a-team is an innovative Microsoft Teams app designed to optimize the creation of new team instances for enterprise organizations. The app promotes standardization and best practices by integrating a wizard-guided request form, an embedded approval process, a request status dashboard, and an automated team build. Built on Power Platform, the app includes a user-friendly Power App frontend and a Power Automate flow for approval. With Request-a-team, organizations can implement repeatable best practices for team collaboration and accelerate response times for team requests.

The **Company Communicator** app is a custom Teams app that empowers corporate teams to communicate efficiently with multiple teams or many employees over chat, ensuring the organization can reach employees where they collaborate most. Whether for new initiative announcements, employee onboarding, modern learning, development, or organization-wide broadcasts, this app provides an easy-to-use interface for designated users to create, preview, collaborate, and send messages. Moreover, Company Communicator is the foundation for building custom targeted communication capabilities, such as custom telemetry on how many users acknowledged or interacted with a message. With Company Communicator, organizations can effectively and efficiently communicate important information to their employees, improving overall collaboration and streamlining operations.

Request-a-guest is a Microsoft Teams app that helps organizations manage guest access to their Azure **Active Directory** (**AD**) tenant. By providing a simple form for employee requests and an in-built approval process, the app ensures that only authorized requests are processed and that guests are only invited from permitted domains. Additionally, the app offers a fully audited workflow that tracks requests and approvals, which can help improve security and compliance. Once approved, guest invites are automatically issued, and the original requestor is added as the manager of the guest, streamlining the onboarding process and making it easier to track and manage guest access. Overall, Request-a-guest is a valuable tool that helps organizations control guest access to their Azure AD tenant and improves operational efficiency, security, and compliance.

The Request-a-guest app template is available on GitHub at `https://github.com/OfficeDev/ microsoft-teams-apps-request-a-guest`.

Co-worker appreciation sees that recognizing colleagues' achievements has always been challenging. By simply clicking to reward a colleague, recipients and team members are instantly notified about the award details in the channel, boosting team morale and creating a positive work culture. In addition, all awards are securely recorded in the team app, making it easy to celebrate team success. It's like a Power Apps-based leaderboard version of the Open Badges app template – fun, engaging, and valuable. The co-worker appreciation template is a game-changer for Microsoft Teams, empowering teams to recognize hard work and build camaraderie.

The **New Employee Onboarding** (**NEO**) solution is an excellent tool for organizations looking to improve their onboarding process. Using SharePoint and integrating with Teams, the app can help streamline onboarding by providing a customizable new employee checklist for HR teams to use to manage relevant content and processes for new hires.

One of the most significant benefits of the NEO app is that it empowers new employees to share feedback and introduce themselves to their managers using helpful bot commands. This feature can help new employees feel more comfortable and engaged during onboarding, leading to higher job satisfaction and productivity.

The ability to share introductions with relevant teams is also a great feature, as it ensures a smoother onboarding experience for all involved parties. Additionally, the app's ability to collect pulse surveys can help organizations gather valuable insights into their onboarding process and make adjustments to improve it.

Overall, the NEO app is a game-changer for organizations looking to create a consistent, productive, and engaging onboarding experience for new employees. By leveraging SharePoint and Teams, the app provides a comprehensive solution for managing the onboarding process, from content and processes to feedback and surveys.

Incentives is a Teams Power Apps app template that rewards employee participation in training and change management initiatives. Admins create activities and rewards, assign points, and set minimum requirements for eligibility. Employees earn points by completing activities and can track their progress on a leaderboard. Points can be redeemed for rewards such as coffee or food. Admins approve reward requests and provide voucher codes for redemption. Incentives help organizations drive engagement and productivity by incentivizing and tracking employee participation.

As mentioned previously, you can review all the templates here: `https://aka.ms/TeamsAppTemplates`.

In the next section, we will talk about the Icebreaker template and learn how to deploy it.

Deploying an App Template

So far, we have discussed what App Templates are and reviewed a few of them to understand more about what functionality they can deliver. As previously mentioned, these are readily available and have end-to-end documentation for deployment and configuration. So, let's take the Icebreaker app and deploy it in your demo tenant.

Icebreaker

Icebreaker is one of the most popular Microsoft Teams bots, which helps team members get closer by pairing two random team members to meet weekly. In addition, this bot makes scheduling easy by suggesting free time that works for both members.

Before deploying the App Template, you need to address the following questions:

- What is this app template?
- Why do you need it?
- How do you deploy it?

Answering these questions will ensure successful deployment and better adoption of the app.

What is this app?

Icebreaker is a popular Microsoft Teams app template and helps your team members to get close by pairing random team members to meet weekly. This bot makes scheduling easy by checking the free time that works for both members. This helps establish connections and build a strong community.

You can also use this icebreaker bot to build interest-based communities within your organization. Again, we will use this app template as an example for you to see how easy deploying these app templates is.

Why do you need it?

Before deploying any app template, make sure you have answered the following questions so that you have a proper business justification for the deployment:

- What is the purpose of this App Template?
- How does the user experience this, and is this acceptable for the organization?
- What are we deploying, and what is the cost estimate for the resource consumption?
- Who manages this, and what do we need to maintain?

How do you deploy it?

Once you understand what you are deploying and why you need to know how to deploy it, the best place to start is with GitHub's documentation and deployment guidance. For the Icebreaker app template, here is the link for the GitHub documentation:

```
https://github.com/OfficeDev/microsoft-teams-apps-icebreaker
```

The architecture of the Icebreaker app

If you review the architecture of the Icebreaker app template from the GitHub documentation, it is evident that this app has two components:

- **Teams Bot**: An Azure App Service web app that functions as the Teams Bot
- **Pair up Logic App**: An Azure Logic App configured to send a request to the bot to initiate the pairing up at the appropriate time.

The following diagram shows the overview architecture for the Icebreaker app template:

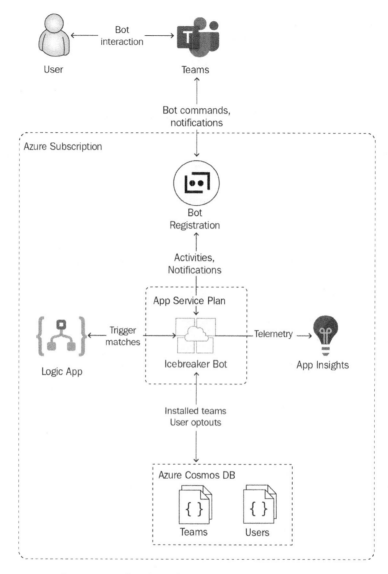

Figure 8.1: Icebreaker solution architecture from GitHub

Based on the architecture, you can see that this application requires you to have an Azure subscription that allows you to deploy the following resources:

- Azure logic apps
- App Service
- App Service plan
- Bot Channels Registration
- An Azure Cosmos DB account
- Application Insights

To summarize, the Icebreaker app is created using the Microsoft Teams app template architecture, utilizing Microsoft Teams, Microsoft Graph, Azure Functions, and Azure Bot Service. Microsoft Teams is the app's user interface, while the Graph API manages user data. Azure Functions power the backend for data processing and storage, and Azure Bot Service provides the chatbot functionality. Additionally, the app integrates with Azure Cognitive Services, such as Language Understanding and Text Analytics, to support **natural language processing** (**NLP**) and sentiment analysis. In the next section, we discuss deploying the Icebreaker app.

Deploying the Icebreaker app

We have two options for deploying the application, one using a PowerShell script and the other as a manual deployment. In this section, I will cover the manual option so that you can understand the components required to run this application.

This is a four-step deployment process, noted as follows:

1. Register an Azure AD application.
2. Deploy a custom template to your Azure subscription.
3. Create the Teams app package.
4. Upload and run the app in Microsoft Teams.

After we review each step, I will also take you through the best practices.

Registering the Azure AD application

The first step of this App Template is to register an Azure AD application. For that, you can go directly to the URL provided here, or you can go to the Azure portal and search for app registration. Either way, ensure you sign into the Azure subscription you would like to use for this deployment:

```
https://portal.azure.com/#blade/Microsoft_AAD_IAM/
ActiveDirectoryMenuBlade/RegisteredApps
```

You will see a screen like the following for app registrations; you can click **New registration** to create the Azure app:

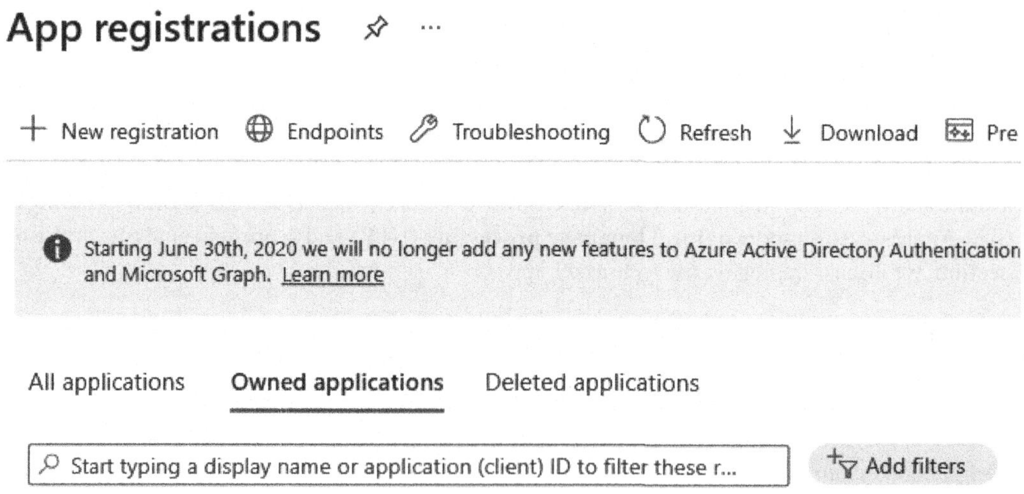

App registrations ⭐ ⋯

+ New registration   ⊕ Endpoints   🔧 Troubleshooting   ○ Refresh   ↓ Download   ⊞ Pre

---

ℹ Starting June 30th, 2020 we will no longer add any new features to Azure Active Directory Authentication and Microsoft Graph. Learn more

---

All applications   **Owned applications**   Deleted applications

🔍 Start typing a display name or application (client) ID to filter these r...   ➕ Add filters

Figure 8.2: Azure AD app registrations

You will now be taken to register your Icebreaker app. Enter `icebreaker` in the **Name** field and select the **Multitenant** account type. That is all you need from the **App registrations** screen:

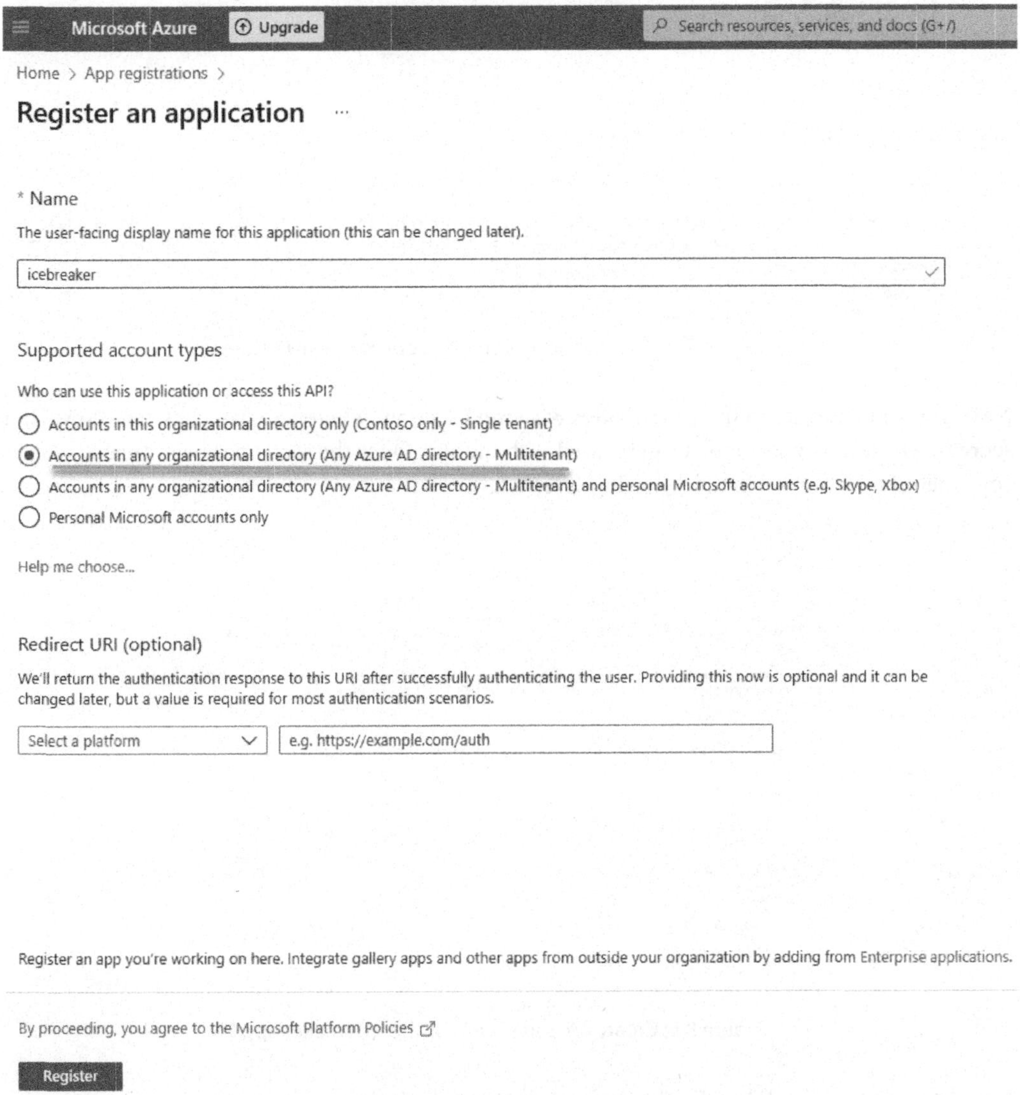

Figure 8.3: Registering the icebreaker app

After you have entered the details and clicked on **Register**, the **Application (client) ID** field will include a value, as shown in the following screenshot. I suggest you keep a note of this ID so you can use it whenever required. Now the app has been created, and you can copy the values in the **Application (client) ID** and **Directory (tenant) ID** fields, as shown in the following screenshot:

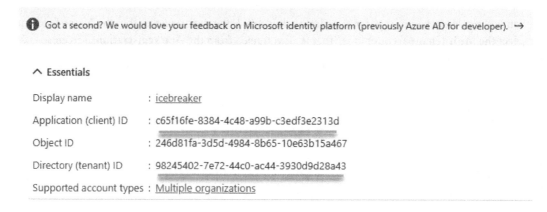

Figure 8.4: Icebreaker app overview, copying the ID values

Next, you can navigate to the **Certificates & secrets** section, where you can click on +**New client secret** to create a new secret that can be used with the app. Once the secret has been created, you can copy the value, as shown in the following screenshot:

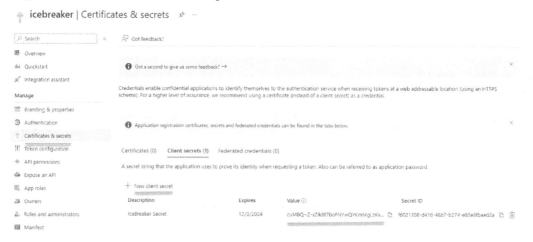

Figure 8.5: Create an app secret for the icebreaker app

Now you have an App ID and a client secret, you can deploy the custom template to your tenant, which we will see in the next subsection.

Deploying a custom template to your Azure subscription

After you have the Azure App ID, you can create the required Azure resources by deploying the custom template for the Icebreaker app template. You can go to the URL directly or the GitHub deployment guide and click the **Deploy to Azure** link.

Here, you can find the custom template to deploy in Azure for the Icebreaker app: `https://tinyurl.com/4t9pnzt5`.

Either way, you will be directed to the screen shown in the following screenshot:

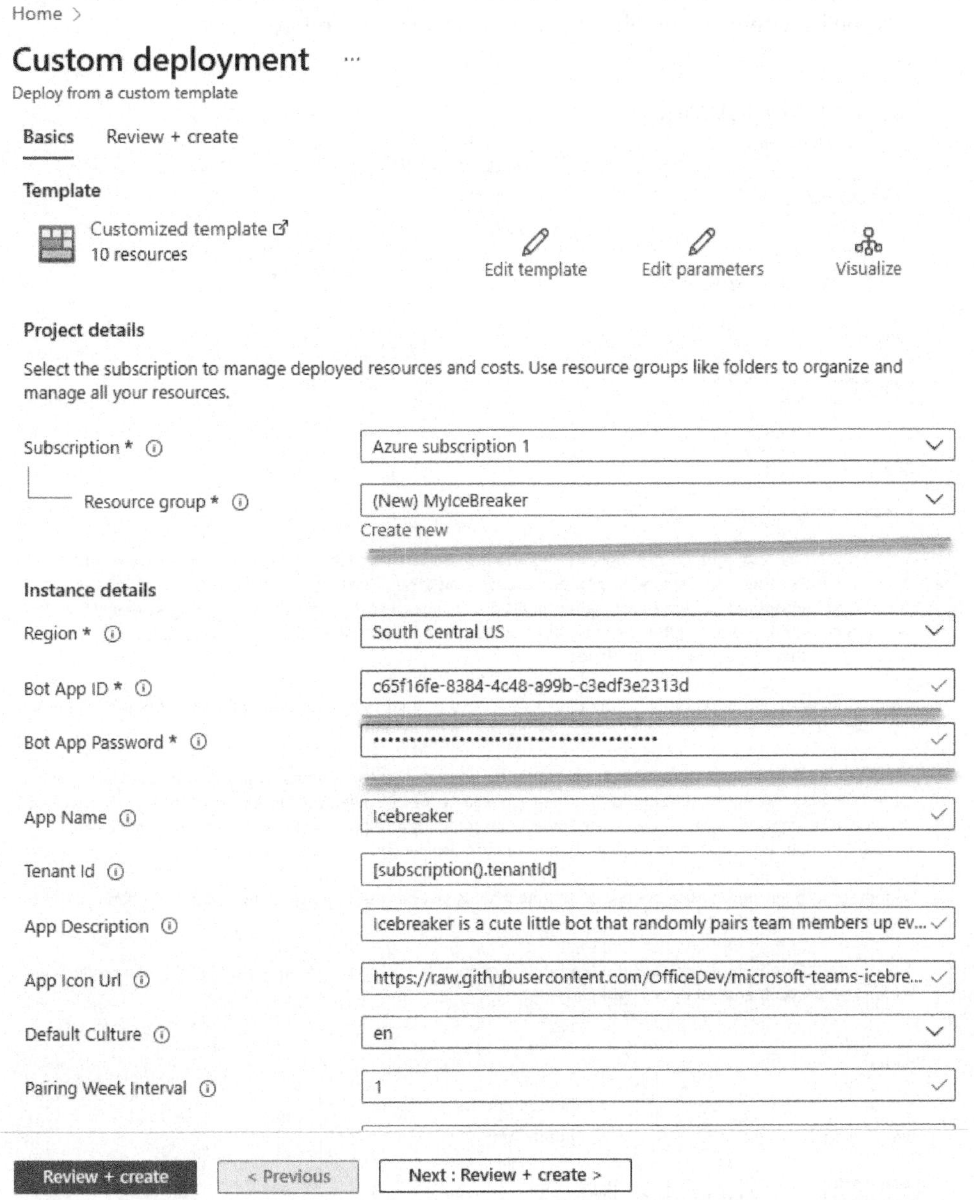

Home >

Custom deployment   ...
Deploy from a custom template

Basics   Review + create

Template

Customized template ☑
10 resources

Edit template   Edit parameters   Visualize

Project details

Select the subscription to manage deployed resources and costs. Use resource groups like folders to organize and manage all your resources.

Subscription * ⓘ	Azure subscription 1 ⌄
└── Resource group * ⓘ	(New) MyIceBreaker ⌄
	Create new

Instance details

Region * ⓘ	South Central US ⌄
Bot App ID * ⓘ	c65f16fe-8384-4c48-a99b-c3edf3e2313d ✓
Bot App Password * ⓘ	•••••••••••••••••••••••••••••••• ✓
App Name ⓘ	Icebreaker ✓
Tenant Id ⓘ	[subscription().tenantId]
App Description ⓘ	Icebreaker is a cute little bot that randomly pairs team members up ev... ✓
App Icon Url ⓘ	https://raw.githubusercontent.com/OfficeDev/microsoft-teams-icebre... ✓
Default Culture ⓘ	en ⌄
Pairing Week Interval ⓘ	1 ✓

Review + create   < Previous   Next : Review + create >

Figure 8.6: Icebreaker app | Custom deployment

As shown in the preceding screenshot, you can either select an existing value from the **Resource group** field or select **Create new**, get the App ID and client secret from the notepad you copied from the previous step, and enter them in the **Bot App ID** and **Bot App Password** fields.

Then, you click **Review + create**, which will redirect you to the validation screen, ensuring that all the details you have entered are valid as per your Azure subscription:

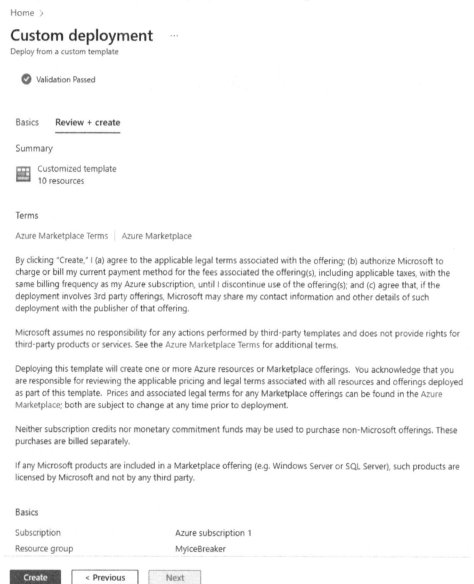

Figure 8.7: Validation of the deployment template

When presented with the **Validation Passed** message, as shown in the preceding screenshot, you can click **Create** to deploy the required resources for this App Template.

When you click **Create**, it will redirect you to the **Deployment is in progress** screen, showing the progress of the various required resources in the template.

You will need to capture the URL for use in the Teams app package that you will create in the later steps. Click on the **Microsoft Web/sites** resource, as shown in the following screenshot:

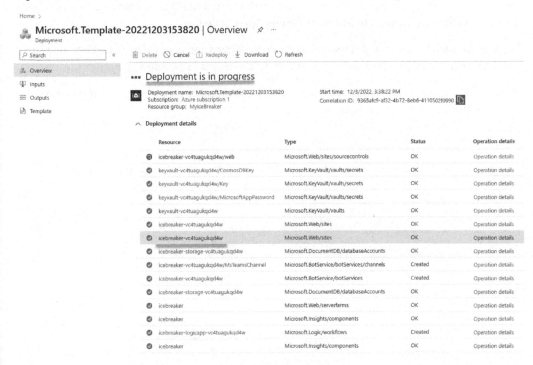

Figure 8.8: Deployment is in progress

Once you click on the **Microsoft Web/sites** resource, it will redirect to the actual resource. As shown in the following screenshot, you can copy the URL from the **Overview** section. It will be presented as `https://icebreaker-XXXXXXXXXXXX.azurewebsites.net`, where the Xs are the hash:

Figure 8.9: Copy the URL of the Microsoft Web/sites

With this, you have successfully deployed the required Azure resources for the Microsoft Teams app template. The next step is creating the Teams app package with the appropriate information from the Bot ID and domain created from the previous steps.

Creating the Teams app package

Now you are ready to create a Teams app package and define the app name, description, icons, accent color, company website URL, privacy policy and terms of use, and URLs by changing the `manifest.json` file before deployment to Microsoft Teams App Catalog.

You can download the required resources to create the Team's app package from GitHub (`https://github.com/OfficeDev/microsoft-teams-apps-icebreaker`).

If you click the preceding link, it will take you to the icebreaker repo, and you can download it, as shown in the following screenshot:

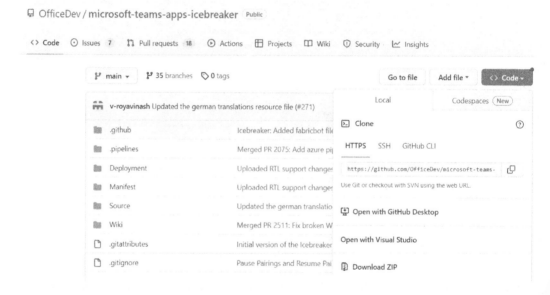

Figure 8.10: The GitHub repo for icebreaker

Once you have downloaded the app from the repo, you can copy the `manifest.json`, `color.png`, and `outline.png` files from the `manifest` folder of the repo:

Name	Date modified	Type	Size
∨ Today			
manifest.json	11/28/2022 4:17 PM	JSON Source File	3 KB
color.png	11/28/2022 4:09 PM	PNG File	7 KB
outline.png	11/28/2022 4:09 PM	PNG File	1 KB

Figure 8.11: Teams App Package for Icebreaker

With these resources, you can create an app package that can be distributed to your Microsoft Teams as a Teams app. The Team's App package is a ZIP file that contains the following items:

- **App manifest**: This includes how the app is configured and its capabilities, required resources, and other essential attributes
- **App icons**: You will require a color and outline icon for your app

If you open the manifest.json file, there are placeholder fields, as shown in the following screenshots, so you can replace the more relevant values for your team.

The following screenshot shows the manifest section which includes the developer information and placeholder values:

```
"developer": {
    "name": "<company name>",
    "websiteUrl": "<website url>",
    "privacyUrl": "<privacy url>",
    "termsOfUseUrl": "<terms of use url>"
},
```

Figure 8.12: The manifest.json placeholder values for developer information

As shown, replacing the values for the developer information in the manifest.json file makes it more relevant to your organization:

```
"developer": {
    "name": "gcTestInc",
    "websiteUrl": "https://www.gctestInc.com",
    "privacyUrl": "https://www.gctestInc.com/privacy.html",
    "termsOfUseUrl": "https://www.gctestInc.com/terms.html"
},
```

Figure 8.13: The manifest.json values after filling in the developer information

The next important thing to do is to replace bot Id with the actual BOT ID you noted previously, as shown in *Figure 8.14*:

```json
"bots": [
  {
    "botId": "<bot id>",
    "scopes": [
      "personal",
      "team"
    ],
    "supportsFiles": false,
    "isNotificationOnly": true
  }
```

Figure 8.14: The manifest.json section with a placeholder for botId

After the `developer` information and `botId`, the last thing in the `manifest.json` file is `validDomains`, as shown in the following screenshot. This should be populated with the domain you copied from the Microsoft Web/sites that was created through the deployment template:

```json
  ],
  "validDomains": [
    "<app domain>"
  ]
```

Figure 8.15: The manifest.json section with the placeholder for valid domains.

Once you have filled in the placeholder values in the `manifest.json` file, you are ready to create the Teams App package, as shown in *Figure 8.16*:

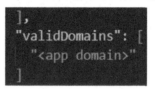

> Downloads > icebreaker

Name	Date modified	Type	Size
⌄ Today			
✓ icebreaker.zip	11/28/2022 4:19 PM	Compressed (zipp…	8 KB
manifest.json	11/28/2022 4:17 PM	JSON Source File	3 KB
color.png	11/28/2022 4:09 PM	PNG File	7 KB
outline.png	11/28/2022 4:09 PM	PNG File	1 KB

Figure 8.16: An icebreaker.zip file

Now the app is ready for uploading, the next step is to perform the upload and run the app in Microsoft Teams.

Uploading and running the app in Microsoft Teams

The `icebreaker.zip` file is ready, and you can upload it into Teams; go to the left rail in Microsoft Teams, as shown in *Figure 8.17*.

Click on **Apps** | **Manage your apps** | **Upload an app**.

Manage your apps provides you with a place to manage your apps and permissions; from here, users can install apps:

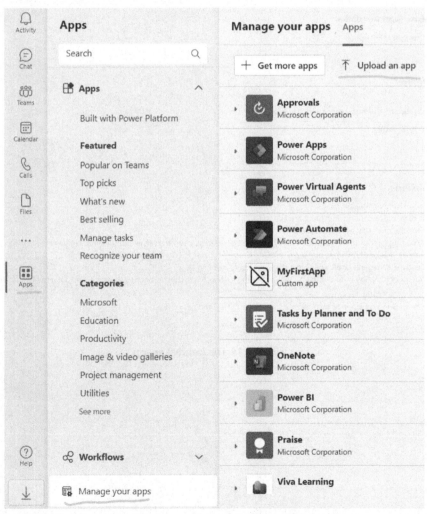

Figure 8.17: Upload icebreaker.zip in Manage your apps

As shown in the preceding screenshot, clicking on **Upload an app** will bring up the following screen for the icebreaker app:

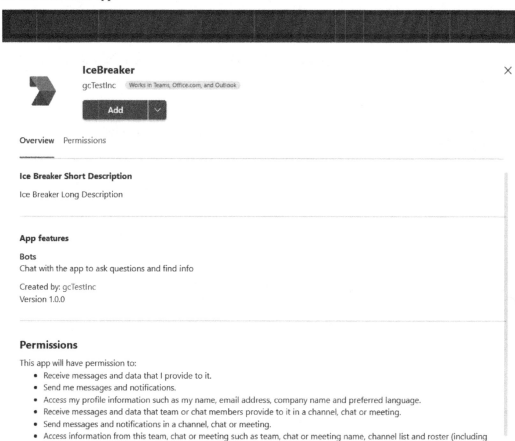

Figure 8.18: The icebreaker app

Click **Add** and select the team you want this bot to be available for. For example, I picked the **Teams App Template Test** team and the **General** channel, as shown in *Figure 8.19*:

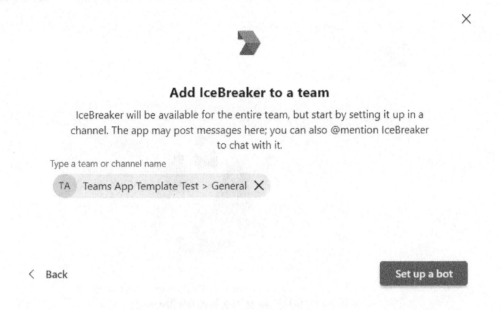

Figure 8.19: Selecting the Microsoft Teams team

Now that the bot is installed for the team that you selected, you will see this Icebreaker welcome message in Microsoft Teams, as shown in the following screenshot:

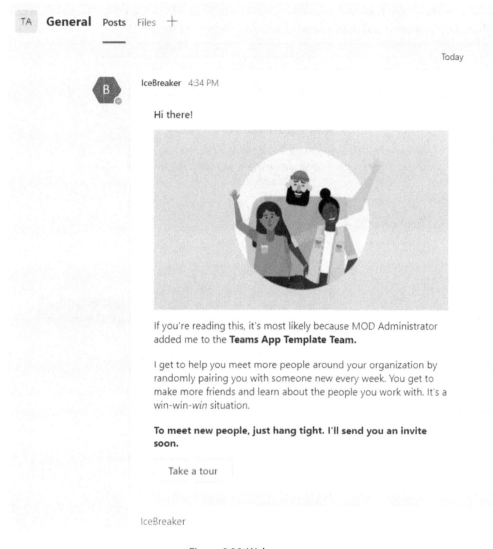

Figure 8.20: Welcome message

With this, you have deployed the icebreaker bot, and you can now invite various team members to this team.

General best practices

Deploying an icebreaker app template can be a valuable way to improve employee engagement and communication within an organization. However, to ensure successful deployment, it's important to follow best practices to maximize the benefits of using an icebreaker app.

Determining your specific use case is critical in deploying an icebreaker app template. Different templates may be more appropriate for different situations, so choosing the one that best addresses your organization's needs is important.

Before deploying the app to a production environment, testing it in a non-production environment is important to ensure that it functions properly and has no bugs or issues. Additionally, most icebreaker app templates allow for customization, so it's important to take the time to tailor the app to your organization's branding and specific requirements.

Also, please refer to the *How to sign up for a Developer Tenant with the Microsoft 365 Developer Program* section for creating a developer tenant.

Once the app is deployed, it's important to provide users with training and resources to ensure they can use the app effectively. In addition, by monitoring usage and engagement metrics and gathering user feedback, you can identify areas for improvement and make necessary changes to maximize the app's benefits.

It's important to keep the app up to date to ensure that it continues functioning properly and that your users can access the latest features and improvements. By following these best practices, you can help ensure a successful deployment and take full advantage of the benefits of using an icebreaker app in your organization.

Creating dedicated teams to use the icebreaker app is important, rather than installing it on your business collaboration teams. This will ensure members can join and leave without interrupting their ongoing collaborations.

It's also a good idea to regularly invite new members to these dedicated icebreaker teams to keep pairing interesting and prevent the same individuals from always being matched with each other. This can help ensure that everyone in the organization has the opportunity to connect with new colleagues and build relationships. Successfully deploying an icebreaker app template in your organization can foster meaningful connections and improve communication and engagement within your organization.

Extensibility in Microsoft Teams

When you deploy an app template for Microsoft Teams, you may need to ensure that the app or bot is installed for each user who needs to receive messages or interact with the app.

To do this, you can use the Microsoft Graph API or the Microsoft Teams admin center to deploy the app to all users in your organization. You can also use Teams app setup policies to install the app for all intended users, which is a convenient way to ensure that everyone in your organization can access the app without requiring them to install it manually.

Teams app setup policies are a powerful way to manage app deployments for large organizations, and they can save a lot of time and effort by ensuring that everyone has the apps they need. By using Teams app setup policies, you can ensure that all the necessary apps are installed for the right groups of users without manually installing each app on every user's device. This can be especially helpful for organizations with many users, where manual app deployment would be time-consuming. The Teams app setup policies are discussed in detail in *Chapter 1*.

Customizing an App Package

When customizing app templates for Microsoft Teams, you can easily change the app name, description, icons, accent color, company website URL, privacy policy and terms of use, URLs, and other properties by editing the app's manifest file before deploying it to the Microsoft Teams app catalog.

The app manifest file is an XML file that contains information about the app, including the previously mentioned properties. You can easily customize the app's appearance and behavior by editing this file to meet your organization's needs. You can also change the the name of the bot that sends messages to end users by updating the settings of the Azure Bot Service used by the app.

Making these changes to the app's manifest file is a simple and effective way to customize and tailor app templates to your organization's specific needs. The Microsoft Teams documentation provides detailed guidance on how to customize the app manifest file and deploy custom apps to the Microsoft Teams app catalog.

Customizing the SharePoint site and Power Automate flows

SharePoint and Power Automate offer a range of customization options that can help organizations tailor their app templates to their specific needs.

With SharePoint, you can customize the site's branding to match your organization's look and feel. This includes customizing the site's theme, adding a logo or header image, and changing the site's colors and fonts. You can also add or remove web parts to create a customized layout for your site and create custom lists and libraries to store and manage your organization's data.

Similarly, with Power Automate, you can modify the pre-built flows of the app templates to meet your specific business requirements. For example, you can add or remove actions, customize data mappings, and create branching logic to control the flow of your business processes. You can also create custom flows from scratch to automate specific tasks or processes unique to your organization.

The Microsoft documentation provides detailed guidance on customizing SharePoint and Power Automate flows, including step-by-step instructions, best practices, and sample code. This can help organizations take full advantage of the app templates and tailor them to their specific needs, making them more effective and efficient for their users.

Summary

In this chapter, we have introduced Microsoft Teams App Templates, which are already available and don't require much effort to deploy in your environment. The key benefits of these apps are that you can deploy them without writing any code, and they are entirely customizable. Also, you have complete ownership as you deploy an Azure subscription in your organization. Lastly, you will have a sample app available with each App Template.

In the next chapter, we will learn about Microsoft Viva, a comprehensive employee experience platform that can be integrated with Microsoft Teams, SharePoint, and other Microsoft applications. It provides various tools and resources to help employees stay connected, engaged, and productive.

9

Microsoft Viva

Microsoft Viva is a new **Employee Experience Platform** (**EXP**) in **Microsoft 365** (**M365**), with various modules, such as Viva Topics, Viva Connections, Viva Insights, and Viva Learning, integrated into a single hub in Microsoft Teams. This platform supports connection, insight, purpose, and growth, empowering people and teams to work to their full potential.

Over the years, the EXP digital platform, helping organizations align and engage employees, has become increasingly popular.

We're going to cover the following main topics in this chapter:

- Microsoft Viva and various modules of Microsoft Viva
- The benefits of implementing Microsoft Viva in your organization
- The detailed implementation of Microsoft Viva Connections
- Customizing the Viva Connections app

Implementing Microsoft Viva

Microsoft Viva supplies a range of features that help organizations improve communication, collaboration, and employee well-being. In addition, Microsoft Viva integrates with Microsoft Teams to supply a single platform for communication and collaboration.

Here are some of the key features of Microsoft Viva:

- **Microsoft Viva Connections**: Microsoft Viva Connections is a gateway for modern experience and provides employees with a centralized location for connecting with colleagues, sharing news, finding information, and accessing resources.
- **Microsoft Viva Insights**: Microsoft Viva Insights provides organizations with valuable data and insights about employee productivity, engagement, and well-being patterns. This feature helps organizations understand how employees are using technology and how they can improve their work experience.

- **Microsoft Viva Learning**: Microsoft Viva Learning provides a centralized learning hub for employees with access to a library of learning resources and courses provided by their organization and partners. This feature helps organizations upskill and reskill employees, improving their performance and productivity.

- **Microsoft Viva Topics**: Microsoft Viva Topics is a content management system that helps organizations curate and manage information and knowledge using AI. This feature allows employees to find the information they need quickly and easily, improving efficiency and collaboration.

- **Microsoft Viva Goals**: Microsoft Viva Goals aligns your organization's teams with strategies and priorities and helps them to achieve the best results. This feature empowers employees to achieve their goals relating to a project's **Objectives and Key Results (OKRs)**.

- **Microsoft Viva Engage**: Starting from March 2023, Yammer will undergo a complete rebranding process, becoming Viva Engage. The rebranding will begin with the mobile apps for iOS and Android, as well as the Outlook Communities app, and will continue to other endpoints throughout 2023. This process will involve updating the app name, icon, and all in-app references to reflect the new branding.

- **Microsoft Viva Sales**: Since October 3, 2022, Viva Sales has been made generally available. This revolutionary application has been specifically designed to enhance the employee experience for sellers. Viva Sales integrates a seller's CRM system, M365, and Microsoft Teams, providing them with a seamless workflow to manage their tasks, save time, and focus on building customer relationships and closing deals.

These are some of the key features of Microsoft Viva, but the platform is constantly evolving with new features. Therefore, I recommend visiting `https://learn.microsoft.com/en-us/viva/` for the latest information and updates.

Now, as discussed previously, Viva helps organizations with communication, collaboration, and employee engagement, but it is essential to follow the best practices to ensure a successful rollout of Microsoft Viva. The following is a list of some of the general best practices to follow:

- **Plan implementation**: Before implementing Microsoft Viva, it is essential to have a clear plan and identify all your goals, assess your current technological landscape, and determine the resources you will need to get the platform up and running.

- **Involve key stakeholders**: Make sure to involve key stakeholders, such as HR, IT, and business leaders, in the implementation process, which ensures that the platform meets the needs of different departments and aligns with overall business goals.

- **Communication with employees**: Good communication is critical to successful implementation. Ensure to keep employees informed about the rollout, what they can expect, and how they will benefit from the platform.

- **Training and support**: Provide employees with training and support to help them get up to speed with Microsoft Viva. This includes online tutorials, in-person training sessions, and ongoing support to answer questions or resolve issues.

- **Integrate with existing systems**: Microsoft Viva integrates with many other systems, including Microsoft Teams and other M365 apps. Taking advantage of these integrations is essential to ensure a seamless user experience.

- **Monitor and evaluate performance**: Regularly monitor and evaluate the performance of Microsoft Viva to ensure it delivers the expected results. This includes collecting employee feedback, analyzing data and metrics, and making necessary adjustments.

- **Continuously improve**: Microsoft Viva is a constantly evolving platform, with new features and updates being released regularly. Make sure to keep up to date with the latest developments and incorporate new features into your implementation as they become available.

By following these best practices, organizations can ensure a successful implementation of Microsoft Viva and reap the benefits of improved communication, collaboration, and employee engagement.

The benefits of implementing Microsoft Viva

Here are a few examples of how organizations can successfully implement Microsoft Viva to improve communication, collaboration, and employee engagement:

- Microsoft Viva provides a centralized communication and collaboration platform, helping employees stay connected and work together more effectively. This results in improved efficiency, faster decision-making, and better outcomes.

- Microsoft Viva provides robust security and compliance features to help organizations keep sensitive data safe, which includes encryption, secure sharing, access controls, file sharing, and task management, among other features.

- Microsoft Viva Learning provides employees with access to training and development resources.

- Microsoft Viva Insights allows for monitoring employee productivity and engagement and making data-driven decisions to improve the work experience.

- Microsoft Viva Topics allows for managing and sharing knowledge across teams in the organization.

- Microsoft Viva Insights provides organizations with access to data and insights to make data-driven decisions, leading to better decision-making, improved outcomes, and more effective and efficient organization.

- Microsoft Viva Learning enhances employee learning and development by providing a modern and personalized learning experience directly within Microsoft Teams.

Every implementation will be unique and tailored to the organization's needs and goals. Still, those few thoughts provide a glimpse into the benefits that Microsoft Viva can offer your teams and organizations.

Microsoft Viva Connections

With Microsoft Viva Connections, you can create a personalized landing page or home site experience for your organization. Supplying the correct information to the right person at the right time is critical for any digital transformation to succeed, and this is the goal of Viva Connections.

Microsoft Teams is a hub for team members to collaborate on a day-to-day basis. SharePoint Online is a platform for modern intranet portals where you can build sites for broader communication of news and valuable information about the organization.

Historically, employees had to leave Microsoft Teams to access their modern intranet portals or informational sites; in the chapters of this book, the focus is to keep users in Teams and not disrupt their work by having them move between apps.

Viva Connections is a Teams app available in Microsoft Teams, with the SharePoint Online landing page and various resources available directly in Microsoft Teams. So, this acts as a singular gateway for employees.

Implementing Microsoft Viva Connections

If you are trying to implement Microsoft Viva Connections in your organization, it is essential to assess your organization's needs and identify your goals for the platform.

Microsoft Viva Connections provides several configuration options to help tailor the platform to meet your organization's needs. This includes customizing the user interface, setting up user accounts and permissions, and configuring the platform to integrate with other systems and apps.

Once the platform is up and running, it is essential to provide employees with training and support to help them get up to speed with Microsoft Viva Connections. This includes online tutorials, in-person training sessions, and ongoing support to answer questions or resolve issues.

Regularly monitor and evaluate the performance of Microsoft Viva Connections to ensure it delivers the expected results, which includes collecting employee feedback, analyzing data and metrics, and making necessary adjustments.

Microsoft Viva Connections is a constantly evolving platform, with new features and updates released regularly. Therefore, it is essential to keep up to date with the latest developments and incorporate new features into your implementation as they become available.

SharePoint home site

SharePoint Online plays a crucial role in Viva Connections, as SharePoint Online is the foundation for creating a modern intranet, which delivers the landing page experience in Viva Connections.

Modern intranet sites are built using the SharePoint communication site template, while collaboration sites are built using the SharePoint team site template. Therefore, you can create multiple sites for your intranet with various purposes, such as news, branding, CEO or leadership connections, design, training, and best practices. First, however, you need to create one site for a customized landing experience and promote that site as a SharePoint home site.

> **Note**
>
> SharePoint Online provides various templates to create sites. Each template has lists, libraries, pages, and other elements or features.

There are two types of templates: classic and modern. Classic templates are outdated and there are no new developments being made to them; most are on the path to retirement. So that just leaves modern templates. With modern templates, you have two groups: modern team sites and communication sites. Modern team sites, which are designed for collaboration and communication, are for sharing news and information with a large audience of users.

This home site serves as a gateway to your modern intranet; once you design the communication site for your organization's brand, set this as the home site in the SharePoint admin center. It would help if you were a SharePoint administrator to set up the home site in your tenant.

Home site

Set the communication site you want to use as the main landing site for your intranet. Setting a site as your home site enables extra capabilities automatically.

Learn about planning, building, and launching a home site

URL of the site you want to use

Example: https://contoso.sharepoint.com/sites/home or /sites/home

Figure 9.1: Set the primary landing site for your intranet

As a SharePoint administrator, you can log in to the SharePoint Online admin center, go to **Settings**, and click on **SharePoint Home site**. Then, it provides a popup to add the customized communication site.

As of the time of writing, you can only set one home site as a landing place. However, Microsoft is working on a feature that will allow multiple home sites per tenant so that you can have multiple distinct connection experiences for different groups or units in the organization.

To design a better home site, use the guidelines at `https://learn.microsoft.com/en-US/viva/connections/create-sharepoint-home-site-for-viva-connections`, as helps to provide the best experience for users across the organization.

In addition to the guidelines, ensure your organization has a good governance plan and intranet information architecture to create effective intranet portals.

Global navigation in the SharePoint app bar

It is essential to set up global navigation in the SharePoint app bar for Microsoft Viva Connections, as it provides quick and easy access to the different components of Viva Connections from anywhere within your M365 environment.

Global navigation in the SharePoint app bar is a feature that displays a set of links or buttons in a consistent location across the top of the screen. By setting up global navigation for Viva Connections, employees can easily navigate to the different modules and features of Viva Connections, such as the Dashboard, Topics, Insights, and My Feed, without having to navigate through multiple pages or menus.

Global navigation improves the overall user experience and increases the adoption of Viva Connections, as employees can quickly and easily access the information and resources that they need to do their job. In addition, it is easier for employees to switch between different components of Viva Connections, increasing their productivity and improving the overall flow of work.

Where is the app bar? The app bar is present on the left-hand side anywhere on any modern site, as shown in the following figure. With the app bar, users can quickly access sites, news, and resources across all your SharePoint sites, helping to improve navigation and productivity by reducing the number of clicks to access commonly used information.

Figure 9.2: SharePoint app bar

The SharePoint app bar shown in the preceding figure is a navigation element that appears at the top of SharePoint pages in M365 and displays a set of links in a consistent location across the top of the screen, allowing users to access standard SharePoint features and functionalities from anywhere within the environment. For example, in the context of Microsoft Viva Connections, administrators can add links to the Viva Connections modules, such as the Dashboard, Topics, Insights, and My Feed, to the SharePoint app bar.

Global navigation complements the home site and expands the resources you can access from the home site, and the same links also appear in the Viva Connections app for Microsoft Teams.

Viva Connections Dashboard

The Viva Connections Dashboard is a component of Microsoft Viva Connections.

The Dashboard in Viva Connections is the main landing page for employees and provides a consolidated view of relevant information, news, and insights. It lets employees stay informed and connected to the latest information and resources and easily access other Viva Connections components, such as Topics, Insights, and My Feed.

The Viva Connections Dashboard is fully customizable, and administrators can add or remove cards and other components to match their organization's specific needs. The Dashboard can also be personalized for each employee based on their role, department, location, or other factors.

How to create a Dashboard

Browse to the SharePoint home site you created using the previous steps, go to the top gear icon (settings), and click on **Manage Viva Connections**. If you have selected the option to add a Dashboard or you already have a Dashboard, you will see the option to view the Dashboard, as shown in the following figure:

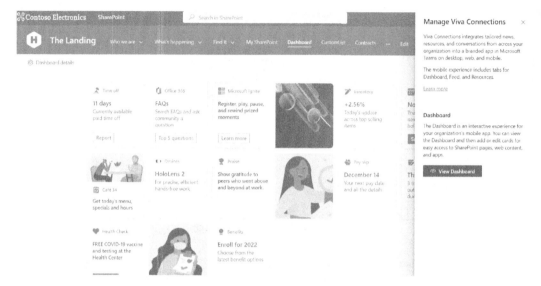

Figure 9.3: Viva Dashboard in the SharePoint home site

If you notice in the preceding figure, a few out-of-the-box cards are already on the Dashboard.

What are cards?

Cards on Viva Connections Dashboards are a type of component that provides quick and easy access to relevant information, news, insights, and resources. They are designed to be compact, interactive, and engaging, providing employees with a personalized and modern digital workplace experience.

Each card typically displays a specific type of information or resource, including text, images, videos, links, and other elements. In addition, cards can be customized to match each employee's specific needs and preferences. They can be configured to display data from various sources, such as SharePoint, Teams, OneDrive, and other M365 services.

For example, a news card might display the latest headlines from the company's internal news site, while a weather card might display real-time weather information for a specific location. An upcoming events card might display a calendar of upcoming meetings and events, while a to-do card might provide employees with a consolidated view of their tasks and to-dos.

The cards on the Viva Connections Dashboard are fully customizable, and administrators can add, remove, and configure cards to match their organization's specific needs. By providing employees with a personalized and relevant view of the information and resources they need to do their job, cards on the Viva Connections Dashboard can help improve the overall user experience and increase employee engagement and productivity.

To modify the Viva Dashboard and add new cards, take the following steps:

1.   Click on **Edit** on the top right of the Dashboard, as shown here:

Figure 9.4: Viva Dashboard Edit

2.   Once you click on **Edit**, you will have the option to add cards, as shown in the following figure:

Figure 9.5: Add a card to the Viva Connections Dashboard

3.   Then, you will be prompted with a card picker.

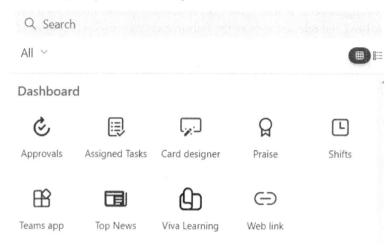

Figure 9.6: Card picker for adding cards to the Viva Dashboard

There are three types of cards available to add to the Viva Dashboard, as follows:

- **Out-of-the-box cards**: These are the cards out there already that you can change the configuration and settings for.

- **Adaptive Extension Cards (ACEs)**: These cards can be customized and extended using code with the **SharePoint Framework (SPFx)**.

- **Third-party cards**: These are cards built by third-party companies and **Independent Software Vendors (ISVs)**.

Common scenarios of cards used in Viva Connections

The Dashboard has cards that engage viewers with existing Teams apps, third-party apps, custom solutions, and various links. The Dashboard can be built without any code, or a developer can create custom cards to meet an organization's specific needs.

There are several types of cards that you can add to the Viva Connections Dashboard, including the following:

- **Benefits cards**: View pay stubs, vacation hours, company holidays, and HR benefits

- **News cards**: Provide employees with a consolidated view of the latest news and updates across the organization

- **KPI cards**: Display **Key Performance Indicators (KPIs)** and other metrics in real time, so employees can quickly see how the organization is performing

- **Weather cards**: Provide real-time weather information for a specific location

- **To-do cards**: Allow employees to track and manage their tasks and to-dos with a single, consolidated view

- **Announcement cards**: Provide a centralized place for employees to view and manage announcements and notifications across the organization

- **Upcoming events cards**: Display upcoming events and meetings and allow employees to RSVP and manage their calendar directly from the Dashboard

- **Quick links cards**: Provide employees with quick access to frequently used links, resources, and applications

These are just a few examples of cards that can be added to the Viva Connections Dashboard. The specific types of cards available will depend on the configuration and customization of your Viva Connections environment.

We now understand the Viva Connections Dashboard, which serves as the main landing page for employees and provides a consolidated view of relevant information, news, and insights. It includes several types of cards, such as news cards, weather cards, to-do cards, announcements cards, and quick links cards, which give employees quick and easy access to the information and resources they need. When you complete the configuration of the Microsoft Viva Connections app in Microsoft Teams, you will see the Viva Dashboard, as shown.

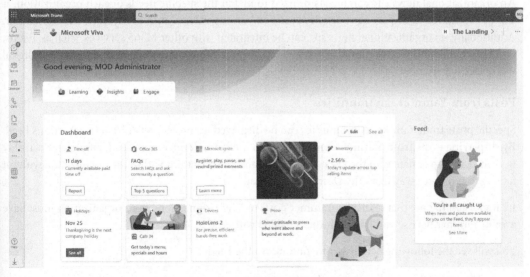

Figure 9.7: Dashboard in Viva Connections

The preceding figure shows the Viva Dashboard in Microsoft Teams. However, we must still complete the Viva Connections app confiiguration to see this in Microsoft Teams.

Before going to Viva Connections in Microsoft Teams, we need to review the last piece of the Viva Dashboard, which is the Feed.

The Feed in the Viva Connections Dashboard

The Feed in Viva Connections is a component of the Viva Connections Dashboard that provides employees with a personalized view of the latest news, updates, and insights from across the organization. The Feed is designed to be a central hub for employees to stay informed and connected and discover and engage with relevant content and conversations quickly.

Primarily, the content of the feed comes from the following resources.

News from organizational news sites in SharePoint

An organizational news site is a SharePoint site used to publish and share news, updates, and information with employees within an organization. The purpose of an organizational news site is to provide a centralized location for employees to access the latest information about the company and its products, services, and initiatives.

An organizational news site typically includes features such as a news article library, a news archive, and web pages displaying news articles. It may also include tools for authoring, publishing, and managing news articles and mechanisms for managing the approval and distribution of news content.

An organizational news site can be customized to match the specific needs of each organization. It can be configured to display news articles based on various criteria, such as keyword, date, or author. Additionally, an organizational news site can be integrated with other M365 services, such as Teams, OneDrive, and Viva Connections, to provide employees with a comprehensive and seamless digital workplace experience.

Posts from Yammer communities

Specific posts from Yammer communities can be displayed in the Microsoft Viva Connections Feed. By displaying posts from Yammer communities in the Viva Connections Feed, employees can stay informed and up to date with the latest discussions and conversations within the organization without having to navigate away from the Dashboard or Feed.

It's important to note that to display Yammer posts in Viva Connections, your organization must have a valid Yammer license and have Yammer enabled within M365.

You will see the following activity from Yammer in the Feed:

- Yammer All Company Featured Posts
- Yammer All Company Announcements
- Yammer All Company Posts

- Yammer Followed Community Featured Posts

- Yammer Followed Community Announcements

- Yammer Followed Community Posts

- Yammer Followed Community Q&A posts

- Yammer Followed Community Praise Posts

- Yammer Storyline posts

Videos in Stream (SharePoint)

Microsoft Stream is a video service integrated with SharePoint, allowing you to embed and share videos within your SharePoint sites easily. With Stream, you can securely upload, store, and share videos and collaborate with others by adding comments, likes, and mentions.

Microsoft Stream videos on SharePoint and OneDrive, shared with your entire organization, will appear in the Feed.

Now we have the SharePoint home site ready with the required global navigation, have set up the Viva Dashboard, added the required cards on the Dashboard, and understood the Feed. So, the next step is to configure the Viva Connections app in Microsoft Teams.

Viva Connections app

Once your landing site is ready, go to the Teams admin center and add the Viva Connections app. You need at least a Teams administrator role to log in to the Microsoft Teams admin center and manage this app.

There is a possibility that Viva Connections in Microsoft Teams is blocked. If it is in the **Blocked** state, change it to **Allowed**, as shown in the following figure.

Figure 9.8: Teams admin center – go to Manage apps to allow the Viva Connections app

In my demo tenant, it already has the **Allowed** status, as shown in the preceding figure.

Pinning the Viva Connections app

You should pin the Viva Connections app to the Teams left navigation bar for all users; it helps all users to access the organization's landing page through the Viva Connections app much more quickly.

You can accomplish this by adding Viva Connections to the pinned apps in the Microsoft Teams admin center, under **Setup policies**, as shown in the following screenshot.

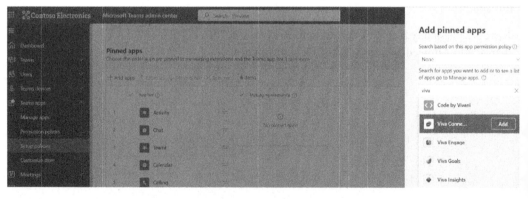

Figure 9.9: Adding Viva Connections to the pinned apps

After adding it to the list, as shown in the preceding figure, the Viva Connections app was added to the list of pinned apps, as shown in the following figure. Here, you can move around the pinned apps based on the order in which you want the apps to be visible on the Teams client to the end user. For example, many organizations like to move the Viva Connections app to be the first one on the Teams app bar.

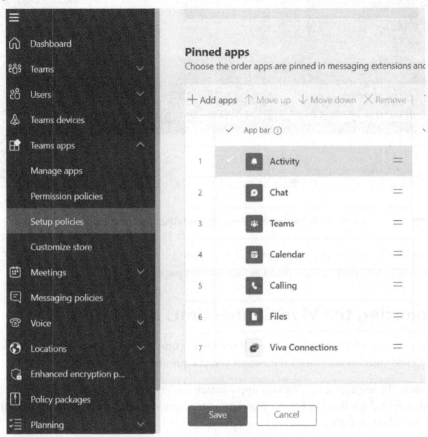

Figure 9.10: Microsoft Teams pinned apps

Click **Save**, as shown in the preceding screenshot, and it will show Viva Connections on the Microsoft Teams client. When you click on the Viva Connections app, it will redirect you to the communication site you had set as the home site in the Teams window.

Figure 9.11: The landing page through the Viva Connections app

As discussed, this will be the gateway to your modern intranet. Users can access any of the other SharePoint sites for collaboration through this landing page.

Customizing the Viva Connections app

Now that you have added the Viva Connections app to your Teams client, you can customize the app settings to add your organization's logo when you pre-pin the app for end users.

To customize the settings, go to **Manage apps**, search for **Viva Connections**, and open the Microsoft app, as shown in the following figure. You can see the option to edit the app settings by clicking the pencil under **Customizable**.

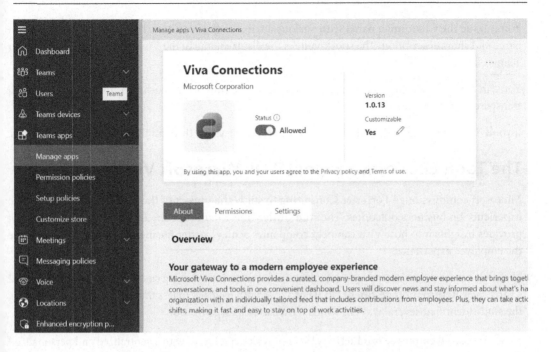

Figure 9.12: Search and open Viva Connections through Manage apps

Once you click the pencil icon under **Customizable** or the actions icon in the top-right corner and then **Customize**, a screen like the following one will pop up with customizable options:

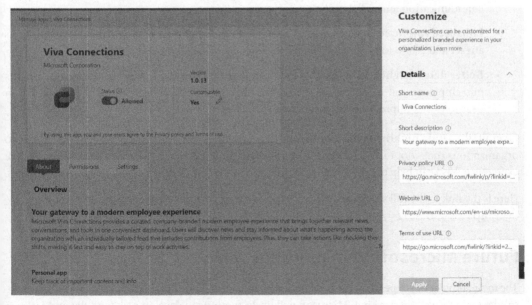

Figure 9.13: Customize the Viva Connections app

You can see the **Customize** panel with various attributes that you can change, including the short name and short description. The short name is the display name of the Viva Connections app in your Teams client.

You can scroll down the **Customize** panel to see an option for uploading a full-color icon and a transparent outline icon.

If you'd like to go live in a phased manner, you can control access through the app permission policies.

The Total Economic Impact™ Of Microsoft Viva

Microsoft commissioned Forrester Consulting to study the impact of the Microsoft Viva employee experience on business outcomes. The study, titled *The Total Economic Impact™ Of Microsoft Viva*, provides insights into how Viva can help companies achieve better business outcomes and improve the employee experience.

The study revealed that a composite organization, based on interviewing customers using Viva, realized a three-year **Return on Investment** (**ROI**) of 327%, with payback in less than six months. In addition, the study identified several ways in which Viva can help organizations:

- **Increased employee productivity**: Viva provides employees with a centralized and personalized hub for accessing the tools to do their jobs more efficiently, reducing the time spent searching for information or tools.
- **Improved collaboration**: Viva's integration with Microsoft Teams and other collaboration tools enables employees to work together more effectively, reducing the time and costs of inefficient communication and collaboration.
- **Enhanced employee engagement**: Viva's focus on the employee experience helps organizations attract and retain top talent and increase employee satisfaction and engagement.
- **Better data insights**: Viva Insights provides organizations with real-time data and insights into employee well-being, productivity, and collaboration, enabling them to make data-driven decisions that improve business outcomes.

Overall, the study highlights the significant ROI and business benefits that Viva can deliver to organizations that adopt it. By providing employees with a personalized and integrated employee experience, Viva can help organizations save time and money while driving better business outcomes.

Here is the link to the full study report – `https://query.prod.cms.rt.microsoft.com/cms/api/am/binary/RE56D0e`.

Future Microsoft Viva modules

The future of Viva will depend on the needs and demands of modern workplaces. As businesses continue to adapt to new ways of working, Microsoft will likely continue to develop new modules and features to support them. Microsoft will continue to invest in it and add more features and capabilities over time. Recently, it has announced a few new features, but we are awaiting complete details.

Microsoft Viva Amplify

Microsoft Viva Amplify is an internal communication application designed to help teams and leaders communicate to create compelling messaging that resonates with employees. The app provides a centralized space where employees can manage their campaigns, publish messages across multiple channels, and analyze resulting metrics.

Microsoft Viva Pulse

Viva Pulse offers smart templates and research-backed questions that allow managers to quickly pinpoint what's working well and where to focus their efforts. The app also provides suggested learning and actions to help address team needs, making it easier for managers to act on the feedback they receive. Using Viva Pulse, managers can gain valuable insights into their team's experience and use that information to drive positive organizational change.

Summary

In this chapter, we have looked at Microsoft Viva. This comprehensive employee engagement platform integrates with Microsoft Teams and gives employees access to various tools to improve the employee experience.

Microsoft Viva includes various apps for learning, insights, topics, and goals, which aim to promote growth and engagement in the workplace.

In this chapter, we have discussed Microsoft Viva Connections and how to set up the Viva Connections app. Microsoft Viva Connections provides a central hub for accessing critical information and resources and promoting collaboration and communication within an organization using the SharePoint Online communications site as a landing page.

The main benefits of the Microsoft Viva Connections app are as follows:

- Provides a landing experience for your organization
- Targets the correct information to the right people at the right time
- Provides navigation links to critical sites
- Provides employee Dashboards

After concluding this chapter, we move to the last chapter, where we discuss various third-party apps on Microsoft Teams and general usage reports of Teams apps.

10
Microsoft Teams Third-Party Apps

This chapter will discuss various third-party apps and will teach you how to integrate Microsoft Dynamics 365 apps with Microsoft Teams. In earlier chapters, we explained that there are three types of apps available on Microsoft Teams; out of them, we discussed built-in apps built by Microsoft and custom apps built by customers with their developers and teams. In this chapter, we'll look at the final type of Teams apps, which are built by **independent software vendors (ISVs)**.

Using various third-party apps on Teams will help users of Microsoft Teams get more productive as they can work on many things from Teams without having to switch back and forth between various apps.

In addition to Microsoft-provided apps, you can also use Microsoft-certified third-party apps.

In this chapter, we will go over the following topics:

- **Third-party apps:** We'll take a few third-party apps such as Workday, Now Virtual Agent, TeamViewer, and Adobe Acrobat and review them to get a deeper understanding of the context of integrating them in Microsoft Teams

- **Integration with ServiceNow Virtual Agent:** We'll explore Now Virtual Agent, a Chatbot from ServiceNow

- **Dynamics 365 apps on Microsoft Teams:** Then, we'll review the Microsoft Dynamics 365 apps on Microsoft Teams and their various integration options with Teams

- **Teams apps analytics and reporting:** Finally, we will end this chapter by reviewing where Teams creates reports from Teams administration

Let's get started.

Third-party apps on Microsoft Teams

Third-party apps can integrate with Microsoft Teams and enhance Teams' functionalities and capabilities with additional features. These apps are available from the Microsoft Teams App Store, which offers various functionalities to support a range of different functions:

- **Customer Service and Support**: ServiceDesk Plus Cloud, Chatra, OfficeAmp, Now Virtual Agent, Freshdesk, and Zendesk

- **DevOps/IT**: Bitbucket, GitHub, GitHub Enterprise, Jenkins, Jira Cloud/Server, Workbot, PagerDuty, and Stack Overflow for Teams

- **Analytics/BI**: Google Analytics, Miro, +BI Collaboration, and Mindomo

- **Education/Learning**: Wikipedia Search and Quizlet

- **Employee Life/Engagement**: Polly and Kudos

- **Human Resources**: Disco, Karma, Envoy, TeamSticker, and Quote Master

- **Meetings**: Calendar BOT, Cisco Webex Meetings, Secretary Bot, SoapBox, Zoom, Team O'clock, and Cronofy Calendar Connector

- **Project Management**: MindMeister, Confluence Cloud, Trello, Workboard, Priority Matrix, Zoho Projects, Asana, TaskList, OpenAgora, and Smartsheet

- **Sales and Marketing**: SurveyMonkey, MailClark, Live Chat, Salesforce, Live Chat Bot, Q, and Woobot

- **Productivity**: RememberThis, YouTube, Adobe Sign, Evernote, and Lucidchart

- **Creative Design**: Adobe Creative Cloud and Freehand (by InVision)

Let's review a few third-party apps again; I have chosen a few apps to explore with you.

Workday for Teams

The Workday app on Microsoft Teams is a third-party app that enables users to access HR and finance data within the Teams environment. In addition, this app integrates Workday into Microsoft Teams, so users can streamline HR and finance processes, making it easier and more efficient to manage employee data while staying within the Teams environment.

This app allows users to quickly accomplish everyday HR and finance tasks.

Figure 10.1: Workday and Microsoft Teams integration

The following are some of the most common actions that the Workday Teams app performs:

- **Finding people**: Quickly find coworker information and direct reports
- **Managing time off**: Check your time off balance and submit a request for time off
- **Streamlining feedback**: Quickly provide your coworker's feedback and choose the audience
- **Managing expenses**: Post your receipt and let Workday create your expense items
- **Accelerating hiring – feedback**: Quickly gather feedback for job candidates and make your hiring process much more manageable

To use the Workday app in Microsoft Teams, you need to have an active Workday account that needs to be configured by your Microsoft Teams administrator.

Now Virtual Agent, a chatbot from ServiceNow

ServiceNow is a leading tool for **IT service management** (**ITSM**) that helps track issues and tickets; it allows all the employees to access ServiceNow to submit their tickets or business approvals when they need help.

ServiceNow is usually available with browser experience; in the context of the Teams app, there is an app called "Now Virtual Agent," a chatbot that helps employees to resolve their issues faster without speaking to a live agent.

Now Virtual Agent is a chatbot integration from Microsoft Teams with a one-to-one association between the ServiceNow instance and the Microsoft Teams tenant.

To use Now Virtual Agent, the user needs to have a user record on the ServiceNow platform, so that the app can provide relevant and accurate information to the right person, track user activity, and provide insights into how the app is being used.

To access Now Virtual Agent, open Microsoft Teams and navigate to the channel or chat where you want to use the Virtual Agent integration. Click on the **Apps** icon in the left sidebar, search for Now in the search bar, and select the app.

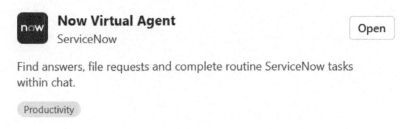

Figure 10.2: Now Virtual Agent in Microsoft Teams

If you don't see Now Virtual Agent as shown in the preceding figure, ensure the Teams administrator allows the use of the app in your tenant.

Although Now Virtual Agent does not require extra licensing; customers must hold a valid ServiceNow license to use this chatbot to connect with the platform. It is worth mentioning that ServiceNow ITSM offers two types of licenses – Standard and Pro – which customers can select based on their specific requirements.

For customers with ServiceNow's ITSM Standard license, the bot can do the following:

- Create a ticket
- Get updates on a ticket
- Search for documentation in the knowledge base

For customers with ServiceNow's ITSM Pro license, the bot can do the following:

- Do everything listed for the Standard license
- Customize the conversation and workflow with Virtual Agent Designer (includes 50+ conversation flows out of the box)

Integrating ServiceNow with Microsoft Teams

So, now you understand the context of Now Virtual Agent, but you have to set up a few things to establish the integration between ServiceNow and Teams. Here's what we need to do:

1. Begin by preparing your organization's Microsoft tenant to grant access and permissions to your ServiceNow instance.

2. Next, connect your ServiceNow instance to your organization's Microsoft tenant to complete the integration.

3. From the ServiceNow portal, log in as administrator, access the **Messaging Apps Integration** screen shown in the following figure, and install **Microsoft Teams**.

Figure 10.3: Integration of Microsoft Teams in the ServiceNow portal

4. After you click **Install**, it will tell you to log in to Microsoft Teams, as shown in the following figure. First, you need to grant your consent:

Permissions requested

Now Virtual Agent
ServiceNow 🏵️

This app would like to:

∨ View your basic profile

∨ Maintain access to data you have given it access to

☐ Consent on behalf of your organization

Accepting these permissions means that you allow this app to use your data as specified in their terms of service and privacy statement. You can change these permissions at https://myapps.microsoft.com. Show details

Does this app look suspicious? Report it here

Cancel	Accept

Figure 10.4: Consent to the Microsoft tenant

5.   Install the ServiceNow **Now Virtual Agent** app on Microsoft Teams:

Now Virtual Agent
ServiceNow

The Now Virtual Agent allows you to perform routine ServiceNow tasks directly in Microsoft Teams, so you can work more efficiently using chat. With Now Virtual Agent you can execute routine...

Figure 10.5: Now Virtual Agent

TeamViewer

The TeamViewer app is an external add-on for Microsoft Teams, allowing users to access and manage devices and computers remotely within the Teams interface. This feature allows for real-time collaboration while providing remote support. The app provides various functionalities, including remote control, desktop sharing, online meetings, web conferencing, and file transfer. It is available across different operating systems, such as Windows, macOS, Linux, iOS, Android, and Windows phones.

Figure 10.6: TeamViewer apps in AppSource

TeamViewer integration with Teams

TeamViewer integration with Teams enables users to enhance their Microsoft Teams experience with various powerful features. These include cross-platform remote control, which allows users to remotely access and control devices from within Teams, regardless of the operating system they are running on. In addition, the integration also includes **augmented reality** (**AR**)-based remote visual support, which enables users to provide immediate visual remote support to frontline workers and engineers on site. Finally, users can also enjoy shared remote access to devices and development environments, seamlessly extending the types of resources shared within Microsoft Teams groups.

Getting on-demand remote support

The TeamViewer app seamlessly integrates with Microsoft Teams to provide cross-platform remote control, AR-based remote visual support, and shared remote access to devices and development environments, enhancing the overall Teams experience. With TeamViewer, users can easily connect to their coworkers', customers', and vendors' devices from within Teams channels to quickly resolve issues and remotely control devices as if they were there in person.

Enhancing collaboration in Microsoft Teams

With TeamViewer integration for Microsoft Teams, users can extend the resources shared within their Teams groups by allowing remote access to development and testing environments, and other necessary devices. This can be done seamlessly within the Teams platform, improving collaboration and efficiency. By enabling remote access to various devices and environments, team members can work together on projects and resolve issues without the need for physical proximity.

Providing fast visual remote support

Issues can be resolved quickly and efficiently by providing immediate visual remote support when users need it most. With TeamViewer integration in Microsoft Teams, you can connect to engineers on-site or on the frontline using AR-based visual remote support. This enables you to provide real-time assistance and quickly solve problems within the Teams platform. TeamViewer consists of the following tabs:

Figure 10.7: TeamViewer in Microsoft Teams

The TeamViewer app consists of several components, including a bot accessible from the **Activity** tab, as well as four static tabs: **Help**, **Settings**, **Active Sessions**, and **Connection History**. It also features a customizable tab called **TeamViewer** for channels and group chats. In addition, messaging extensions are available in both the command box and compose area, providing users with additional functionality within the app.

For more details on this app, navigate to https://appsource.microsoft.com and search for TeamsViewer, or you can go to https://appsource.microsoft.com/en-gb/product/office/WA200002046?tab=Overview.

TeamViewer Remote Management for Microsoft Teams

TeamViewer Remote Management can be integrated with Microsoft Teams to enhance IT efficiency and keep the IT infrastructure stable and secure. This integration enables IT admins to receive instant alerts for device issues within Teams and provides remote management capabilities for faster issue resolution. Additionally, it offers comprehensive device and network monitoring to detect and react to. The integration includes a bot in the **Activity** tab, four static tabs for **Help**, **Settings**, **Active Sessions**, and **Connection History**, and a configurable tab for **TeamViewer** in channels and group chats. Messaging extensions are also available in the command box and compose area.

Fully integrated remote management solution

TeamViewer Monitoring monitors your IT infrastructure. With its help, you can keep track of critical aspects of your devices, including those running on Windows, macOS, and Linux, as well as network devices such as routers and printers. In case of any issues or anomalies, you will receive instant alerts directly in Microsoft Teams, allowing you to promptly address the situation.

By integrating TeamViewer Remote Management with Microsoft Teams, you can leverage the full range of features and capabilities of both tools to enhance your IT efficiency and improve your IT infrastructure's health, stability, and security. For example, you can quickly and securely connect remotely to devices to resolve real-time issues, ensuring faster resolution and minimal disruption to your workflows. Additionally, with comprehensive device and network monitoring capabilities, you can anticipate and address problems before they occur, ensuring your IT infrastructure stays healthy and optimal.

Secure remote access

TeamViewer Monitoring is an essential tool that integrates with Microsoft Teams and allows users to initiate a remote control session from within Teams, making it easier for coworkers to work together and resolve alerts or issues on their devices. With the integration, users can share their screens with others, collaborate in real time, and troubleshoot problems faster.

For example, a coworker experiencing a technical issue on their device can send an alert through Teams. Another coworker with the necessary expertise can then use the TeamViewer integration to access the troubled device remotely and help resolve the issue without being physically present. This can save time, reduce frustration, and increase productivity in a remote or distributed work environment.

Instant setup for immediate use

TeamViewer offers a range of features, making it an ideal solution for fast implementation and intuitive use. For example, the software allows users to connect to remote devices quickly and easily, even over low-bandwidth connections. It also offers a range of security features, such as end-to-end encryption and two-factor authentication, to ensure that remote connections are secure and protected. For more details on TeamViewer Remote Management, go to `https://appsource.microsoft.com/en/product/office/WA200004343?tab=Overview&exp=ubp8`.

These apps are available on Microsoft Teams; however, you need a licensed TeamViewer account to use these solutions. You can get more information about these licenses from `https://www.teamviewer.com/en/customer-support`.

Overall, TeamViewer can be an excellent tool for organizations looking to improve their remote support capabilities, collaborate more effectively, and enhance productivity.

Adobe Acrobat Sign

Adobe Acrobat Sign is an e-signature solution that provides the most direct signing experience for both the sender and the signer. In addition, it is an e-signature solution that runs inside Microsoft Teams, making it easy to deploy and use.

You can add Acrobat Sign from Microsoft AppSource and install it to the Teams app or work with your administrator to deploy it across the organization.

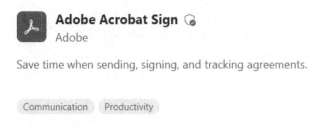

Figure 10.8: Adobe Acrobat Sign from Microsoft AppSource

Adobe Acrobat Sign is the e-signature solution that lets you send documents for e-signing, approvals, or other processing without leaving Microsoft Teams.

Launch the Acrobat Sign for Teams app and look for the **Request signatures** tab, as shown in this figure:

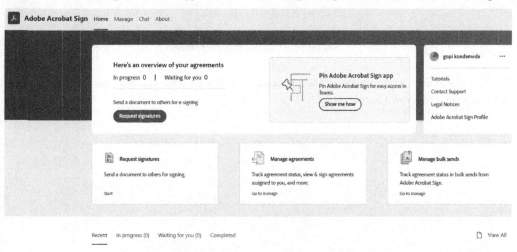

Figure 10.9: Adobe Acrobat Sign | Request signatures

Once you click on **Request signatures**, you can request a signature for a document and send it to the recipients that are required to sign it.

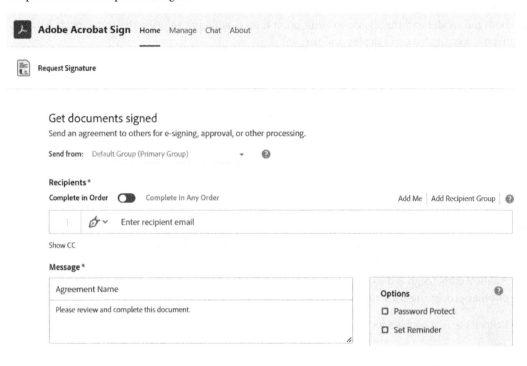

Figure 10.10: Get documents signed

With Acrobat Sign, you can access and use templates directly from the **Manage Agreements** page within Teams, as shown here:

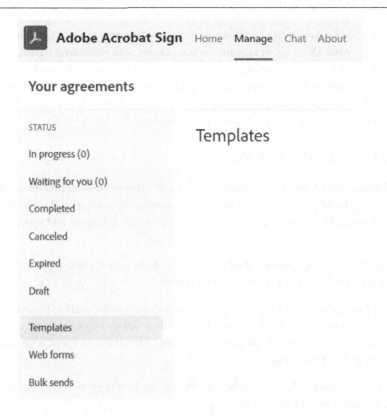

Figure 10.11: Various options presented in Manage Agreements

From here, you can manage agreements and fully see their status directly within Teams. You can also open or download documents from the **Manage Agreements** page.

With Acrobat Sign, you can manage reusable web forms you share or embed on your website for visitors to quickly fill in and sign.

You can send the same document to many recipients. For example, you can type their email addresses or upload a CSV file with signer-specific data. Every signer will receive a copy of the document.

You can find **Bulk sends** on the **Manage Agreements** page within Teams.

Adobe just embedded Acrobat Sign within the new Microsoft Teams approvals engine, so it's also available without downloading extra code or plugins.

This brings secure e-signatures embedded as a native solution. That way, users can manage all their required approvals, including those that require e-signatures, without leaving the Teams platform.

Learn more about the Microsoft Teams integration at `https://adobe.ly/teams-sign-guide`.

The **Microsoft Teams Approval** app allows users to create, manage, and share approvals within the Teams platform. Also, the app offers seamless integration with electronic signature solutions such as Adobe Sign and DocuSign, enabling users to sign and approve documents electronically. The Approvals app feature helps to increase productivity, particularly in remote work environments, by saving time and resources. Additionally, the app provides real-time approval tracking, allowing for greater visibility and collaboration between team members.

Dynamics 365 on Teams

Dynamics 365 is a cloud-based service that predominantly involves **customer relationship management** (**CRM**), developed and maintained by Microsoft. However, depending on the nature of the product, it can help to maintain various business functions such as sales, finance and operations, marketing, field service, project service, talent, and customer service.

Dynamics 365 strongly integrates with other Microsoft products such as Power Platform for customizations, Microsoft Teams for collaboration, and AI for insights.

Dynamics 365 integration with Microsoft Teams allows easy collaboration for meetings, chats, and calls from the Dynamics 365 workspace or from within Teams and lets you seamlessly access the business process or records and collaborate from Teams. However, our focus is on Teams consuming Dynamics 365 and collaborating.

For better results, strong collaboration is required for any functions of Dynamics 365 such as sales, marketing, customer service, and so on.

Adding Dynamics 365 app to your team

To get started, you can add the Dynamics 365 app to your team by accessing the App Store within Microsoft Teams.

Dynamics 365
Microsoft Corporation

Collaborate on Dynamics 365, share files, and easily get info via chat. Note: Your team and channel name will be visible to others on connected records in Dynamics 365, and files will be synced...

Figure 10.12: Dynamics 365 app in Microsoft Teams

The preceding figure represents the Dynamics 365 app in the Microsoft Teams App Store. After selecting the Dynamics 365 app, you will be prompted to choose the channel and team to which you want to add the app, enabling you to integrate Dynamics 365 into the selected channel easily.

✕

Add Dynamics 365 to a team

Dynamics 365 will be available for the entire team, but start by setting it up in
a channel.

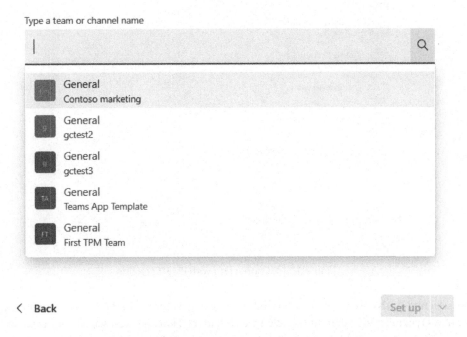

Figure 10.13: Adding Dynamics 365 to a Teams channel

Entity Selection or View Selection

After you pick the channel from the previous figure, the **Set up** button shown in the figure will become available. Once you click **Set up**, the next step is to select an entity or view. See the following criteria to decide which one to choose:

- **Entity Selection**: You can select an entity to connect by picking a recently viewed record or searching

- **View Selection**: You can pick an entity and see the list of views

In the following figure, I picked the **Account** entity, which brings all the views of **Account**; from the views, select **Active Accounts** to view, and click **Save**.

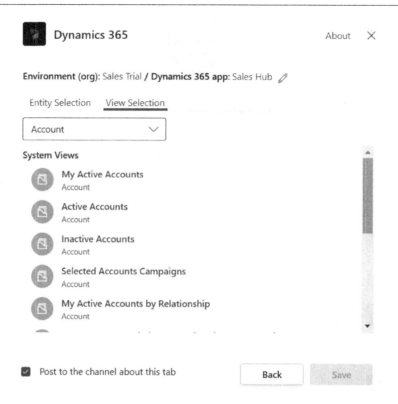

Figure 10.14: Connecting with View Selection

After selecting **Active Accounts** to view and then saving, as shown in the preceding figure, you will see a new Dynamics 365 tab in the selected team channel. Here, you can see all your active accounts and schedule a meeting with them directly or even use the **Meet now** feature of Teams. You can also select an account to open and make changes directly in Teams:

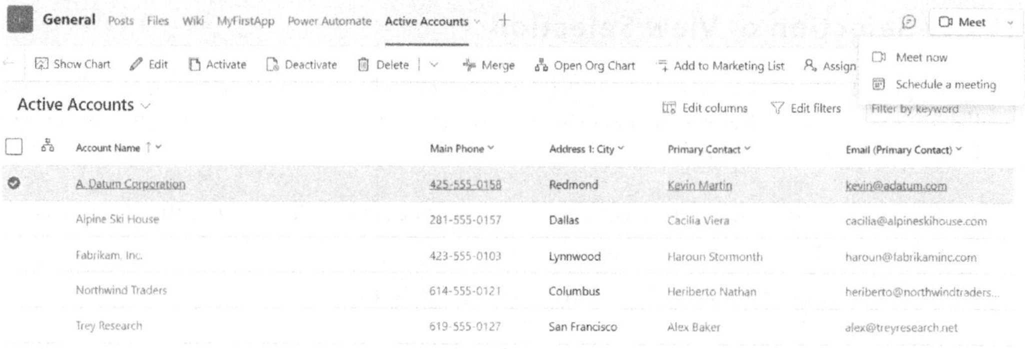

Figure 10.15: Adding Dynamics 365 to a Microsoft Teams team

After adding the Dynamics 365 Teams app to your Teams client, you need to connect the Teams app to the environment and the appropriate Dynamics 365 app you want to connect.

Now you have added the Dynamics 365 app and set up a tab in the Microsoft Teams channel, you can set up a personal dashboard for Sales Hub or Customer Service Hub.

My Dashboard with the Dynamics 365 app for Microsoft Teams

With this, you can set up a personal dashboard to interact with Dynamics 365 apps directly in Microsoft Teams.

Once you open the Dynamics 365 app, you can go to **Settings**, as shown in the following figure, and select the environment so that, in the next dropdown in Dynamics 365 app, it will only bring the app modules licenses for the selected environment.

On the **Environment (org)** dropdown, you can only see the environments that are in version 9.x or later.

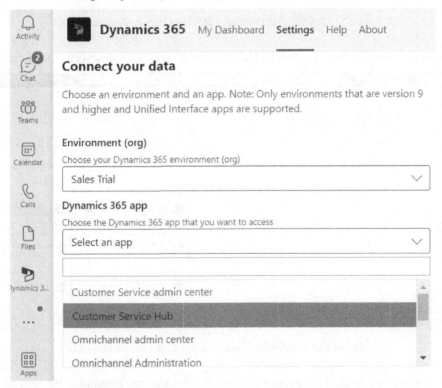

Figure 10.16: Dynamics 365 app selecting the required app

In the preceding figure, I picked **Sales Hub** and saved it. If we go to the dashboard, you can access your Dynamics 365 Sales Hub in Teams, as shown here:

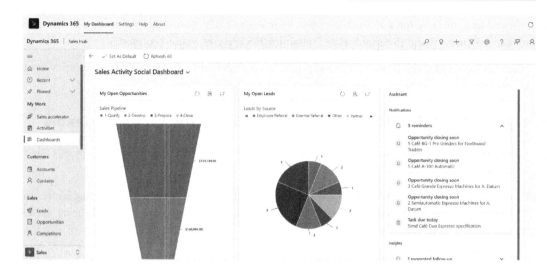

Figure 10.17: Accessing Dynamics 365 Sales Hub in Microsoft Teams

You can also connect with **Customer Service Hub** and see Customer Service Hub in the Teams environment:

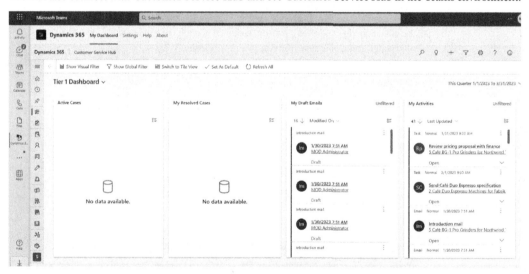

Figure 10.18: Accessing Dynamics 365 Customer Service Hub

Now that you have checked the personal dashboard through the Dynamics 365 app, we can see another scenario of chatting with an individual user through a Teams Chat and the records directly related to chatting with users.

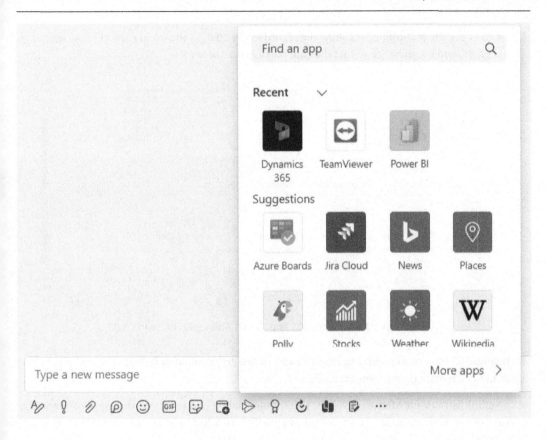

Figure 10.19: Dynamics 365 app in a Teams Chat

Click on the Dynamics 365 app; it opens the app and will allow you to choose the record that you want to share in Chat. It opens the most recent record by default, but you can search in **Accounts**, **Opportunities**, **Cases**, **Contacts**, and **Leads**, or search in the **All** category.

In this case, I have picked the recent **Alpine Ski House** account, as shown here:

Figure 10.20: Dynamics 365 app search for the record to share in Chat

Once you click the account, it will show the record in the chat, as shown in the following figure, and you need to send the message so that the chat participant can see it:

Figure 10.21: Dynamics 365 app shared Alpine Ski House in Chat

Dynamics 365 integration with Microsoft Teams in one-to-one chat or Teams channel chat helps to view and collaborate on customer records.

As an administrator for Microsoft Teams, you should analyze and report on the usage of Teams apps across your organization. In the next section with Teams Admin Center, we review the options to accomplish this.

Reporting and analytics of Teams app usage

Microsoft Teams Admin Center is a one-stop shop for all Teams administration policies and settings at various scopes such as **User**, **Teams**, and **Tenant** levels. In addition to these configurations, we have various reports available for you to understand the general usage and analyze the tenant.

First, you need to be a global administrator, global reader, or Teams service administrator to access the reports.

We have several usage reports in Teams Admin Center such as Teams user activity reports, Teams app usage reports, Teams device usage reports, PSTN reports, audio conferencing usage, live event usage, and so on. However, this book on Teams apps will focus on understanding the Teams app usage report.

In the Teams app usage report, you will find out which apps users are using in Teams and also understand the activity and app utilization data.

This report will help you understand the number of apps installed in your environment, how many are used actively, and the platform. If you understand the usage of apps in Microsoft Teams, it is easy to prioritize and plan your apps for new scenarios and acquire third-party apps.

How to access the Teams app usage report

As said previously, all these reports are in Teams Admin Center (`https://admin.teams.microsoft.com`); go to **Analytics & reports** in the left navigation pane and click on **Usage reports**, as shown in the following figure:

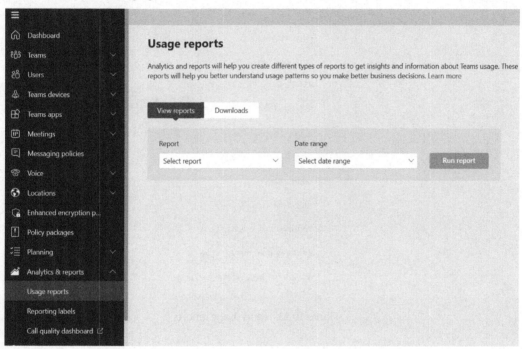

Figure 10.22: Teams Admin Center | Usage reports

Click on the **Report** dropdown, which will have various reports, as shown in the following figure:

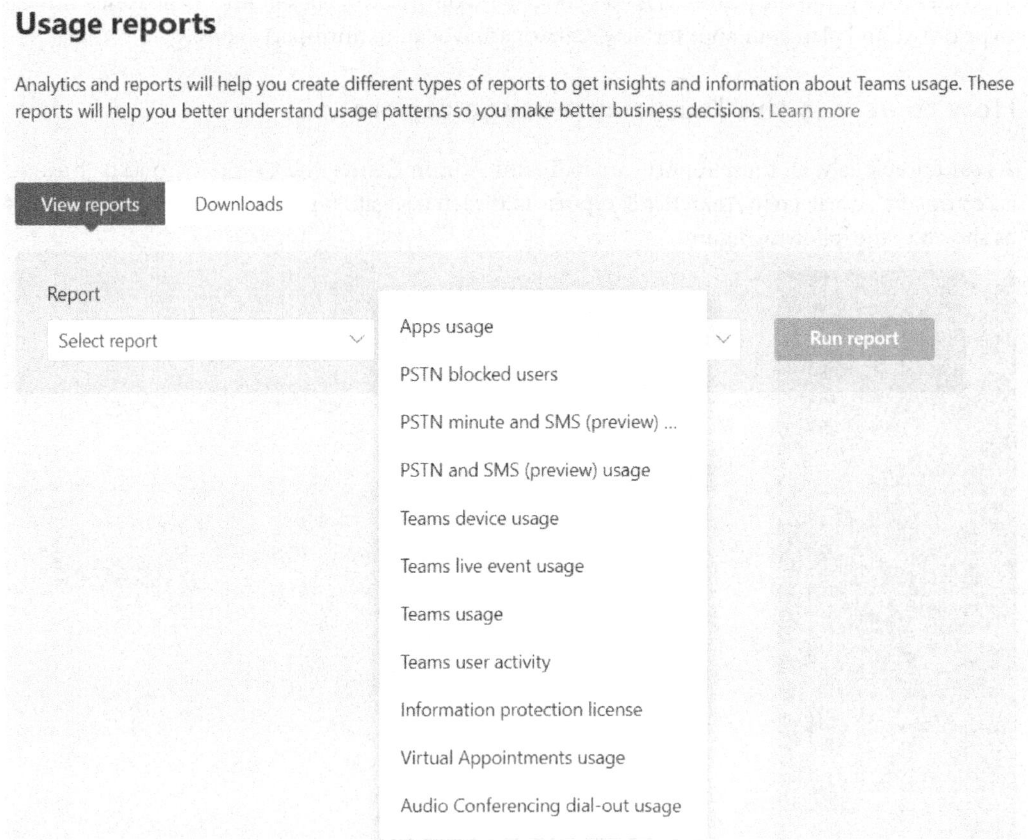

Usage reports

Analytics and reports will help you create different types of reports to get insights and information about Teams usage. These reports will help you better understand usage patterns so you make better business decisions. Learn more

View reports   Downloads

Report

Select report

Apps usage

PSTN blocked users

PSTN minute and SMS (preview) ...

PSTN and SMS (preview) usage

Teams device usage

Teams live event usage

Teams usage

Teams user activity

Information protection license

Virtual Appointments usage

Audio Conferencing dial-out usage

Run report

Figure 10.23: Teams usage reports

There are various usage reports available, and as a Teams administrator, it is always good to review these reports from time to time to understand the Teams usage. For example, click **Apps usage** and select the date range (7, 30, 90, and 180 days) in which you would like to see Teams app usage.

It will generate the app usage report, as shown in the next figure. If you look at the chart, the x axis represents the report's date range, and then the y axis reports the count of apps.

You can filter the chart with a few options, such as **Active Microsoft apps** (number of Microsoft apps used across the tenant), **Active third-party apps** (third-party apps), **Active LOB apps** (line-of-business apps), and then with total active, inactive, and installed apps.

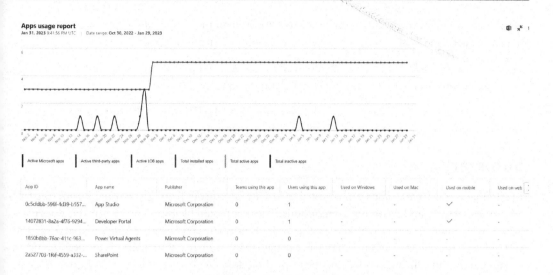

Figure 10.24: Apps usage report

Below the chart, we have a breakdown of all apps with the details of the apps.

We have a few other usage reports from the **Microsoft 365 (M365)** admin center (`https://admin.microsoft.com/`); it would be interesting to look at Microsoft Teams-related usage reports.

When you log in to the admin center, in the left navigation, go to **Reports**, expand the reports, and click **Usage**. You need to be in a global admin, report reader, global reader role, or product-specific admin (Exchange admin, SharePoint admin, Skype for Business admins, Teams Service administrator, Teams Communications administrator, etc.) role to access these reports.

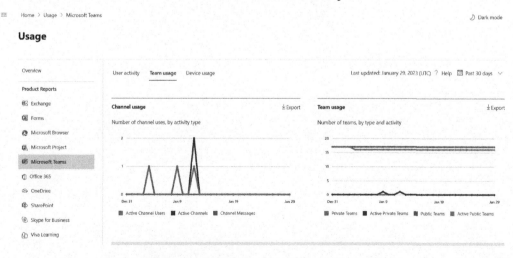

Figure 10.25: M365 admin center Microsoft Teams usage reports

Also, there is a lot of work adding the usage reports through the Graph API; Graph acts as a gateway to provide access to M365. You can make these Graph calls in any script or PowerShell.

There are various APIs already available, but for Teams, we have Microsoft Teams device usage, Microsoft Teams user activity, and Microsoft Teams team activity.

You can also use PowerShell to query the Graph API, a RESTful web API that provides access to various Microsoft services through which you get various usage reports.

Summary

In summary, third-party apps can be integrated with Microsoft Teams, providing businesses with additional features and customization options. These apps can be grouped into various categories: productivity, communication, customer engagement, security and compliance, learning and development, and industry-specific. As a result, businesses can tailor Microsoft Teams to their specific needs, improve collaboration, and enhance productivity by using these apps. With a vast selection of third-party apps, businesses can find a solution that works best for them and boosts their performance.

We have discussed various third-party apps built by ISVs on various occasions. We have also reviewed a few third-party apps and the path to integrating them into Microsoft Teams. This discussion will give you a general idea of how third-party apps add value to the existing functionality.

Dynamics 365 is a set of intelligent applications that can run all of your business. In this chapter, we have discussed its integration options with Teams.

Lastly, we reviewed Teams usage reports but mainly the usage of the app, as so far you have worked with various types of apps in Teams and it will review the usage of the apps in your Teams environment.

Index

Packtpub.com

Subscribe to our online digital library for full access to over 7,000 books and videos, as well as industry leading tools to help you plan your personal development and advance your career. For more information, please visit our website.

Why subscribe?

- Spend less time learning and more time coding with practical eBooks and Videos from over 4,000 industry professionals

- Improve your learning with Skill Plans built especially for you

- Get a free eBook or video every month

- Fully searchable for easy access to vital information

- Copy and paste, print, and bookmark content

Did you know that Packt offers eBook versions of every book published, with PDF and ePub files available? You can upgrade to the eBook version at packtpub.com and as a print book customer, you are entitled to a discount on the eBook copy. Get in touch with us at customercare@packtpub.com for more details.

At www.packtpub.com, you can also read a collection of free technical articles, sign up for a range of free newsletters, and receive exclusive discounts and offers on Packt books and eBooks.

Other Books You May Enjoy

If you enjoyed this book, you may be interested in these other books by Packt:

Hands-On Microsoft Teams - Second Edition

João Ferreira

ISBN: 9781801075275

- Perform scheduling and manage meetings, live events, and webinars
- Create and manage Microsoft Teams templates to streamline company processes
- Deal with permissions and security issues in managing private and public teams and channels
- Extend Microsoft Teams using custom apps, Microsoft 365, and PowerShell automation
- Build your own Teams app with the Developer Portal without writing any code
- Deploy helpful chatbots using QnA Maker and Power Virtual Agents
- Explore Teams use cases for education, frontline work, and personal life
- Bring together knowledge, learning, resources, and insights with the new employee experience platform, Microsoft Viva

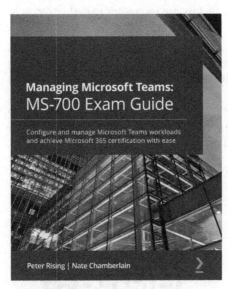

Managing Microsoft Teams: MS-700 Exam Guide

Peter Rising, Nate Chamberlain

ISBN: 9781801071000

- Explore Security Compliance configuration options for Teams features
- Manage meetings, calls, and chat features within Microsoft Teams
- Find out how to manage phone numbers, systems, and settings in Teams
- Manage individual team settings, membership, and guest access
- Create policies for Microsoft Teams apps and features
- Deploy access reviews and dynamic team membership

Packt is searching for authors like you

If you're interested in becoming an author for Packt, please visit `authors.packtpub.com` and apply today. We have worked with thousands of developers and tech professionals, just like you, to help them share their insight with the global tech community. You can make a general application, apply for a specific hot topic that we are recruiting an author for, or submit your own idea.

Share Your Thoughts

Now you've finished *Customizing Microsoft Teams*, we'd love to hear your thoughts! Scan the QR code below to go straight to the Amazon review page for this book and share your feedback or leave a review on the site that you purchased it from.

`https://packt.link/r/1801075387`

Your review is important to us and the tech community and will help us make sure we're delivering excellent quality content.

Download a free PDF copy of this book

Thanks for purchasing this book!

Do you like to read on the go but are unable to carry your print books everywhere?

Is your eBook purchase not compatible with the device of your choice?

Don't worry, now with every Packt book you get a DRM-free PDF version of that book at no cost.

Read anywhere, any place, on any device. Search, copy, and paste code from your favorite technical books directly into your application.

The perks don't stop there, you can get exclusive access to discounts, newsletters, and great free content in your inbox daily

Follow these simple steps to get the benefits:

1. Scan the QR code or visit the link below

https://packt.link/free-ebook/9781801075381

2. Submit your proof of purchase
3. That's it! We'll send your free PDF and other benefits to your email directly

Made in the USA
Las Vegas, NV
04 November 2023

80220852R00162